SO-BHU-954

DATE DUE

THE RING OF FIRE

THE
RING OF
FIRE

David Ritchie

ATHENEUM · 1981 · NEW YORK

The illustrations following page 106 have been provided courtesy of The American Museum of Natural History (1,2,4,6,7,11), The U.S. Geological Survey, Department of the Interior (3,5,8,9), and The National Oceanic and Atmospheric Administration, U.S. Department of Commerce (10).

Library of Congress Cataloging in Publication Data

Ritchie, David——
The ring of fire.

Bibliography: p.
Includes index.
1. Volcanism—Pacific area.   I. Title
QE524.R57   1981   551.2'099   80–69391
ISBN 0–689–11150–9   AACR2

Composition by American–Stratford Graphic Services, Brattleboro, Vermont
Manufactured by Fairfield Graphics, Fairfield, Pennsylvania
Designed by Mary Cregan
First Edition

To my father,
who assumed I knew what I was doing

Contents

Contents

Preface

Science magazine has called our time the "golden age of the earth scientist." That is no understatement. Geology and its related sciences are more important to our daily lives than ever before, and indeed to our future on this planet. We would all do well to learn at least the basics of geology—the internal structure of the earth, the distribution and motions of crustal plates, and so forth—because this information can be a great help in understanding the daily news.

If the average American knew a little more about the earth under his or her feet, society would benefit in countless ways. The self-styled "earthquake prophet" would be unable to raise panic (and riches) with his bizarre forecasts of doom. Greedy developers would be less likely to entice home buyers to settle on disastrously quake-prone land. Voters would have a more constructive understanding of energy-related issues. And so on.

In short, we all suffer from our ignorance of the earth

sciences. For this ignorance, I think the schools are largely to blame. Geology has long been taught unimaginatively, presented as a science second only in dullness to economics. Most students are turned off to geology for life.

In fact, geology is one of the most vibrant and exciting fields of knowledge. What other science takes in the whole earth and its whole history? What other science offers a glimpse into long-vanished worlds full of strange and wonderful animals? And what other science lets us peer far into the future, to see an earth where the continents and seas have rearranged themselves almost past recognition?

This is what teachers should be trying to communicate to students—not just the dry lists of minerals and the dull facts about plutons.

There is excitement in geology, and I hope this book conveys some of that feeling, while giving the reader a better understanding of the violent and fascinating planet we live on.

Boston, Massachusetts, October 1, 1980

Acknowledgments

This book began as a suggestion from Thomas Stewart of Atheneum Publishers in the fall of 1979. That suggestion grew into more than 400 pounds of notes and sketches, prior to the writing of the manuscript. So much information is available on the circum-Pacific Ring of Fire that it would require a set of 20 or 30 volumes to do the subject justice; all I can do in a book of this length is focus on a few interesting topics and vignettes, and let the interested reader go on to explore the subject further. A list of suggested readings is given at the end of the book.

So many persons have helped with the making of this book that it would be impossible to list them all here. Chief among them, however, are Thomas Stewart; my literary agent, Barbara Bova; Dr. Raymond Sullivan of San Francisco State University, who provided many valuable leads to follow in library research on earthquakes; Thom Willenbecher, who helped greatly with research for the chapter on the Mount St. Helens eruption; and George

ACKNOWLEDGMENTS

Androvette, who gave me a place to stay out of the rain while working on the manuscript.

The libraries of Tufts University, Northeastern University, the University of Virginia, the University of Massachusetts at Boston, the University of California at Berkeley, and the cities of Boston and San Francisco all provided much useful information for this book. I would like to thank especially the library personnel at Old Dominion University and the College of William and Mary, who went out of their way to help locate obscure books, articles, pamphlets, and government reports.

The California Division of Mineral Resources supplied a great deal of valuable material (about 50 pounds of it!) for the chapters on earthquakes and the geological history of California.

James Burke's book *Connections* gave me many ideas for the discussions of how the Ring of Fire has affected civilization, and for those ideas I am deeply indebted to him. Special thanks also to Dr. Reiko Schwab for her help and advice.

David Kogut of the New Bedford, Massachusetts, *Standard-Times* provided moral support when I needed it.

Finally, my father, Virgil S. Ritchie, was an unfailing source of encouragement during the long process of writing the manuscript. He also provided some particularly useful facts about the eruption of Krakatoa, and this book would be less exciting without his assistance.

THE RING OF FIRE

I

The Fiery Cascades

JOHN WESLEY HILLMAN had an unusual distinction. His name went down in history one day in 1853 when his mule saved his life.

Hillman was a prospector and he had heard stories of lost gold mines in the Cascade Mountains of the Pacific Northwest. Could it be, he wondered, that the stories were true?

Gold had been discovered in California a few years earlier, and all kinds of wild tales were circulating in the hotels and saloons farther east. There were, so rumor had it, parts of the American West where one could pick one's fortune off the ground in a few hours.

Most prospectors viewed such tales with skepticism. The chance of any individual prospector striking it rich was extremely small. For every thousand seekers after gold, there was perhaps one who found more than enough to buy a cup of coffee. As for prospectors who made their fortunes, the figure was nearer one in 10,000.

There were a lucky few who found paying ores or spectacular nuggets. Some of those nuggets—or, rather, identical models of them—are on display at the offices of the California Division of Mines in San Francisco. But the chance of such a discovery was exceedingly small.

Still, the chance existed, and it drew thousands of fortune seekers westward in the mid-1800s. One of them was Hillman, who thought there must be a fortune, or at least a tidy profit, for the taking in the Western mountains if one only looked for it long enough. So he acquired a mule and some provisions and set out with several companions, looking for anything that might lead to golden riches. Fortunately for Hillman, his mule had good eyesight.

On June 12, 1853, Hillman was riding up the flank of a mountain when the mule halted suddenly and Hillman found himself at the edge of a precipitous cliff. Had he been riding a blind mule, Hillman wrote years later, he would probably have ridden over the brink and fallen to his death.

The cliff looked out on the last thing the prospector ever expected to find on top of a mountain: a deep blue lake seven miles wide. The lake rested in a great natural bowl some 36 miles in circumference. At one end, a few hundred feet offshore, an odd-looking conical mountain with a flat top rose what later proved to be 760 feet above the waters. Though it stood ten times taller than the highest office building then in America, the cone-shaped island looked almost lost in the vast waters of the lake—waters of a deep sapphire blue, a dozen times more intense than the blue of the Oregon sky.

When Hillman recovered from the shock of his discovery, he told his companions farther down the slope what he had found. Some members of the party wanted to climb down to the lake for a close inspection, but the slopes were steep and covered with a layer of crumbly rock fragments that would make a return ascent difficult. Discretion prevailed, and the men decided to observe from the safety of the rim. Today a plaque marks the spot where Hillman was saved by his mule.

The place needed a name. After some debate, the travelers decided on Deep Blue Lake. (Perhaps it was Hillman's prerogative, as the discoverer, to name the lake after himself, but he did get his name on a promontory on the rim, now called Hillman Peak.)

Hillman was puzzled by the lake's location. Ordinarily, lakes are found in valleys between mountains, not on the summits. Also puzzling was the fact that local Indians seemed ignorant of the mountaintop lake. Later Hillman learned that it was a sacred place, and only a few shamans had seen it before him.

The Klamath Indians believed the lake was once the domain of a god-king named Llao, who set up his throne on the rim of the basin. His subjects included a race of giant crayfish that lived in the deep, cold waters of the lake.

Llao's reign came to an unhappy end when his arch-enemy Skell caught up with him, had him dismembered, and cast the pieces of his body into the waters. The crayfish ate the bits of flesh, not knowing they were devouring their king. Then Skell tossed Llao's head into the lake. The crustaceans saw the sacrilege they had committed and began to weep copiously. Their tears raised the lake to its present level, and Llao's head became the conical island.

Today Llao's head is known as Wizard Island. Deep Blue Lake is called Crater Lake and is part of a national park. There is a ring road around the rim of the basin where John Wesley Hillman once stood with his mule. And in the years since Hillman's discovery, geologists have replaced the legend of Llao with a more plausible and even more violent model of Crater Lake's birth.

Crater Lake is just an infant on the geological time scale.

It was formed only about 6,500 years ago. The lake's formation was a complicated process, but essentially it happened when a mighty mountain lost its underpinnings.

The mountain that once stood on the site of Crater Lake was some 12,000 feet high. Geologists call it Mount Mazama. Volcanic in origin, it built itself up over the centuries, layer on layer of lava and brownish ash, until it stood equal in stature to any of the Cascade peaks today. A secondary cone grew on the mountain's western slope.

Snow fell on Mazama's summit and formed glaciers. Slowly the rivers of ice oozed down its sides, scoring and scratching the rocks as the ice moved along. Thousands of years later, geologists would find these rocks nestled between layers of volcanic rock—a sign that from time to time, during eruptions, the glaciers were wiped out. Forests also grew on the slopes of Mazama and were destroyed in the mountain's periodic outbursts. But after each eruption, quiet returned, and so did the ice and the trees.

The last ice age buried Mazama under thick glaciers. If anyone inhabited the area around the mountain at this time, Mazama must have been an awe-inspiring sight, wrapped in white from base to summit, with winds whipping plumes of ice crystals off the crown. But white is the color of old age, and Mazama's life was almost over. In a few more centuries, the mountain's lofty peak would be gone forever.

Death came for Mazama as the ice age was ending. The glaciers were retreating northward when Mazama, awakening after a long sleep under its icy cover, began to stir again.

Earthquakes shook the mountain as molten rock—magma —oozed upward from deep inside the earth, displacing rock layers on its way to the surface. The quakes were gentle at first, then grew stronger almost daily. Mazama was building up to its own destruction.

Then Mazama erupted. The initial blast must have

been heard more than 100 miles away. A cloud of gas and ash shot upward from the riven summit of the mountain and rose into the upper atmosphere. The plume spread out, covering the land and blocking the sun. Lightning sparkled high in the cloud and darted between the cloud and the earth as ash fell to earth in a rain of gritty gray dust.

At the same time, clouds of hot ash were roaring down the flanks of the mountain, leveling trees like grass under a mower. The superheated ash flows roared along the valleys cut in the mountain's side by glaciers, and traveled thirty miles or more before coming to rest.

Lava poured out of the mountain—but not for long. As Mazama roared, the molten rock that fed the eruption was draining away rapidly into fissures in the rock underground. Thus the vast subterranean pool of magma beneath Mazama was soon depleted, and lava burst no longer from the mountain.

The molten rock did more, however, than exit through Mazama's throat. The magma had actually helped to support the tremendous weight of the overlying rocks, and now with it drained away from its inside, Mazama was suddenly a great hollow shell of stone, unable to support its own weight.

Mazama collapsed like a dynamited building. The mountain's fall was over in a few hours. When the smoke and dust cloud dissipated, the towering top of Mount Mazama was gone. What remained was a crater lined on the bottom with rubble, the debris of the collapsed peak. Snow and ice gradually filled the crater (known to geologists as a caldera) up to its present level. The lake is 1,900 feet deep. One could sink the Empire State Building in Crater Lake, and there would still be more than 400 feet of water over the television mast.

But the fires under the mountain were not yet dead. After Mazama collapsed—perhaps as little as a thousand years ago—a new volcano rose from the ruins of Mazama:

Wizard Island. The symmetrical cinder cone, which took its name from its likeness to a wizard's hat, is dotted with trees and has a neat circular crater on top, some 300 feet wide. Wizard Island is quiet today. But will it remain so forever? No one can say. Mighty Mazama itself was once no bigger than Wizard Island, and the literature of geology is full of stories of volcanic mountains that destroyed themselves, only to rebuild later on the same site. Perhaps Mazama will rise again, and fall again. Time will tell.

Crater Lake is part of the Cascade range, a chain of volcanic mountains extending from northern California to British Columbia. The Cascades are a northern extension of the Sierra Nevada and lie, on the average, about 100 to 150 miles from the Pacific Ocean.

A low-lying, broad mass of rock, the Cascade Range is topped by more than a dozen magnificent volcanic peaks, from Lassen Peak in north central California to Mount Garibaldi near Vancouver, British Columbia. The Cascades are penetrated by three rivers: the Fraser in the north, the Klamath in the south, and the Columbia in between. The Columbia has cut down almost to sea level through the mountain range, but not quite. There is a sudden hundred-foot drop at The Dalles on the Columbia, and here one finds the magnificent rapids that gave the Cascades their name.

With only a couple of exceptions such as Mount Garibaldi, the Cascade peaks have strangely dull names for such majestic mountains. They have either bland impersonal names, like Three Sisters, or bland personal names, like Mount Hood and Mount Adams. The early English-speaking visitors (starting with Lewis and Clark in 1805) who named the natural landmarks of the Pacific Northwest were generally an unimaginative lot—in contrast to the French-Canadians, who put colorful and sometimes ribald names on the landscape. (Wyoming's Grand Teton Range, for example, was named by French-Canadian trappers in honor of the female breast. The name surprises some

French visitors, who expect Americans to be more puritanical in naming mountains.)

The Cascades also contain the only active volcanoes in the lower forty-eight United States. These tall, snow-covered mountains have spat out smoke and ash on dozens of occasions since the Pacific Northwest was settled.

Southernmost of the Cascade volcanoes is Lassen Peak, a 10,500-foot volcano in northern California. The beautiful peak can be seen from Sacramento on clear days and is a popular tourist attraction. Earlier in this century, however, Lassen Peak was considerably less attractive; the mountain started erupting near the beginning of World War I and destroyed much of the surrounding countryside.

Lassen Peak rumbled to life and belched ash and smoke from 1914 to 1921. Glowing lava in the volcano lit the cloud of ash and steam from underneath at night, and hot mud poured down the volcano's sides. Chunks of pumice —a lightweight gray volcanic rock—rained down on the surrounding countryside. Finally the volcano gave out with a blast of vapor, ash, and superheated air that flattened everything before it within a radius of four and a half miles. The flaming torrent destroyed more than five million board feet of timber and felled trees five feet in diameter. Any animals caught in the path of this fiery surge were incinerated on the spot. Temperatures in the blast wave may have reached 1,000 degrees Centigrade. What remained after the holocaust was a scorched wasteland where nothing bigger than a bacterium remained alive. People in the communities near Lassen Peak called it "the devastated area."

This kind of calamity has happened often in northern California. Some towns and highways there are built on thick layers of cinders, ash, and carbonized wood laid down when avalanches of fire swept down the sides of volcanoes.

The effects of Cascade vulcanism can be seen clearly at Lava Beds National Monument, not far from Lassen Peak,

9

in Siskiyou County. Here bizarre formations of lava stand as silent reminders of volcanic violence in California's past.

About 80 square miles in area, Lava Beds National Monument is a basalt formation several thousand years old. Scattered about the landscape are large conical formations, two or three times the height of a grown man, that look like giant anthills or termite mounds. These are called "spatter cones." They were formed when extremely fluid lava burst out of the ground through fissures in the rock. The lava was so full of gases that it bubbled and spattered rather like boiling mud, and bits of lava built up to form the anthill-like formations one sees today. It is easy to imagine some giant insect crawling up out of these cones to seize unwary passersby.

Lava Beds played an interesting role in the Indian wars of the late nineteenth century. The lava deposits are full of large tubes, which formed as surrounding lava cooled while lava inside continued to flow. These tubes are large enough to accommodate humans, and the Modoc Indians used them as hiding places during their war with the United States military in 1872 and 1873.

The extent of lava flows in the Northwest is staggering. They cover some 130,000 square miles of Washington, Oregon, and Idaho—an area equivalent to the whole state of Montana, or France and Great Britain combined. Hills a mile high were submerged in molten rock. This deluge of lava did not happen all at once, of course. Hundreds of individual flows, about 30 to 35 feet thick on the average, piled on top of one another to create the massive flood basalts of the Pacific Northwest.

Nothing quite so spectacular has happened in the Cascades in the last few thousand years. Newberry Volcano in Oregon and Medicine Lake Volcano in California have both erupted in the last 2,000 years (just yesterday, on the geologist's time scale), and Mount Baker in Washington State has vented steam occasionally in the last decade. The most notable eruption of recent years, however, took place in the southwestern corner of Washington, about 50 miles east of Portland, Oregon. The place: a little-known volcano named Mount St. Helens.

Mount St. Helens rose, symmetrical and white, from the timber country in the foothills of the Cascades. The mountain stood alone in the midst of the gently rolling landscape, and looked so much like a smaller version of Japan's famous Mount Fuji that Mount St. Helens was called "the Fujiyama of America." The Yakima Indians of Washington called the mountain Si Yeet, meaning "woman." Yakima legends said Si Yeet was a beautiful young woman dressed in white, who was put on earth by the Great Spirit to guard the Bridge of the Gods, on the Columbia River, and to protect the bridge from damage by the brawling male warriors Wyeast and Pahto, whom the white men called, respectively, Mount Hood and Mount Adams. There were variations on this legend. Si Yeet was called Loo-Wit in some versions. The Klickitat Indians called her Tah-one-lat-clah, meaning "fire mountain."

Whatever they called the mountain, however, the native Americans took a moral view of its eruptions. They believed an outburst from the mountain was a sign that the Great Spirit was angry. The Indians were especially fearful of Loo-Wit after the whites arrived in the Pacific Northwest, with their mines and saws and huge steaming locomotives. White men, it seemed, were bent on raping the earth in all ways possible: cutting the trees, disemboweling the mountains, fouling the air with smoke, and assaulting the ear with noise. Such meddling with nature, the Indians thought, was bound to kindle the Great Spirit's anger in the form of an eruption.

The white men reached the same conclusion, though for different reasons. Some years ago, a U.S. Geological Survey (USGS) geologist was studying the strata around 14,410-foot Mount Rainier, the giant volcano that looms over Seattle. To his surprise, he found a layer of yellow-brown volcanic ash, two feet thick, unlike any ash ejected from Mount Rainier.* Following this layer of ash back to its source, he was astonished to find it originated from the much smaller (9,677 feet) Mount St. Helens. Later it was learned that the ash from this one eruption—about 4,000 years ago—could be traced deep into the Canadian province of Alberta. Estimates showed the volcano had cast out more than half a cubic mile of solid material on this one occasion. That much ash would fill a cube 4,225 feet tall, or over three times the height of the World Trade Center in New York City. Furthermore, there was evidence of other violent eruptions in the history of Mount St. Helens. The stratigraphic record showed many thick layers of pumice and ash, as well as mudflows (caused when heat from eruptions melted snows on the summit) and avalanches of once red-hot rock. There were signs of eruptions about once per century, for the last 1,000 years. Most of the imposing peak appeared to have been built up in the last 2,500 years. So when Julius Caesar was assassinated, Mount St. Helens probably stood little taller than Wizard Island in Crater Lake. In 1980, Mount St. Helens was still a young and boisterous mountain; and as Caesar might have said, such mountains are dangerous.

That was the message of an article in *Science* magazine in 1975. Three geologists predicted Mount St. Helens would erupt again before the end of the century. And three years later, two USGS vulcanologists foretold ominously: "In the future, Mount St. Helens probably will erupt violently and intermittently just as it has in the recent geologic past, and these future eruptions will affect human life and health, property, agriculture and general economic welfare over a broad area." Just how broad an

---

* The "tephra," or solid material ejected from a volcano, can identify the source of an eruption as surely as a fingerprint marks a criminal. Every volcano puts out a characteristic kind of tephra, just as every person has a unique fingerprint. By studying the composition of the ash, a researcher may trace the contents of beds of volcanic ash back to the volcano that spewed them out.

area, and how serious the effects would be, Americans would soon find out.

Virtually all we know about the history of Mount St. Helens we have learned by studying the geology of the mountain and its environs. Native Americans seem to have kept no records of eruptions, except in stories passed down orally from one generation to another. The first eruption of Mount St. Helens to be documented by early settlers occurred in 1842, and it seems to have been a spectacular event. An eyewitness account of the eruption mentions "vast columns of lurid smoke and fire" which rose from the volcano, flattened on top after reaching a high altitude where the hot gases cooled, and then spread out parallel to the horizon and "presented the appearance of a vast table, supported by immense pillars of . . . flame and smoke." The ash cloud from this eruption reached The Dalles, Oregon, some 60 miles southeast of the mountain.

The eruption continued, on and off, for the next 15 years. The volcano puffed smoke and steam as if to remind residents of nearby Portland and other communities that the "fire mountain" was not dead, but only sleeping lightly. The last reported eruption took place in 1857. Then the volcano settled into silence for more than a century.

Meanwhile, the Washington territory grew toward statehood. The first permanent U.S. settlement, at Tumwater on Puget Sound, acquired a neighboring community two years later, in 1847. This new town was called Smithfield. Later its name was changed to Olympia (an appropriate name, in view of the Olympuslike mountains to be seen all around), and it became the territory's capital. Americans settled rapidly in western Washington, but settlement was more difficult in the eastern part of the territory, because of Indian resistance. Eventually the lure of gold in the eastern mountains brought droves of miners, however, and the Indians were overwhelmed by force of numbers.

By the late 1880s, Washington was a bustling, prosperous state with a rapidly increasing population, thanks partly to the mines in the eastern mountains and partly to the Northern Pacific Railroad, completed in 1883. Statehood was granted in 1889. Less than a decade later, a rich gold strike in the Klondike set gold fever rippling through the Western states once again, and Washington's port cities prospered from the brisk new trade with the Far North. Washington started the twentieth century as a vigorous land with tremendous natural wealth, from minerals to timber. A mild climate and a diversified economy, not to mention magnificent scenery, make Washington a pleasant habitation, and by the 1970s the state—particularly the cities on Puget Sound—had a reputation as perhaps the best place to live in America. All this time, the mountain slumbered.

The past eruptions of Mount St. Helens were a dim memory by 1980. Then, on the afternoon of March 20, a jumping needle on an instrument at the University of Washington in Seattle indicated the mountain was stirring again.

The instrument was a seismograph, a sophisticated vibration sensor designed to detect and record the jolts and rumbles made by quakes far underground. It had picked up an earth tremor centered about 20 miles north of Mount St. Helens. The earthquake was not severe. No one felt anything, and in most cases such a "mini-quake" would barely have been worth noting.

But this quake was special. It occurred near a potentially active volcano. And with the recent prophecies of eruption still fresh in mind, geologists specializing in earthquakes and volcanoes turned their attention to the mountain, to see if the quakes increased in strength and number.

They did. Three days after the first tremor was recorded, some 40 earth tremors were rocking the area around the volcano every hour. Yet geologists were not ready to predict an eruption. The quakes, they noted, were still well below the surface. But the tremors had also moved to within almost a stone's throw of the volcano, suggesting that molten rock underground was oozing toward the vents in the volcano's summit. Were the "burps" that issued from Mount St. Helens, as one geologist called them, a prelude to eruption?

The suspense was brief. A loud explosion on March 27 indicated the mountain was indeed preparing to erupt. Ash and vapor rose more than 20,000 feet into the air from the volcano's throat. When the smoke and steam cleared, a crater 250 feet wide could be seen on the summit, ringed with black ash.

Residents of the area around Mount St. Helens were nervous about the volcano in their backyard, but they were also fascinated and more than a little proud. This was, after all, the first volcanic eruption in the United States since Lassen Peak's display some 60 years earlier, and the mountain's rumbling was putting this quiet corner of Washington State on the front pages of newspapers all over North America. It was pleasant to be the center of attention for once, and the people who lived near Mount St. Helens saw the eruption as a cause for celebration.

Students at local schools wrote songs praising the eruption and calling for an outburst of lava. T-shirt printers had a field day. Shirts with mottoes like "Mount Saint Helens is hot" and "Survivor—Mount Saint Helens, 1980" appeared in Kelso and Longview, less than 50 miles from the volcano, and the Longview *Daily News* ran an editorial saying that a minor eruption "would be great."

The people of the nearby communities hoped Mount St. Helens would stage a spectacular but harmless eruption. Such outbursts of nature are always good for the tourist business. Besides, at least one well-known volcano expert had said this eruption would probably be minor, compared to what Mount St. Helens had done in the past. But there was a chance that the eruption would be worse than expected. Not even the most optimistic person could dismiss that fear entirely. And if this eruption was like the one 4,000 years earlier, then Longview and Kelso might become the modern Pompeii and Herculaneum.

Journalists covering the eruption had a more immediate worry: how to get near the volcano for close-up pictures after the Forest Service had barred them from the vicinity of the mountain. The Forest Service warned that fines and jail terms might be in store for anyone who ventured onto the volcano's slopes above the timberline. This ban puzzled some journalists, who wondered why they should be allowed to cover natural disasters such as hurricanes on the spot but be kept away from a volcano. Despite the ban, however, some correspondents did get onto the mountain. One magazine's helicopter had the good luck to develop trouble with its fuel line, and was forced to land in the forbidden area. A party from Seattle somehow reached the summit of the mountain and filmed a beer commercial on the very rim of the crater. And three free-lance journalists sneaked into the restricted area on skis, at night, to avoid detection by the Forest Service. It took them two days to reach the top. On the way, they were shaken by a series of relatively mild outbursts from the mountain, but they persevered and finally reached their goal. They found the summit covered with sandy ash and pockmarked with depressions left by boulders the volcano had expelled. But the rim looked unstable, and the journalists left quickly.

Most residents immediately around the volcano obeyed official orders to move. But one man refused and, as a result, became a local legend and something of a national hero in the weeks that followed.

His name was Harry Truman. Eighty-three years old and a widower, he owned the Mount St. Helens Lodge, on the slopes of the volcano near Spirit Lake. Truman was a wiry man with red cheeks and sparse gray hair. Though he was no relation to the former President, the two men shared many traits. Both were devoted to colorful language, both were well-read and opinionated, and both liked to raise their spirits with a small libation now and then.

Harry Truman lived in his lodge—painted a strange combination of pink and pastel green—within five miles of the volcano. Stenciled signs on the front porch said unmistakably "NO MINORS." He rented cabins, boats, and outboard motors to the tourists who came to his resort every year to look admiringly at the mountain and to fish for trout. Tourists with guidebooks learned the lake bed was lined with white pumice from an ancient eruption that had created the lake itself.

High above the dark evergreens on the south shore, the mountain loomed, huge and white. One could trace the paths of ancient glaciers by the channels they had cut on the volcano. Sometimes icy winds blew down off its sides. Other times the mountain was hidden completely in cloud. Even when weather concealed it, however, one knew the mountain was there, a colossal, silent presence that never went away.

No one knew the mountain better than Harry Truman; or so he said. He had lived at its doorstep for half a century. He had walked all the trails—sometimes in the company of Supreme Court Justice William O. Douglas, an occasional visitor to Mount St. Helens. For company at the lodge, Truman kept sixteen cats. He seemed unafraid that the mountain might erupt and kill him. Mount St. Helens, he said in one of the many interviews he gave reporters, "didn't dare" explode and hurt him and his lodge. He even had a plan to make the volcano calm down. Like President Truman, he favored dropping a bomb. One magazine quoted him as saying the best plan was to lob a bomb into the crater and "tear the thing out of there."

When he came down off the mountain to visit with schoolchildren in Brooks, Oregon, on May 14, Truman maintained he had no fear of an eruption. He admitted, however, that the earthquakes worried him, and he had moved into the basement of the lodge, where he apparently thought the danger from quakes was less. The children were delighted with him. They raised their fists in friendly salute, and dubbed him "Volcano Harry." He had four days to live.

All through late March and the month of April, while Harry Truman talked to reporters, sipped whiskey, and prepared to receive the first tourists of summer, Mount St. Helens had been building up to a massive eruption.

Just after noon on March 27, the mountain emitted a loud boom, and an ash plume rose a mile and a half over the summit. An earthquake followed an hour and a half later. Fissures in the volcano could be seen reaching three miles to the smoking peak, and there was a new crater 150 feet deep and 200 to 250 feet wide.

Two days later, early in the morning, the volcano spewed out a cloud of ash and vapor that reached 150 miles south to the town of Bend, Oregon. The earthquakes were getting ever stronger and more frequent, and on April 7 scientists noticed "harmonic tremors"—earthquakes that indicated molten rock was flowing under the mountain. Governor Dixy Lee Ray of Washington declared a state of emergency two days later, and the National Guard moved in to keep curiosity seekers from getting too close to the volcano.

The next eruption, on April 8, was the longest to that date: more than five and a half hours. The crater on the summit was now a third of a mile across and 850 feet deep. And shortly thereafter an even more ominous sign appeared: the mountain's north flank was starting to bulge outward, like a blister on an overinflated tire. The hot magma and gas inside the mountain were building up pressure and trying to escape. As the bulge grew, vulcanologists called it the single biggest potential danger posed by the eruption. Scientists feared the bulge would explode and send a fierce blast wave roaring over the north flank of the volcano.

It looked as if that fear might become reality on May 7.

After more than two weeks of mere rumbling, Mount St. Helens erupted violently. But the bulge remained intact.

There was little doubt by this time that a still larger eruption was coming. USGS scientists moved out of a camp they had set up on the slope of the volcano 4,300 feet above Harry Truman's lodge. No one, however, could tell exactly when the eruption might occur. One University of Puget Sound geologist, in a scientific echo of ancient astrological theory, thought an eruption was likely on or around May 21, because the gravitational tug from the sun and moon would reach a maximum then.

That prediction was off by only three days.

At 8:30 A.M. on May 18, 1980, the Geosynchronous Operational Environmental Satellite (GOES) was orbiting 22,000 miles above the earth. It was designed to watch the Western states for signs of pollution and other environmental problems. GOES matched the earth's speed of rotation so that the satellite remained always over a particular spot in the Pacific Ocean.

GOES had its camera trained on the Pacific Northwest. The field of view included Washington and Oregon and parts of the surrounding states and British Columbia. White wisps of cloud drifted across central and western Washington and northern Oregon.

Then, suddenly, another cloud appeared, in the southwestern corner of Washington near the Oregon border.

This cloud, darker than the others, was dome-shaped and surrounded by a low-lying white ring, like the ground-hugging cloud that ripples outward from a nuclear bomb explosion.

In fifteen minutes, the cloud was as broad as nearby Puget Sound. Silently, GOES transmitted its photos back to the National Environmental Satellite Service.

Winds were from the west in Washington that morning. As GOES watched impassively from space, the cloud swept eastward toward the Rocky Mountains. It moved rapidly. By 10:15 A.M., the cloud was halfway across the state of

Washington. By early afternoon, it had crossed the Idaho border and was also spilling southward, into northern Oregon; tendrils were reaching for Montana. The cloud lay like a great gray apostrophe over the Pacific Northwest.

Viewed from the perspective of a satellite in space, it was a small event. For persons on the ground, however, it was one of the greatest natural catastrophes in American history. Mount St. Helens had finally blown up.

At that moment, a 30-year-old geologist named David Johnston was on the very side of Mount St. Helens. Volcanoes were his specialty—a specialty that had brought him close to death in 1976, when he had been trapped on Alaska's Mount Augustine and was rescued only a few hours before the volcano erupted.

Johnston had warned reporters once about approaching the volcano closely during an eruption. Mount St. Helens, he said, was like a bomb with a lit fuse, but no one could tell how long the fuse was.

He had already been forced to move his camp on the mountainside. The original location, geologists feared, might be buried in snow and ice falls if a strong tremor shook the mountain. So Johnston and his associates moved five miles away, to a site on the north side of the mountain where danger seemed less.

On the night of May 17, he was alone at the new camp. He talked to his colleagues by radio in Vancouver, Washington, 40 miles southwest of the mountain, and said he had nothing new to report. He awoke at dawn the following morning and talked to Vancouver again, giving the same message. Had he been able to see inside Mount St. Helens, he might have had a quite different message.

Johnston's camp faced the huge bulge on the mountain's north face, where magma inside had been building up pressure for weeks. Now the bulge was more than 2,000 feet long and 500 feet high—and getting ready to explode.

Johnston called again at 8:32. He was shouting: "Vancouver! Vancouver! This is it!" Those were his last words.

But observers did not need Johnston's warning. They could see Mount St. Helens blowing up.

First a strong earth tremor shook the mountain. Other quakes followed. The ground shook steadily. Then, all at once, the bulge on the northern face of the mountain crumbled. Countless tons of rock debris slid down the mountainside, and the gas and magma inside the mountain were free at last. They burst out of the volcano with a force equivalent to a one-megaton nuclear explosion.

The blast wave from Mount St. Helens fanned out toward the north with the impact of a pile driver. The 200-mile-per-hour blast leveled trees up to 20 miles away. Some were ripped out of the ground, roots and all, and hurled through the air; all lay in the same direction, away from the volcano that felled them.

Chunks of rock and ice, some of them weighing tons, sailed out from the site of the explosion, tracing graceful parabolas in the air and coming to rest in what had been a forest. Finer material rose from the volcano in a towering black plume of smoke and ash, shot through with lightning. The plume rose to 12 miles' altitude and spread out over the landscape, blotting out the sun. Suddenly the whimsical T-shirt mottoes and the cries of "We want lava," a few weeks earlier, no longer were amusing.

The dark cloud from the mountain roared across the land toward the few observers left in the vicinity of the mountain's north flank. Many of them had just enough time to reach their cars and speed away to safety. But some died where they stood. One man, who had been photographing the eruption with a movie camera, was found afterward, covered with gray ash, his camera to his eye, seemingly still shooting even in death.

Mount St. Helens's north flank had disintegrated in the explosion, and now was falling downslope in a mammoth avalanche. The torrent of debris took a left turn and flowed into the southern fork of the Toutle River. The avalanche struck Spirit Lake at about the same time. Tons of rock and soil, plummeting downhill into the lake, displaced an equal weight of water and sent millions of cubic feet of water surging out of the lake and down the northern fork of the Toutle River. This instant flood raced down the river valley, gray and turbid from the rock and soil added to the water. On the way, the water picked up whatever else it could carry: rocks, soil, trees, cars, a railway locomotive, pieces of buildings. A railroad bridge on the river withstood the flood briefly, but the water's load of debris, like a hundred battering rams, proved too much for even the steel bridge; its girders groaned and buckled, and it was carried away by the runaway river. Meanwhile, ash was raining all around out of the sky, a gritty gray downpour of finely ground volcanic rock from the mountain's throat.

The flood poured into the town of Toutle, more than 20 miles from the peak. Anything near the river was swept away or buried in mud. Fortunately for the locals, many houses were built on higher ground, and their occupants remained alive to watch the torrent roll by, full of rock and earth and dead animals and the many artifacts of humans, from bricks to bulldozers. The temperature of the river was rising. Steam rose from the heated water and hung in the cool spring air. The heat killed all the fish in the nearby Cowlitz River, of which the Toutle is a tributary. And when the Cowlitz finally emptied into the Columbia River, navigation on the Columbia virtually ceased. Freighters were trapped miles from the sea as the material in the water settled and filled in the ship channel. For weeks after the eruption, ships would go aground in the Columbia. Sometimes a ship's master would be unaware of his vessel's grounding, so soft and fine was the ash laid down on the riverbed. The captain might think his ship was moving, then look at the shoreline and see its relative motion had stopped.

Meanwhile the ash fallout from Mount St. Helens was spreading. Carried southeast by winds in the upper atmosphere, the cloud from the volcano reached Montana on the first day. The following day, it was over South Dakota, Nebraska, and Kansas. After moving as far south as northern Mississippi and Alabama, it then curved back northward, following the jet stream, and toward the Northeastern states. Three days after the eruption, ash from Mount St. Helens was over the Virginias, the Carolinas, and all the Eastern states to the north of them. It was raining over much of the Eastern seaboard that night, and here and there one saw children putting out white plates and saucers, hoping the rain would wash a bit of the volcano out of the air for study.

For people in the East, the volcano was a curiosity and an exciting news story. Nearer the volcano, however, life was becoming a hazard.

The gray cloud from Mount St. Helens turned noon into midnight in Yakima, Washington. Ash with the consistency of confectioner's sugar piled up on the streets. In photographs it looked like New England snow blowing about. But the ash, unlike snow, would not simply melt away. It would have to be removed somehow. And how does one sweep up almost a million tons of ash?

Some could be bulldozed away, or scraped off rooftops, or shoveled out of the way. Much of it, however, had to be hosed away. This colossal bath put a severe strain upon water supplies and sewage systems in the buried towns and cities. Moscow, Idaho, used nearly its entire water supply for the cleanup, and found that only half the streets had been washed when the town reservoir was almost empty.

Some effects of the eruption were almost comical. Two newlyweds in Yakima had their picture taken wearing tuxedo and white bridal gown and veil—and surgical masks over their noses and mouths, to keep from inhaling the dust. White masks were so common on the streets of Yakima that one bank placed a sign in its front window asking customers to remove them for security reasons before coming inside.

For a few days, "ash jokes" became an art form in the Pacific Northwest. A signboard appeared beside an inn in Plummer, Idaho: "Isn't this a pain in the ash?"

Less amusing was the view from the air when rescue helicopters first flew into the area devastated by the eruption. "It looks like the bottom of an ashtray," one official commented. Indeed, it did. There was no color to be seen. Everything was gray. Near Camp Baker, on the north fork of the Toutle River, stood a battered pickup truck. In the back of the truck was the body of a young child who was probably overcome by heat and stifling gases from the volcano. The body, the truck, and the ground about them were all the same shade of gray, like a statue cast in cement.

The most frightening sight, however, was the mountain itself. Nearly 2,000 feet of the summit had vanished. Where the shining white peak of Mount St. Helens, "the Fujiyama of America," had stood only a few days before, there was a gaping crater one mile wide and two miles long, facing northward toward the vast acreage devastated by the blast. The northern rim of the crater stood 3,000 feet lower than it had before the explosion. One and a half cubic miles of solid material had been cast out from the mountain.

What had been Spirit Lake was a steaming wasteland of rock and mud and silty water. Underneath the debris was the Mount St. Helens Lodge, and with it Harry Truman and his sixteen cats. The mountain had dared to blow up on him, after all.

The Yakima Indians were philosophical about the disaster. They told reporters they had known a castastrophe was coming eventually. The white men had brought down ruin on themselves. The Indians, confident the Deity had not directed the holocaust at them, said they would "take what God gives us."

Equally philosophical was *The New York Times*. In an editorial about the eruption, the *Times* pointed out that the volcano was different from a man-made catastrophe such as the atomic bomb. The volcano was just a mindless force and product of nature, doing what the laws of geology and physics said it should. "You can't," the *Times* said, "blame a volcano."

The results of the eruption, in summary, were: at least 100 persons dead or missing; 150 square miles of timber blown down and destroyed; rivers and harbors clogged with mud carried down from the volcano; more than $100 million in damage to crops covered by ash; and $1.5 billion or more in total damage.

Mount St. Helens became the symbol of a troubled year in America. Urban riots and high inflation were bad enough; but it seemed nature itself had turned against America, sending a volcanic eruption and, later, a killing drought to add to the nation's misery. And damage from Mount St. Helens was psychological as well as physical and economic. Americans had believed themselves safe from this particular kind of natural disaster. Eruptions happened in Italy, or Japan, or Indonesia, but not in the United States. Now it was clear that volcanic violence could happen here. The eruption of Mount St. Helens was one more increment to the nation's sense of insecurity. What next?

For all its magnitude, the eruption of Mount St. Helens was only a small incident in the long and turbulent history of the Cascades. So, for that matter, were all the mountain's past eruptions, and the catastrophic birth of Crater Lake as well. And the fiery Cascades themselves are only a sideshow in a much greater production called the circum-Pacific "Ring of Fire."

II

The Misnamed Ocean

THE FIRST European sailors to round Cape Horn successfully were surprised and delighted at what they found just past the tip of South America. Before them stretched a vast expanse of calm water, blue and sparkling under the sun. This quiet scene presented such a contrast to the violent storms around the cape that the mariners named the great sea the Pacific—or peaceful—Ocean.

Few things on earth have ever been so grossly misnamed. The Pacific has its tranquil moods, to be sure, but it is also the scene of nature's most awful tempests. Sunlight beating down on the tropical Pacific creates a heat surplus in the low latitudes. That heat must be exported northward and southward to the cooler areas near the poles, and one mechanism of export is among the most terrifying and destructive phenomena on earth: the tropical cyclone, or typhoon.

The origin of the typhoon's name is a mystery. It has

been suggested that "typhoon" is a phonetic version of the sound of the storm's fierce winds. And if one is caught in one of these cyclones, the imagination can easily transform the noise of the wind into some cosmic voice booming: *Tai-fun!*

By any name, these storms would be impressive. A typhoon may be 500 miles wide and have winds near its center approaching 200 miles per hour. The typhoon feeds on heat and water vapor, two insubstantial things; but nothing about a typhoon is insubstantial. In the broad Pacific, it gathers strength over thousands of miles of ocean. The results are rains capable of washing away entire communities, and winds capable of driving a straw through the trunk of a palm tree. Anyone who takes this force of nature lightly may be likely to die. A U.S. Navy task force steaming across the Pacific during World War II was forced to pass through a typhoon. Two destroyers were capsized by the winds. Water poured down the funnels and put out the boilers. The ships sank almost immediately, with no known survivors.

Even hundreds of miles away, typhoons are a force to be feared. The winds create a giant swell that ripples out from the storm and can batter a ship to pieces. A vessel may be sailing under a clear sky, with no bad weather in sight, and find itself under assault by moving mountains of water. This is the same eerie swell Joseph Conrad describes in *Typhoon,* where the ship *Nan-Shan* plows through mountainous seas under an incongruously clear blue sky.

Ships are not the only things in danger from typhoons. Shorelines anywhere near one of these tremendous storms may be in double peril: first from the winds and rain, and second from the "storm surge," water pushed onshore by the power of the typhoon's winds. The typhoon is actually stacking up water against the coast. Superimposed on this surge, then, are the waves whipped up by the winds. This combination of surge and waves may reach miles inland in some places and demolish communities far from the normal shoreline. And even in the mountains, where waves cannot reach, the typhoon may still bring destruction. Runoff from the rains may send flash floods roaring through valleys, and the rains may soak soil to the saturation point, so that it loses coherence and peels away from the mountains in great avalanches. One moment a mountainside is there, and the next moment it is gone.

If the air can be violent in the Pacific, however, the earth can be even more so.

The Pacific Ocean is surrounded, from the Aleutian Islands in the north to Tierra del Fuego in the south, by a narrow band of intense earthquake and volcanic activity. This band is known as the Ring of Fire. It contains some 75 percent of all the active volcanoes in the world, and has been the site of the most destructive earthquakes and volcanic eruptions in history. The Ring's influence on human history and culture has been profound, and it is safe to say that our civilization would have been vastly different if the Ring of Fire had never existed.

The Ring generally follows the shoreline of the Pacific: from Tierra del Fuego at the southern tip of South America, northward past the volcanoes of the Andes and Central America, the San Andreas Fault of California, the Cascade Mountains in our Pacific Northwest, the fiery Aleutians of Alaska, westward to Russia's Kamchatka Peninsula, and southward to Japan and eastern China, the Philippines and Indonesia, New Guinea and New Zealand. The Ring makes a few detours into other seas and even into continental interiors—the quake-prone Caribbean, for example, is considered a part of the Ring of Fire, even though separated from the Pacific by Central America, and the Ring is responsible for earthquakes hundreds of miles from the ocean, in the Western United States. As a rule, however, the Ring of Fire is the Pacific's coast, and vice versa.

Because it is so huge, the Ring of Fire is hard to visualize in its entirety. From the tip of South America, around the Pacific basin to the geothermal fields of New Zealand, the Ring measures more than 30,000 miles in length. It encloses an area of some 69 million square miles—more than the area of the planet Mars and its two moons combined.

The energies stored—and occasionally released—along the Ring of Fire are also practically too great to comprehend. It is not uncommon for a volcanic explosion or an earthquake along the Ring of Fire to release as much energy as a nuclear war would. Some eruptions have cast whole cubic miles of solid material into the air.

Perhaps the most sobering statistics about the Ring of Fire, however, are its casualties. No one knows exactly how many lives have been taken in the natural violence along the Ring of Fire since civilization began, but the total probably runs well into the millions. In one earthquake alone—the famous 1976 Tangshan quake in China—650,000 persons were killed. That is roughly the population of Boston, or of Bremen or Frankfurt.

China has no monopoly on devastating "superquakes," however; they occur at other points along the Ring as well. One such earthquake, in December, 1803, destroyed the city of Edo, Japan (now called Tokyo), and killed 200,000. Tokyo was visited by another killer quake in 1857 and lost 107,000 persons. Probably one of the most destructive of all was the Tokyo-Yokohama earthquake of 1923, in which more than 140,000 persons were killed.

Here is a partial list of some of the more destructive earthquakes and volcanic eruptions that have taken place along the Ring of Fire in the past few centuries.

1556, China. We have very little historical information about this earthquake, but it is said to have shaken three provinces and taken more than 800,000 lives.

1596, Japan. An earthquake somewhere near shore created a huge seismic sea wave, or tsunami, that completely destroyed the island of Uryu-Jima and killed more than 4,000 persons. A few hundred survivors escaped to the mainland on board fishing boats.

1616, Philippines. Mayon, an 8,000-foot volcano on Luzon Island, is one of the most destructive volcanoes in the world. Situated in the densely populated Philippines, Mayon has been erupting every few years for at least the last three and a half centuries, and every major eruption has brought death and devastation to the surrounding area. In 1616, shortly after the Spanish conquest of the islands, Mayon erupted with terrific force. There were few survivors, so we have no way of knowing the full extent of the catastrophe, except that scores of villages near the volcano were overwhelmed by ashfalls and ribbons of molten rock. Another eruption, in 1766, was better documented. More than 2,000 persons died in this eruption, which sent rivers of hot mud (probably created when lakes in the caldera of the volcano spilled over) cascading down the slopes of Mayon, wiping out several towns along the way. Another 2,000 persons died in the 1814 eruption, which completely buried at least two towns under ash. Mayon was relatively benign during the first part of the nineteenth century; fewer than 2,000 persons died as a result of its eruptions. But in the last part of the century, the volcano made up for those years of comparative quiet. Major eruptions occurred in 1886, 1888, and 1897. The eruption of 1897 was the most intense. It lasted a week and sent lava streaming down the slopes toward Libon, a nearby village, burning 100 persons to death. Some 400 persons in all died in this outburst of the volcano. Other eruptions occurred in 1914 and 1928; the death tolls were low.

1737, Japan. Japan has a long coastline and thus is in particular danger from tsunamis, which often accompany earthquakes near the shore. The northern shores of Japan, and part of Russia's Kamchatka Peninsula as well, were inundated by a tsunami in 1737. This seismic wave was estimated to be more than 200 feet high just before it broke.

1757, Chile. The port city of Concepción is visited often by earthquakes, and one severe tremor in the summer of 1757 reportedly wiped out half the city with a tsunami. About 5,000 persons were killed and 10,000 injured.

1759, Mexico. Though Mexico is not as prone to volcanic eruptions as the Philippines or some other nations, volcanoes do appear in Mexico from time to time. Jorullo Volcano, named for the landowner in whose fields it rose, started forming in late September, 1759. The earth spouted ash and smoke and steam, and soon there was a 1,300-foot volcano where previously there had been only a flat plain. (Some reports say the volcano was built up entirely in one night, but such stories are probably exaggerations.) Although the estimate of deaths and damage is uncertain, 200 deaths is a figure often quoted. Jorullo erupted for four decades before subsiding.

1772, Java. The islands of the Javanese archipelago are a region of intense earthquake and volcanic activity. In 1772, inhabitants of the densely populated Papandayang area on Java were jolted by a series of earthquakes that started early in the year and culminated some weeks later in a mighty tremor that split apart a mountain and created a huge depression, 6 miles wide and 15 miles long, which swallowed an entire town and killed some 2,000 persons. Imagine Manhattan Island sinking suddenly beneath the water and you have some idea of the scale of the subsidence at Papandayang.

1793, Japan. Only a decade after an eruption at Asamayama, in which 5,000 persons were killed, the island volcano of Unsen exploded. This eruption was accompanied by a series of powerful earthquakes that destroyed the island completely. Pumice was deposited on the sea in layers thick enough to walk on. More than 50,000 persons died.

1812, Venezuela. On Thursday, March 26, a major earthquake destroyed Caracas, killing 10,000 persons there and several thousand more in surrounding communities. Many of the casualties occurred well after the quake, as water supplies contaminated by the earthquake spread disease among the survivors. This earthquake, which was seen as a sign of God's wrath toward the independence movement in Latin America, cost the revolutionary forces much of their support and made Spain's control over its colony more secure for a time.

1815, Indonesia. The date of April 5, 1815, is one of the most famous in vulcanology. That was the day Tambora erupted. Tambora (also called Tomboro or Tamboro in various histories) was a 13,000-foot volcano on the island of Sumbawa, near Java. In the week of April 5–12, Tambora spewed out 36 cubic miles of solid material, making it the single greatest eruption ever, in terms of matter ejected from the earth. Tambora will be discussed at length later in this book, because its long-term effects were even more destructive than the eruption itself, and killed hundreds of persons half a world away from Indonesia, months after the volcano ceased erupting.

1822, Java. A few years after Tambora erupted, and only a few miles away, the Javanese volcano Galung Gung roared into activity. The eruption began with colossal mudflows and ended with a massive explosion and a series of earthquakes that altered the landscape drastically. More than 100 communities were wiped out by Galung Gung's unexpected outburst; 4,000 is a conservative estimate of deaths.

1822, Chile. About a month after Galung Gung erupted, an earthquake killed 10,000 persons across the ocean in Valparaiso, Chile, on November 19, 1822. This earthquake pushed up the shoreline about four feet, according to one report, and exposed half-sunken wrecks on the sea bottom offshore.

1835, Chile. Concepción and Santiago were virtually leveled on February 20, 1835, by an earthquake that shook down Concepción's great cathedral and killed some 5,000 persons. A British naval vessel was visiting a small harbor near Concepción at the time, and the officers and men—who came from one of the least seismically active countries in the world—were stunned to see the extent of the destruction. One of the British visitors wrote later: ". . . no one dared approach the shattered ruins; and no one knew whether his dearest friends and relatives were not perishing from the want of help. . . . The thatched roofs fell over the fires, and flames burst forth in all parts. Hundreds knew themselves ruined, and few had the means of providing food for the day."

The sailors also had the terrifying experience of seeing a tsunami sweep in from the sea and inundate the villages along the shore. A few minutes after the earthquake, the wave was observed about four miles offshore, heading toward the land. As it swept along the sides of the bay where the British ship was anchored, the wave "tore up cottages and trees," and at the far end of the bay the tsunami rose into a breaker "twenty-three vertical feet above the highest spring tides." Several more waves followed, lifting boats out of the water and depositing them on land, then picking up the grounded boats again and returning them to the sea.

1854, El Salvador. Like many other Latin-American nations, El Salvador is shaken periodically by quakes along the Ring of Fire. The earthquake of 1854 shattered the capital city and killed 5,000 persons. Fortunately, there were mild "foreshocks" before the main tremor, so many people had enough warning to get out of buildings. Without that warning, the death toll would probably have been many times higher. Another earthquake, in 1878, is said to have swallowed up several entire villages.

1855, New Zealand. In January, 1855, an extremely powerful earthquake struck southeastern New Zealand, uplifting the Rimutaka mountain range by 10 feet! A block of the earth's crust 90 miles long and more than 20 miles wide was raised and tilted toward the west by this earthquake. To do this artificially would require several thousand atomic bombs.

1857, Japan. Tokyo was destroyed by earthquake and fire in March, 1857. What buildings remained standing after the earthquake were consumed in a blaze started by the numerous charcoal braziers used for cooking food. More than 100,000 persons died in the resulting "fire storm," which was similar to that created in Hiroshima by the first atomic attack, in 1945.

1868, Northern California. An earthquake hit California on the morning of October 21, 1868, causing extensive damage in San Francisco and neighboring communities. The cause was slippage along the now notorious San Andreas Fault, which, several years later, would give San Francisco its most devastating earthquake ever. Most of the deaths reported were due to the collapse of poorly designed buildings.

1877, Ecuador. One of the most beautiful volcanoes in the world, 19,500-foot Cotopaxi, looms above the highlands of northern Ecuador and has been erupting intermittently ever since the area was settled. Cotopaxi's most violent recorded eruption took place in 1877, destroying much of the mountain's summit and killing some 1,000 persons.

1883, Sunda Strait. Many geologists associate the year 1883 with a single event: the explosion of the volcanic island Krakatoa, in the waters between Java and Sumatra. The destruction of Krakatoa, one of the most famous natural disasters in history, is covered thoroughly in another chapter.

1891, Japan. More than half the area of Japan was rocked on October 28, 1891, by one of the most severe earthquakes in history. The half-minute earthquake killed some 7,000 persons and injured more than twice that many.

1899, Alaska. For reasons we will explore in the next few chapters, the Alaskan shore is an area of intense earthquake and volcanic activity. One of the most powerful quakes in Alaskan history took place in 1899, near Yakutat Bay. Quakes began to shake the area late that summer and built up to an intense tremor on September 10. A mountain range near the bay was elevated almost 50 feet by the earthquake, which was felt to the extent of 200,000 square miles, an area equivalent to the states of Wyoming and Colorado combined, or West Germany and the United Kingdom.

1902, Guatemala. On the evening of April 18, 1902, Guatemala City was destroyed and more than 12,000 of its inhabitants killed by an earthquake and a resulting fire. A highly destructive tsunami rippled out from the focus of the tremor, and the same day Guatemala's Tacaná Volcano erupted, followed in October by nearby Santa María Volcano.

1906, Taiwan. The Taiwan earthquake of 1906 destroyed more than 6,000 buildings and took 1,300 lives. While quakes are not ordinarily associated with Taiwan, it lies along the same Ring of Fire that gives so much seismic and volcanic discomfort to Japan and the Philippines.

1906, California. The San Francisco earthquake of 1906 is probably the most famous natural disaster in American history. More than four and a half square miles of the city were destroyed by a fire which followed the earthquake. The deaths were few by Chinese or Japanese standards—some 700 persons—but damage was estimated at half a billion dollars.

1906, Chile. Valparaiso was partially destroyed by an earthquake in 1906 that killed some 1,500 persons.

1907, Jamaica. Jamaica has a long history of strong earthquakes, one of which destroyed Kingston on January 14, 1907. Fourteen hundred persons perished in the earthquake and the fire which followed.

1919, Java. Volanic explosions are not unusual on Java, but the eruption of Keluit Volcano was a catastrophe even by Javanese standards. The eruption sent a lake that had collected in the caldera roaring down the volcano's sides as a torrent of hot water and mud. More than 5,000 persons were killed.

1920, China. In December, 1920, one of the most destructive earthquakes in history rocked Kansu Province in China, killing almost 200,000 persons. Huge fissures appeared in the ground, and landslides created vast deposits of soil and rock that had to be cleared away before they could trap water and cause floods.

1923, Japan. The "great Kwanto earthquake," as it is known today, struck the area of Tokyo and Yokohama on September 1, 1923, killing 143,000 persons and leaving 500,000 homeless.

1927, Japan. The Tango Peninsula borders Wakasa Bay on Japan's western shore. A quake almost equal in strength to the 1923 Kwanto quake occurred here on March 7, 1927. About 3,000 persons were killed and 14,000 buildings destroyed.

1928, Netherlands East Indies. Rokatinda, a volcano on the island of Paloeweh, started having earth tremors in July, 1928. The quakes built up to an eruption on the night of August 4. Some 100 persons were crushed to death by falling pieces of rock ejected from the volcano, and landslides killed 128 more.

1931, Java. Long-suffering Java was buried by ash over half its area by the eruption of Merapi Volcano in 1931. The eruption lasted three weeks and killed more than 1,000 persons.

1933, California. The Long Beach earthquake of 1933 took more than 100 lives and did an estimated $50 million in damage. The earthquake also produced an interesting story about Albert Einstein. The physicist was visiting the University of California at Long Beach and was talking with one of the school's geologists. The two men walked around the campus while Einstein listened to his companion talk about seismology, the science of earthquakes. Suddenly they looked up to see students and faculty dashing out of the buildings around them. The two scientists had been so engrossed in discussing earthquakes that they had not noticed the Long Beach quake taking place where they stood!

1939, Chile. A three-minute earthquake, starting just before noon on January 24, 1939, once more wrecked the city of Concepción and damaged nearby towns severely. Fifty thousand persons died, and almost three-quarters of a million were left without shelter.

1946, Japan. An undersea earthquake shook the island of Honshu and neighboring islands in the small hours of December 21, 1946, leveling buildings and sending men, women, and children rushing out into the streets in freezing weather. The quake caused huge tsunamis, which swept across the Inland Sea, destroyed several thousand ships, and wiped 50 coastal towns off the map. Half a million persons were homeless after the sea retreated, and 2,000 had been drowned.

1949, Ecuador. Early in the morning of August 5, 1949, the central highlands of Ecuador shook under the force of an earthquake that killed 6,000 persons and injured 20,000. This earthquake was the most destructive to hit Ecuador since the Spanish conquest more than 400 years ago.

1952, Japan. Early in the autumn of 1952, fishermen at sea noticed the ocean bubbling and steaming at a spot about 300 miles off the southern coast of Japan. Later examination revealed a small island was at the site. About 100 feet high, the tiny island—actually the emerging summit of a submarine volcano—was erupting several times a minute, ejecting red-hot blobs of lava (called "bombs" by volcano experts) along with ash and steam.

The island played peekaboo with its discoverers, first building itself up and then being torn back down to sea level either by the eruptions themselves or by wave action.

Geologists were eager to see what the volcano would do, and so two ships were sent to the spot to keep an eye on the eruption. The volcano was named Myozin-syo, and was located in the Bonin Islands, an island chain stretching almost due south from the vicinity of Tokyo.

When the two ships arrived on the scene, a spectacular eruption was under way. Scientists watched from what they thought was a safe distance. One of the ships, *Kaiyo-Maru,* however, strayed over the top of a vent and was blown up when the volcano erupted shortly after noon on September 24. There were no survivors.

1960, Hawaii. An earthquake in Chile in May, 1960, created a tsunami that moved across the Pacific at the speed of a jetliner and struck Hawaii. Hilo City was devastated by a tsunami for the second time in less than two decades. This wave was not quite as destructive as that of 1946; the 1960 tsunami killed about 60 persons in Hilo City. The wave continued on to the far side of the Pacific, however, and killed a total of 438 persons in Japan and the Philippines.

1964, Alaska. The most powerful and destructive earthquake in the history of the United States occurred on Good Friday, March 27, 1964, along the shores of the Gulf of Alaska near Anchorage. Damage was estimated finally at half a billion dollars. One hundred and eighteen persons were killed in the earthquake and in the tsunami which later struck shores all along southern Alaska. The seismic sea wave from the quake damaged coastal towns as far as away as Oregon and California.

1968, Chile. Almost 500 persons were killed in a series of quakes that hit central Chile in March, 1968. Most of the deaths resulted not from the earthquake itself, but rather from the failure of dams that burst, released their stored water, and buried several villages in mud.

1971, California. The San Fernando earthquake, near Los Angeles, killed 60 persons and did almost three-quarters of a billion dollars in damage. Freeway overpasses collapsed, and supposedly quake-resistant buildings fell apart like cardboard constructions. Had the quake lasted a little longer, a dam near Los Angeles might have given way and flooded the valley downstream.

This is, remember, only a *partial* list of the major quakes, eruptions, and tsunamis that have taken place along the Ring of Fire in the last few hundred years. Rarely does a year go by without some natural catastrophe occurring along the Ring. The Pacific shore is shaken and blasted almost continually by the movements of tortured ground and ascending magma.

The Ring is so huge, however, that it was many years before geologists had it mapped out, and still longer before they had an adequate explanation for its nature and behavior. The scientific study of the Ring began in China, where an ingenious machine and a lucky accident combined to make an obscure scholar the first paid seismologist in history—and set geologists on a long trail of inquiry that would eventually yield rich rewards.

III

Frogs and Dragons

THE CHINESE have always had trouble with their borders. "Barbarian" armies have tried to invade China frequently over the centuries, and some of the more despotic Chinese emperors knew they could not always count on their subjects in the provinces to resist invaders. So the emperors built a wall to keep the invaders out. This approach, which General George Patton once called "a monument to human stupidity," was ineffective. The Great Wall shut out potential invaders only so long as the guards who manned the gates were loyal to the emperor; and invaders soon discovered that the guards could be persuaded, for the right price, to forget about loyalty and open the gates so that an army could pass through.

But invasions were not the only troubles China faced along its borders. China is bounded on two sides by belts of strong earthquake activity. In the south is the Himalayan belt, where two colliding chunks of crust are pushing against each other, raising up tall mountains and generating earthquakes at the same time. And along the eastern side of China is the Ring of Fire, with its frequent destructive tremors.

As a result, the history of China sometimes may seem little more than a long list of earthquake disasters. Early records of Chinese earthquakes tend to be short on detail, but tremors with fatalities in the thousands or tens of thousands are common events in Chinese history. As already noted, the earthquake in 1976 killed more than half a million persons, and there are reports of earlier earthquakes taking more lives than that in densely populated areas.

The Chinese, then, have always had an incentive to learn about earthquakes—what causes them, how to avoid damage from them, and so forth. The problem was, the Chinese had a philosophy of nature that discouraged them from making what Western peoples would consider scientific experiments with quakes.

According to Chinese thought, everything in nature was possessed of a spirit *(shen)*, which was basically beyond human understanding and not to be meddled with. So the Chinese seldom thought to look at earthquakes in the rational, hardheaded Western way, and try to figure out what made them occur. Quakes were quakes; they just occurred; and if you were unlucky enough to get caught in one—well, that was just too bad. Better luck in the next world.

There were exceptions to this rule, however, and among them was a scholar named Choko. We know very little about him except that he was interested in earthquakes; and his name has come down to us only because of a device he put together, in the second century A.D., to detect earth tremors.

Choko assumed that waves rippled out through the earth from the source of an earthquake, just as waves do from a spot where a stone is tossed into a pond. Therefore an earthquake wave had a specific direction; and if one could determine that direction, then it would be possible to figure out where an earthquake had occurred. With two or more of these earthquake "direction finders," one could tell the source of a quake by triangulation.

Choko's device looked more like a hallucination than a scientific instrument. It comprised a round copper drum about eight feet wide. At eight points around the drum's circumference, equidistant from one another, were dragon heads. Each dragon held in its mouth a ball. Directly underneath each dragon was a frog, head turned upward and mouth wide open to catch the ball if the dragon should drop it.

This bizarre contraption worked as follows. According to Choko's theory of earthquake waves, the device should rock back and forth in a certain direction as an earthquake wave passed. So one could, in theory, tell the direction of the wave—and the earthquake that generated it—by checking the dragons to see which of them had dropped its ball into the waiting mouth of the frog below.

Choko's friends and neighbors are said to have taken a dim view of his invention. Their skepticism only increased when Choko checked the machine one day and found one of the dragons had released its ball, even though no one had felt an earthquake in that area.

The scholar's reputation was saved, however, by news that arrived several days later. There had indeed been an earthquake, several hundred miles away, on the very day Choko's device detected it, and in the direction his machine indicated. Suddenly, Choko acquired the reputation of a genius, even though his success was due partly to pure chance; it was only a lucky accident that his device indicated the correct direction, because it was not nearly sensitive enough for such a determination. The Chinese government named Choko the world's first official seismologist, and today he is widely recognized as the founder of scientific earthquake study.

Frogs and Dragons

Seismology had been notably unscientific before Choko's day. Earthquakes were a total mystery, and some bizarre theories were invented to explain them. Many of these theories were put forth by Europeans.

The ancient Greeks invoked the four classical elements —earth, air, fire, and water—to explain earthquakes. Thales, who lived around 600 B.C., thought quakes were vibrations from mighty waves striking the shore. The problem with this explanation was that quakes sometimes occur far inland.

What about fire? Anaxagoras (500–428 B.C.) believed that fires deep inside the earth produced vast clouds of super-hot vapor that shook the ground as they rose up to the surface. (Stated in slightly different terms, this theory is remarkably similar to one put forth recently by Dr. Thomas Gold of Cornell University, who suggests earthquakes may be caused, in part, by gases escaping from the earth's interior. Gold's idea is discussed in detail in a later chapter.)

Another writer, Anaximenes, came very close to the modern view of why earthquakes occur. He suggested the earth itself caused quakes as chunks of rock underground struck each other violently. Anaximenes seemed to think these impacts were from large rocks falling from the roofs of subterranean caverns, however, and that view was untenable.

A windy theory of earthquake generation was offered by the philosopher Archelaus. He thought winds were sucked down into the earth's interior somehow, compressed by the weight of overlying rocks, and then expelled with terrific force, creating earthquakes where the winds spewed out of the ground. This phenomenon was blamed for the volcanic eruption at Pompeii in A.D. 79, which was accompanied by an earthquake that reportedly killed the naturalist Pliny the Elder. (It probably did kill Pliny, but not directly. He was grossly overweight and is said to have died of a heart attack.)

Across the continent in Siberia, peasants had an interesting explanation for the quakes that shook eastern Siberia occasionally. They blamed the *mamut,* a mysterious creature that was said to spend its long life tunneling underground like some giant mole. Some storytellers said the *mamut* traveled in herds, and the vibration of their passage underground caused earthquakes. The *mamut* was either a shy, otherwise harmless animal or a beast that devoured whole villages by tunneling under them and opening its huge jaws; the *mamut*'s reputation depended on who was recounting the legend. If the *mamut* saw sunlight, it turned to stone.

As it happened, there was more than a little truth in the *mamut* legend. During the last ice age, Siberia was inhabited by mammoths, shaggy cousins of the modern elephant. Occasionally a mammoth would fall into a crevasse in a glacier and die there, unable to climb out. The creature was buried by snow and ice and then frozen. Thousands of years later, when the surrounding ice melted, the mammoth's body was exposed. This, thought the frightened peasants who saw the mammoth's body sticking out of the ground, must be the monster that makes the ground shake!

The legend of the *mamut* seems rational indeed compared to some ideas that arose in Europe during the Christian Era. Sexual immorality was seen as a contributing factor to earthquakes. This idea seems to have come from a study of the Sodom and Gomorrah episode in the Bible—even though those cities of sin were destroyed by fire from the skies, not earthquakes. The fanatical Emperor Justinian the Great, monarch of the eastern Roman Empire, thought homosexuality brought God's wrath down on a land in the form of earth tremors, and this strange notion. is far from dead, even today. In 1979, a gay-rights bill was being considered at a civic meeting in San Francisco when a mild earthquake shook the building. Fundamentalist Christians, who opposed the measure, were delighted with the timing of the tremor, and claimed the earthquake showed "God is on our side."*

Seismology began to make serious progress in the eighteenth century. Much of this progress consisted of separating empirical facts from mere legends and superstitions; and the sorting process could be difficult. But gradually a large body of reliable information about earthquakes—their characteristics, distribution, and so forth—was assembled, and by the mid-nineteenth century the time was right for someone to become the first modern seismologist.

The person who did so was not a geologist but, rather, an engineer. His name was Robert Mallet, and he was born in the virtually quake-free country of Ireland, in 1810. Mallet, a highly talented and successful engineer, specialized in heating and ventilation systems. He also designed bridges and railway stations. His hobby was earthquakes, and in 1857 he had a glorious opportunity to study one.

That year, Naples was struck by a destructive earthquake. (Naples is, of course, no stranger to seismic and volcanic violence; the eruption of nearby Vesuvius in A.D. 79 buried the towns of Pompeii and Herculaneum, killing several thousand persons and providing a playground for archaeologists eighteen centuries later.) Mallet investigated the quake as thoroughly as the methods available to him would allow. His report, *The Great Neopolitan Earthquake of 1857,* is still considered a classic of research and scientific reporting. Mallet went on to collect all the information he could about earthquakes all over the globe, and at last he sat down to draw a world map of earthquake distribution.

Mallet shaded the parts of the map where quakes oc-

* Earthquakes are a favorite topic of conversation among America's fundamentalists, who interpret the Bible to say that Christ's return will be preceded by devastating tremors around the world. Other alleged signs of his imminent return include television, Women's Liberation, artificial birth control, unisex haircuts, and the formation of the European Economic Community.

curred most frequently. Several parts of Europe were dark, notably Italy. A smudge along the northern border of India showed where the formation of the Himalayas was being accompanied by earth tremors; and geologically unstable Iceland appeared as little more than a dark blot.

The most notable feature of Mallet's earthquake map, however, was a dark band of intense seismic activity running around the rim of the Pacific Ocean: the Ring of Fire.

Mallet was one of the first researchers to see the Ring as part of a global network of high-intensity quake zones. If he had been more of a theorist, he might have come up with a coherent and comprehensive explanation for the distribution of those zones. But Mallet was not much of an "ideas man," and that explanation had to wait until the first part of the next century, when another amateur geologist—a weatherman this time—would offer a revolutionary theory of geology that would account for the pattern of smudges on Mallet's map, and turn the earth sciences upside down in the process.

While Mallet searched the libraries of Europe for earthquake data and puttered with his maps and reports, a boy in Lancashire, England, was planning a career as an engineer. The boy was John Milne. Unlike Mallet, who spent most of his life in Britain and seemed disinclined to travel except to the sites of truly spectacular quakes, Milne loved to travel and satisfied his wanderlust in 1875 by voyaging to Japan to accept a teaching post at the Imperial College of Science and Engineering in Tokyo.

A few days after his arrival, Tokyo was shaken by an earthquake. Before then, quakes had been a matter of academic interest to Milne. Now they seemed a very practical concern indeed, and Milne's training as a mining engineer made him well suited to studying earthquakes. He was in the ideal spot for it: Japan is shaken by several hundred earthquakes every day, most of them too weak to be felt but strong enough to register on sensitive recording instruments.

In Milne's time, however, such instruments did not exist. There were a few crude devices for detecting earthquakes, but most of them told the observer little more than what he or she could tell already: that the ground was shaking. So Milne went to work on a new and sensitive machine for detecting and recording quakes. We call it the seismometer.

Milne's early seismometer was crude by modern standards. It used a pendulum to detect the motions of a quake. The vibrations set the pendulum swinging, and the pendulum's motions could be recorded. Modern seismometers are far more sophisticated and use a weight suspended by a spring, rather than a dangling pendulum, to pick up quake vibrations and transfer them to paper. But Milne's machine was a quantum leap forward in the study of earthquakes, and the grateful Japanese government awarded him the Order of the Rising Sun, an unprecedented honor for a foreign barbarian. And he deserved some kind of official recognition, for Milne, with his seismometer and his devotion to the scientific study of earthquakes, had brought seismological research—"hard," quantitative study of earthquakes and what causes them—back to the place where it had originated centuries before: the Oriental segment of the Ring of Fire.

Milne returned to Britain after his stay in Japan, and concentrated on improving his instruments. Meanwhile, his colleagues in Japan were busy exploring the mysteries of earthquakes. Seismology has thrived in Japan ever since, and now the Japanese are among the world's leaders in the study of earth tremors.

The Japanese have explored many avenues of seismological research, often with surprising results. Japanese researchers, for example, were among the first to document the relationship between earthquakes and magnetism. For some reason not fully understood, earthquakes affect magnetic fields and can make magnets lose or regain their magnetism. During an earthquake in the mid-1800s, nails were seen to fall off of magnets to which they had been firmly attracted only a moment before. Strange fluctuations in the earth's magnetic field were seen before and during the great earthquake of 1923. Just how magnetism is connected with earthquakes remains a mystery, but Japanese geologists are working on it.

The Japanese have also made extensive studies of the other geological phenomenon that ravages their land: volcanoes. There is no lack of volcanoes to study in the Japanese archipelago. Much of the land of present-day Japan was created during an episode of intense volcanic activity during the Cenozoic,* when volcanoes were clustered in southern Japan almost as tightly as apples in a crate. Mount Fuji, the beautiful Fujiyama that has become a symbol of Japan, is a product of this Cenozoic vulcanism. So are the less spectacular Bonin Islands, a chain of nearly submerged volcanoes running south from the vicinity of Fiji, into the Pacific Ocean. The land under Japan is hot and churning with volcanic energy, and so it provided an excellent natural laboratory for the study of the Ring of Fire. Japanese geologists were among the first to establish, among other things, that earthquakes and volcanic eruptions are definitely related to each other, and that "harmonic tremors" may signal the imminent eruption of a volcano. During the nineteenth and twentieth centuries, Japanese geologists have had an outstanding record of accomplishment in the study of the Ring and all its destructive natural phenomena.

But until the early twentieth century, what science lacked was a single, unifying theory that would explain

* The Cenozoic is one of the three great divisions of geological time, based on the fossil content of rocks. First came the Paleozoic, shortly after life appeared on the planet. Next came the Mesozoic, the so-called age of dinosaurs; and finally the Cenozoic, our "age of mammals." The Cenozoic is usually said to have started with the extinction of the dinosaurs about 60 million years ago. Our species, *Homo sapiens,* is an extreme latecomer on this time scale; the big-brained modern humans, who took the world away from their hominid competitors such as the Neanderthals, appeared less than a million years ago.

the Ring's existence and why it followed the course it did around the Pacific basin. Why was this small segment of the earth's surface—a fraction of 1 percent, altogether—the site of more than half the world's active volcanoes and many of its most devastating quakes? And why was all this activity concentrated on the shores of one particular ocean, while other oceans, such as the Atlantic, had much quieter coastlines?

The answer had to wait for a man whose contempt for tradition was equaled by his imagination—though, unfortunately, not always by his common sense. His career is a good illustration of how science progresses, and sometimes fails to progress, through a combination of vision, accident, ignorance, experiment, and mudslinging.

IV

The Dance of the Continents

H A L F   A   W O R L D away from the Pacific Ocean lies Greenland, the world's largest island and one of the places least hospitable to life on earth. A Danish possession, Greenland is a reminder of what northern Europe and America were like during the last ice age. The land lies buried under a blanket of ice two miles thick. Only 15 percent of Greenland is unglaciated. If one could lift up the ice and see the land underneath, it would look like a vast "C" of mountain ranges, surrounding a central depression the size of Florida. The ice on Greenland is so heavy that it has actually pressed the crust in the island's heart down below sea level.

That ice cools the air above it so intensely that the cold, dense air flows downslope under its own weight, creating gale-force winds along the way. Exposed flesh will freeze solid within seconds on the Greenland icecap during the winter. Nothing can survive here for long without artificial help. Even bacteria go dormant in the natural deep-freeze that is Greenland. This is the hell of ancient Norse legends, a land of eternal and unrelenting cold, where no warmth can last for long.

Somewhere on the Greenland icecap lies buried the body of a 50-year-old man. He is tall and muscular, with light hair and a thin slash of a mouth. He wears full arctic clothing and is shrouded in sleeping-bag covers. Since nothing decays in the arctic cold, the man probably looks just as he did on the day he died, in 1930, from heart failure while on a scientific expedition.

His name is Alfred Wegener. Once derided as a crank and a dilettante, he is now revered as one of the greatest figures in the history of science. The trail which brought him to death on the icecap was long and exhausting, made him one of the most controversial scientists in Europe, and led him to solve the mystery of the Ring of Fire.

Alfred Wegener was born in Berlin in 1880. His father was an evangelical clergyman. Preachers' children were expected to be brighter than average, and Alfred appears to have lived up to expectations. He did well enough in secondary school to get himself admitted to Berlin University, and after his undergraduate years there he went on to do graduate work in astronomy.

Wegener's contributions to astronomy were minor. As part of the work for his Ph.D., he recast an ancient set of astronomical tables into decimal notation for the convenience of modern astronomers. He also wrote a highly praised article about his studies in the history of astronomy. But Wegener was too restless to confine himself to one particular science, and while at the university he became interested in the science of upper-atmosphere meteorology, then in its infancy.

The air above the troposphere—the layer where most weather occurs—was still largely a mystery when Wegener was in school. The stratosphere, the next layer above the troposphere, had been discovered only a few years before.

There were countless mysteries to explore in the upper air, and Wegener threw himself into this study with the enthusiasm that would mark his undertakings all through his life.

Rather than sit on the ground and study the upper air from a distance, Wegener took to the air himself. In the company of his brother Kurt, he set a world record for long-distance balloon flight in 1902: fifty-six consecutive hours in the air.

Photos taken of Wegener at this time of his life show a lean young man with cropped hair and a sharp nose. In one picture, he smokes a pipe and looks like a Teutonic Sherlock Holmes. He has close-set eyes and seems to be trying to stare down the camera. He looks athletic and was, in fact, a master of Alpine skiing. He liked winter sports and had plenty of opportunity to practice them. Wegener had physical energy and intellectual curiosity in abundance, and that combination made him one of the most dynamic and controversial figures in European science.

He was unconventional. He dismissed mathematics, the "queen of sciences," as so much arcane gibberish, a kind of cabalistic padding scientists used whenever they wanted to "fill out a few pages with formulae." Yet he knew mathematical physics inside out, and wrote a book called *Thermodynamics of the Atmosphere*.

Perhaps the strangest thing about Wegener, however, was his passion for Greenland.

While still in his teens, Wegener developed an interest in the huge bleak island. The interest became fascination, and then an obsession. He studied everything he could find about Greenland—the land, its people, its climate—and finally won his heart's desire when he was allowed to travel with a Danish meteorological expedition to Greenland in 1906. He stayed there for two years.

After he returned to Germany, Wegener joined the faculty of Marburg University. He taught meteorology and is said to have been friendly and popular with his students, in sharp contrast to the aloof Herr Doktor Professors who were typical of his day. But Wegener's heart was still in Greenland, and he longed to return there.

About this time, Wegener turned his attention from the air to the solid earth. Long interested in geology, Wegener began to think that the supposedly fixed continents might really be mobile, sliding about the surface of the globe and constantly rearranging themselves. This idea would one day turn the obscure weatherman into one of the most important figures in the history of geology.

There are some romantic stories about how Wegener came by the hypothesis of moving continents. According to one account, he was gazing at a map of the world when he noticed that the eastern coast of South America was almost a jigsaw-puzzle match for the western coast of Africa. Then the vision of drifting continents supposedly sprang fully formed into his mind. Another story has Wegener sitting atop a mountain in Greenland, looking out over a fjord where ice floes are drifting and bumping into one another. All at once, inspiration strikes him. Eureka! The ice floes are drifting like the continents!

Appealing as these stories are, they are, like the story of Newton and the apple, probably just colorful fiction. Wegener actually seems to have thought of his drifting-continents hypothesis after reading a paper by a British colliery manager named Pickering, in 1909. Pickering was trying to work out a mechanism to account for the birth of the Pacific Ocean. He suggested the Pacific basin was a huge scar left behind when the moon was ripped away from the earth ages ago. What interested Wegener was Pickering's observation that the continents on either side of the Atlantic seemed to fit together neatly at the edge of the continental shelf. Wegener used this idea in his first paper on the subject of "continental displacements." His ideas about the behavior of the earth's crust during these "displacements" were still vague, however, and he might have forgotten about them and gone back to meteorology had it not been for the work of an American 20 years his senior.

The American was Frank Bursley Taylor. Much of Taylor's life was a study in creative idleness. Born in 1860 in Indiana, he had a wealthy and indulgent father who sent him to Harvard. The younger Taylor left school, ostensibly for reasons of health, after two years, and spent the next two decades traveling around the Great Lakes country, studying the landforms left behind by glaciers during the ice ages. He was accompanied by his personal physician, who left him in 1899 when Taylor married. In 1900, at the age of 40, Taylor joined the U.S. Geological Survey—his first paying job.

Taylor's father seemed convinced his son was a genius, and he talked him into writing a book about his "great ideas." Five years later, in 1908, Taylor produced a paper with the dry title "The Bearing of the Tertiary Mountain Belt Upon the Earth's Plan." The paper presented Taylor's idea that the continents were moving with respect to one another. He used the voluminous data collected by an Austrian geologist, Eduard Suess, to reconstruct the original landmass that, according to Taylor, had split apart long ago and formed the Atlantic Ocean.

Wegener read Taylor's writings on the subject of shifting continents, borrowed some of Taylor's ideas, and applied Taylor's theory to his beloved Greenland. Using inaccurate measurements, Wegener thought Greenland was sliding westward several kilometers a year. On that point it turned out that he was mistaken, but gradually his theory was coming together.

Early in 1912, Wegener's theory was published in the *Marburg University Science Journal*. His paper was called "The Horizontal Displacement of the Continents." Wegener might have proceeded to expand the article into a book at once, but war and marriage were imminent distractions.

In 1913, just before war broke out in Europe, Wegener

married Else Köppen. It was the perfect marriage for a meteorologist, for Else was the daughter of Vladimir Köppen, "grand old man" of meteorology and the inventor of a climate classification system still widely used. Köppen liked his energetic young son-in-law and had corresponded with him long before Wegener's marriage to Else. After Wegener returned home from the war—in which he served as an officer and was wounded twice—he succeeded Köppen as head of the Meteorological Research Department of the Marine Observatory in Hamburg. Wegener also started assembling his earlier writings on the subject of continental drift into a book called *The Origins of Continents and Oceans.*

The book contained very few original ideas. Most of Wegener's thoughts about drifting continents were borrowed from Taylor and other geologists. But Wegener had a special talent for teaching, and he put those ideas together in such a way that they became fascinating reading.

Wegener's theory of continental drift can be summed up in a few basic points:

· The continents are not fixed in position, but rather are floating, like icebergs in water, atop denser rocks just under the crust. (The light crustal rock was called the "sial," short for silicon and aluminum, two of its principal components. The denser rock underneath, on which the crust rides, was called the "sima," silicon and magnesium.)

· Originally the continents were all grouped together into a single giant landmass, which Wegener called Pangaea, meaning "all land." This supercontinent broke up ages ago, and its fragments drifted to their present positions and became the continents we know today.

· The energy for the continents' movement came from two sources. One was tidal activity. Wegener believed that tides in the earth caused a net westward motion of the landmasses. Also (and here Wegener was borrowing from Taylor again), the continents were supposedly "running away" from the poles toward the equator as centrifugal force from the earth's rotation drew the drifting land-masses toward the bulge at the planet's midriff.

· Wegener rejected the traditional view of what caused large-scale changes in the earth's surface features. There seemed reason to think, at least before Wegener came along, that the earth was shrinking slowly, rather like an apple drying up, as volatile material escaped from the planet's interior and the inner rock cooled. This shriveling was supposed to be the force that pushed up mountain ranges and caused other major geological events. There was also an opposing school of thought that said the planet was expanding, like a balloon being inflated, and that great fault lines visible in the crust were "stretch marks," one might say, on an ever-fattening world. Wegener, how-ever, saw no reason to think the planet's size was changing.

· Wegener suggested that some old riddles of geology, such as fossils of the same species found at widely separated sites (say, the same kind of dinosaur fossils an ocean apart) might be explained by the breakup of an original super-continent.

· Mountain ranges, Wegener claimed, were raised where the crust "crumpled up" at the collision of two or more crustal plates. The Rockies were a good example. So were the Himalayas and the Andes.

What Wegener said was of course more complicated than this brief summary, but these were the basics of his theory. The book and his ideas were received coolly. British geo-physicist Sir Harold Jeffreys was perhaps Wegener's harsh-est critic. He claimed the rocks of the earth would never flow and deform as Wegener's theory required. Jeffreys was wrong. Several years earlier, Canadian researchers had put rock samples into special testing devices and discovered the rocks were not as rigid as previously thought, but could be "squeezed"—that is, "deformed plastically"—in a way con-sistent with the requirements of Wegener's continental drift theory. But Jeffreys was a powerful voice among geologists, and his criticisms put Wegener's work in a bad light.

Also, Wegener was working at a disadvantage. He was not a professional geologist. He was a meteorologist, and geologists took a dim view of a weatherman trying to tell them that their ideas about the earth were wrong. (The borders between the sciences were much more sharply defined and jealously guarded in the early twentieth century than they are today. Nowadays it is not unusual for a physicist to make outstanding discoveries in biology, or for a biologist to team up with computer scientists in research on cybernetics; but in the early 1900s such collaborations were exceptional.)

Much of Wegener's information, on which he based his vision of Pangaea splitting apart and opening up the Atlantic Ocean, turned out to be wrong. His early estimates of Greenland's rate of drift were several orders of magnitude too high. Rather than sliding along at a rate of several kilometers per year, Greenland's annual drift was closer to several centimeters. Greenland appeared to be practically standing still, and suddenly Wegener's estimate of the time since the Atlantic opened—just a few thousand years—looked absurd.

Wegener made an abominable mess of his time scales. He claimed the opening of the Atlantic, some 100,000 years ago, was the same event that pushed up the Rocky Mountains 100 *million* years ago. He was off by a factor of 1,000. His arithmetical errors damaged his credibility greatly, because a careful scientist at least makes sure his figures add up correctly.

Finally, Wegener sometimes tended to oversimplify his theory. He said, for example, that because of the way Pangaea split down the middle, we should be able to match geological features on one side of the Atlantic with features on the other side. He used the analogy of a torn newspaper. By matching up the words on one side of the tear with those on the other side, we can see, said Wegener, that the page was once a single whole. This was a slippery analogy, since the geological record is not nearly as easy to read as a newspaper. One paleontologist happened to find half of an adult trilobite on one side of the Atlantic, and a matching half on the other side. The halves, by chance, fitted together perfectly. The paleontologist was amused, and claimed jokingly that the fossil supported Wegener's theory. The trilobite had been torn in half by the breakup of Wegener's supercontinent!

Ideally, scientists should carry out debate in a polite and reasonable spirit. But scientists sometimes fall short of that ideal, and in this controversy they fell far short indeed. The sarcasm of his colleagues distressed Wegener, even though he had deliberately made himself something of a lightning rod by publishing such an unconventional theory; and he was probably relieved when, in 1928, he was able to start planning another trip to his beloved Greenland. He had no way of knowing that the expedition would be his last. Apparently the ugly controversy over his theories was exhausting him; pictures of Wegener taken about this time show a tired-looking man, the corners of his mouth turned down in a way that suggests great bitterness and fatigue.

Wegener hoped to make longitude measurements in Greenland that might vindicate his theory of continental drift. Perhaps his opponents' evidence was incorrect after all, and Greenland was drifting at a rate fast enough to acquit his theories. The principal business of the expedition, however, was to make weather observations and measure the thickness of the ice sheet, using new echo-sounding techniques similar to sonar.

Preparations were finished early in 1930, and the expedition set out for Greenland. For Wegener, approaching 50, it was an extremely strenuous enterprise. Temperatures on the icecap fell to 80 degrees below zero Fahrenheit, and working under such conditions put tremendous strain on the human body. There were also supply problems. A manned outpost in the heart of the icecap needed more provisions than were on hand to last the winter of 1930–31; and on the morning of his 50th birthday, November 1, 1930, after celebrating by eating an apple, Wegener started out from the station toward the expedition's camp on the west coast of Greenland, 250 miles away. He was accompanied by an Eskimo guide and traveled with two sledges and seventeen dogs. Neither Wegener nor the guide ever arrived.

About six months later, Wegener's grave was discovered midway between the coastal station and the inland outpost. He had died of a heart attack. The guide had buried him and marked the spot with Wegener's skis. Then the Eskimo took Wegener's pipe and diary and continued on his way toward the coast. Presumably he died en route and was buried by drifting snow, because his body was never found.

Rumors of murder circulated briefly in Germany after Wegener died. After all, he was a controversial figure in the scientific world, and might conceivably have been a target for homicide. The rumors soon ceased, however, and Wegener was ruled to have died of natural causes. He suddenly became a hero in his homeland, and it is tragic that he had to die before he could see his theories of "continental displacement" vindicated.

That vindication was more than twenty years in coming. Continental drift was seen as a quixotic notion during the 1930s and 1940s, and it would have been difficult for a geologist to get an impartial hearing on Wegener's ideas. But science is such that any valid theory or hypothesis will eventually be proved true by the facts. That process may take a long time, and in Wegener's case it did. As geologists gathered more and more information about the earth's surface and interior, the world began to look more and more like Wegener's model of it. The basically correct but clumsy model of drifting continents that Wegener presented in his book was modified by later geologists, notably the legendary Harry Hess of Princeton.

Hess, a geologist with a taste for unconventional theories, saw as early as World War II, when he served as a naval officer, that many unusual features of the earth's surface might be explained either by Wegener's theory or by some revised version of it. There was, for example, a chain of mountains running down the length of the Atlantic Ocean, midway between the New World and the Old. This submerged mountain range showed up for the first time on sonar charts of the Atlantic. Iceland and the Azores, it turned out, were just two places where the range broke surface.

Looking at this newly discovered mountain chain, Hess came up with the theory of "sea-floor spreading." Molten rock, he suggested, might be oozing out along this ridge and forming new crust, which was then pushed out to either side as more magma welled up from underground.

This theory, if proved correct, would supply the driving force for moving the continents—a much more tangible force than Wegener's ideas about tidal motions and "flight from the poles." Hess's theory was confirmed a few years later by researchers studying the Mid-Atlantic Ridge, as the undersea mountains were called. Suddenly the last big piece of Wegener's theory fell into place, and he was vindicated after more than a quarter-century of ridicule.

New techniques for mapping the sea bottom were developed in the 1950s and 1960s, and soon it was clear that a mid-Atlantic mountain range was not the only surprise the ocean floor had to offer. That range of mountains extended all the way around the globe. The mountains marked a zone of sea-floor spreading which, somewhat like the seams on a baseball or soccer ball, divided up the crust of the earth into vast pieces or "crustal plates." Where these plates collided, big things happened: earthquakes, volcanoes, and "orogenesis," the geologist's expression for mountain building. There were also deep trenches in the sea floor, in places such as the Japanese and Alaskan coastal waters, where ocean crust was apparently being sucked down into the mantle, the rock layer under the earth's crust. These miles-deep trenches were called "subduction zones," and marked the sites where crustal rock was being destroyed.

In short, the crust was behaving very much as Alfred Wegener, in his books and articles, had said it would. There were discrepancies between Wegener's theory and the observed events, of course; for one thing, the continents did not all appear to be sliding down toward the equator, as Wegener had proposed, nor did his notion of a westward drift owing to tidal forces explain the motions of some blocks of the crust. But geologists soon saw how these discrepancies could be accounted for. In the last analysis, they concluded that Wegener had been basically right. The face of the earth was not a static mass of unyielding rock, but rather an ever-changing mosaic of shifting plates.

Soon the geophysicists had gone so far beyond Wegener that a new name was needed for the study of earth's shifting crustal blocks. "Continental drift" became "plate tectonics," and from about 1965 to the present, plate tectonics has dominated geology much as Einstein's theory of relativity has dominated physics. In fact, those two revolutionary theories are alike in many ways. For one thing, they are both simple in their basic assumptions but staggeringly complex in their applications. For another, they are both full of highly practical uses. Relativity, through Einstein's famous energy-matter equation, gave us a new source of energy: splitting the uranium atom. Plate tectonics has also added to our energy resources, by increasing our knowledge of how fossil fuels—coal, oil, gas, and so forth—are formed and distributed. Plate tectonics has many other valuable applications, in mining and other earth-related industries, as we will see in later chapters.

According to the modern theory of plate tectonics, the earth's crust (known to geologists as the lithosphere) is divided into about a dozen major plates. These plates do not necessarily coincide with the shores of the continents. The

Indian plate, for example, is a long scimitar-shaped block of crust that underlies India as well as Australia, Tasmania, and parts of New Zealand.

Wegener extrapolated the movements of these plates as far back as the time of Pangaea, his huge supercontinent. Modern geologists, armed with computers and much more extensive data than Wegener had available, have gone even farther. We now have a history of plate movements going back almost half a billion years; and a strange history it is.

Far from starting out as a single supercontinent and then going their separate ways, the continents appear to have been alternately coming together and sliding apart for the last 500 million years in a colossal square dance.

The continents 500 million years ago bore almost no resemblance to those of today. Our chilly Siberia was a crescent-shaped island near the equator. China was a sliver of land to the north of Siberia (just the opposite of the situation today), on about the latitude of modern Florida. There was one large continent called Gondwana,* which occupied about the same latitudes South America does now. And there were a few other, smaller landmasses—Kazakhstania, Laurentia, Baltica—scattered around the equatorial zone and the Southern Hemisphere. The continents as we know them simply did not exist.

Things changed greatly in the next 70 million years or so. Gondwana had slid south to about the site of present-day Antarctica. Laurentia had all but vanished, and Siberia and Baltica were neck and neck in a race for the northern latitudes. China was a small island on the equator, as was tiny Kazakhstania.

Gondwana inched back northward over the next 100 million years. It was still the single largest landmass, but had started to acquire a tattered appearance. Long strings of land extended southward from the continent toward the

---

* Actually, no humans were there to call it anything. The names of these ancient continents have all been assigned by modern scientists.

South Pole, and Gondwana surrounded a large inland sea bigger than all the modern American Great Lakes combined. Laurentia and Baltica were no more. In their place stood a large landmass: Laurussia. Kazakhstania kept its independence, as did China, which was then at approximately its current latitude.

The age of dinosaurs was about to begin, some 250 million years ago, when the separate landmasses were merging. China and Siberia were still isolated islands, but only a few miles of water separated them from the growing bulk of the supercontinent created by the merger of Gondwana with Laurussia. Gradually, the earth was taking on the appearance of Wegener's Pangaea.

All the continents came together roughly 225 million years ago. Pangaea appeared at last.

Pangaea was a vast curved mass of land reaching from pole to pole. It was surrounded by a world ocean called Panthalassa—literally, "the whole ocean." A tongue of that ocean, the Tethys Sea, reached into the indentation on Pangaea's eastern shore. Land that now forms parts of the Himalayas was washed by warm Tethys waters in those days; and if Shakespeare had been writing his plays 225 million years ago, he might have been perfectly accurate in saying that Bohemia *did* have a seacoast.

Pangaea began breaking up about 200 million years ago, still early in the age of dinosaurs. The supercontinent split horizontally down the middle, into two large pieces. The northern piece was Laurussia (sometimes called Laurasia), and included parts of what had been Laurentia; this giant landmass split apart to become the continents of the Northern Hemisphere. The southern fragment of Pangaea was still called Gondwana. Generally speaking, it became the southern continents, with two notable exceptions: Africa, which has since slid northward until most of its area lies north of the equator, and India, which broke off from Gondwana and then slid rapidly northward and out of the Southern Hemisphere entirely. The finished product was our familiar arrangement of continents and oceans today.

The modern crustal plates vary in thickness, from perhaps 5 miles to 50 miles, and are thicker under the continents than under the oceans. And instead of simply drifting along like icebergs in the sea or clouds in the air, as Wegener imagined, the crustal blocks are carried along like goods on a conveyor belt, impelled by churning currents of magma deep inside the earth.

Just under the earth's crust is the mantle. The top layer of the mantle is the asthenosphere. This layer is hot and full of "convection cells." You have probably seen convection cells in a pan of hot water on the stove. Heat applied at the center of the pan makes water rise at that point. As it nears the surface, the water cools and is pushed out to all sides, then finally falls around the comparatively cool edges of the pan. What you get is a circulation cell of rising and falling water. Much the same thing happens in the asthenosphere, where the heat source is the earth's interior.

One may think of the rock in the asthenosphere as liquid, but it is not. It is a solid, but under such intense heat and pressure the rock may, as we have noted, be deformed plastically—made to flow like a thick liquid. It exists somewhere on the borderline between solid and fluid, a condition rather hard for us to visualize.

In certain areas, the rock in the asthenosphere rises slowly toward the surface. Sometimes the molten rock breaks through the crust. The intense pressure is released, and the rock expands and flows. Depending on its composition, the magma—molten rock inside the earth—may flow quickly, almost like water, or as slowly as cold molasses. Once the magma oozes out onto the surface, it is known as lava. This is the stuff volcanic peaks are made of.

Volcanoes tend to appear in long chains along cracks in the crust called "mid-ocean ridges." That name is often misleading, though still widely used, because the first ridge of this kind was found running down the midline of the Atlantic Ocean. The ridges can actually run into the continents, or just about anywhere. At many points along these ridges, lava flows out and builds volcanic mountains. The Azores are a good example of volcanoes along a mid-ocean ridge. So are the Galápagos Islands off the western coast of South America. The whole country of Iceland is made of lava that poured out from volcanoes on a mid-ocean ridge.

Mid-ocean ridges are the site where new crust is formed. Molten rock oozes up from underground, cools, and solidifies. The resulting rock formations can be bizarre. Deep-sea submersibles have visited the dark depths where lava flows from rifts in the ocean floor, and photos taken from these subs show an eerie landscape. Here and there the lava has billowed out in great dark-gray rounded formations like a frozen cascade of discolored shaving cream. There are "bubbles" of rock where the molten lava has frozen solid just as expanding gas inside it was about to escape. There are cylindrical masses of "toothpaste" lava, so called because it rose up like a viscous mass squeezed from a tube. There are turrets and pinnacles, blisters and flood tides of lava, frozen in their tracks by contact with the near-freezing waters at the bottom of the sea. This weird scene seems as alien to humans as the barren moon or the surface of Mars.

But these depths are hardly dead. Exploration teams from the Woods Hole Oceanographic Institution and the Scripps Institute of Oceanography, in 1977, visited the mid-ocean ridge near the Galápagos Islands and found, at 9,000 feet, a veritable undersea zoo. Clinging to the rocks near volcanic vents in the sea floor were giant mussels a foot long, with white shells and bright-red meat. Scrambling over the mussels were hordes of white crabs, adapted perfectly to the intense pressures of the ocean bottom. (The crabs seemed exceptionally hardy: though they died if removed into the relatively low-pressure waters near the surface, they survived for months if maintained in high-pressure vessels that simulated conditions on the sea floor.) There were even brightly colored polychaete worms, the size of grown boa constrictors, that lived in tubes on the bottom. These creatures were able to survive because water near the volcanic vents was much warmer than usual for these depths. Marvelously adapted to this unearthly environment, these species were able to extract chemicals directly from the water and use the chemicals for food.*

The "clambakes," as one biologist called them, were an unexpected discovery. So were strange undersea formations photographed at another site, off the western coast of Mexico. Rising up from the volcanic rock on the ocean floor were tall, thin chimneys, black and white and gray in color, from which hot water was spurting up out of the sea bottom. The chimneys had been built up, layer on layer and inch after inch, by minerals precipitating out of the hot water. All around the vents were rich deposits of metallic ores. These ores might provide a quick fortune to anyone who, in the future, has the technology to mine them at a depth of 9,000 feet. For the moment, however, the ores remain just a scientific curiosity.

The magnitude of water sent through these vents is awesome. Dr. John Edmond of the Massachusetts Institute of Technology has suggested that sea water is cycled through the vents, over the entire globe, at a rate of more than a million gallons per second: more than a hundred billion gallons per day. If that estimate is correct, then the world ocean may be recycled through the undersea vents roughly once every eight million years, or perhaps 500 times since the oceans appeared. Edmond has also suggested the dissolved material spurted out of the undersea

* This kind of adaptation to extreme environments is not unusual. Life finds ways to invade even the most unpromising places. During the Vietnam War, for example, U.S. jet mechanics on aircraft carriers discovered a strange material in the fuel systems of their planes. It turned out to be masses of bacteria living on the jet fuel!

chimneys may play an important role in determining ocean chemistry. Clearly, there is plenty of research to be done on the bizarre world of the mid-ocean ridges.

When lava oozes out along the ridges and solidifies, it does not remain in place there forever. New lava is always rising from underground and flowing out. The effect is to push older strips of solidified lava outward, away from the ridge. As the rock solidifies, it acts as a kind of natural tape recorder. The pattern of the earth's magnetic field is preserved in the rock, just as electronic signals are preserved on magnetic recording tape. And much as the tape can be used to reconstruct the music recorded on it, the magnetic patterns in the sea floor can be used to reconstruct the history of the earth's magnetic field, which reverses itself occasionally for reasons that are still unclear. The magnetic strips on either side of the spreading zone may indicate how fast new crust is being generated at the ridge and pushed out to either side. The spreading rate is slow in the North Atlantic between France and Nova Scotia: only about an inch per year. The figure is slightly higher—two and a half inches per year—off the western coast of Mexico, where a mid-ocean ridge runs north along the coast toward California. Near the Galápagos Islands, a bit farther south, the rate increases to four inches per year, and the annual spreading off the coast of Chile is a whopping seven inches per year. While these figures may not seem impressive, a spread of even an inch per year, along a mid-ocean ridge thousands of miles long, adds up to a huge amount of new crust formed annually.

As the new crust forms and is pushed aside by still younger crust, the crustal plate is moved along, in part, by the swirling convection currents far below. The currents rise at the mid-ocean ridges, then spread out to either side, carrying the crust along with them. This is the "conveyor-belt" system mentioned earlier.

The crustal plates cannot, however, keep spreading out indefinitely. There is only so much room on the earth's surface, and eventually a crustal plate is bound to collide with another plate. What happens then depends on several different factors.

The crustal blocks may meet head on and crumple and buckle upward, resulting in a mountain chain. The Alps in Europe were formed in this way as Italy pushed north into Switzerland. The Himalayas, the highest peaks on land, resulted when the Indian subcontinent moved north and collided slowly with Asia. (The Alps and the Himalayas are still relatively young mountains. Earlier collisions between crustal plates have pushed up mountains as impressive as those of Nepal or Switzerland, but wind and water have worn down those older chains over the millennia. The Ural Mountains of the U.S.S.R., which mark the border between Europe and Asia in the Soviet Union, were once much taller than they are today. So were the Appalachians of the Eastern United States, which once divided Europe from America.)

The meeting crustal plates may grind sideways against one another. This is happening in southern California and Baja California, where a plate of crust is sliding northward along the western margin of the North American plate, creating earthquakes and small mountain ranges as it goes.

Alternatively, one plate may simply ride up over the other. One plate remains at the surface, while the loser in this conflict is pushed down—subducted—into the mantle of the earth. As this plate descends, several things happen.

First, a trench is formed where the subducted plate is warped downward. This is how the deep ocean trenches of the Pacific, off the coasts of Alaska and the western Pacific, were formed. These trenches have a characteristic crescent shape, because they follow the curve of a plane— the crustal plate—intersecting the surface of a sphere; namely, the globe. This pattern accounts for the neat arcuate chains of islands in Japan and the Aleutians.

Second, the subducted plate starts melting as it passes into the hot rock of the mantle. Not all parts of the plate

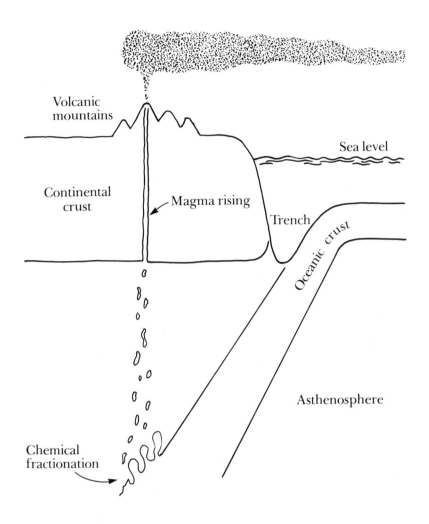

Volcanic mountains

Sea level

Continental crust

Magma rising

Trench

Oceanic crust

Chemical fractionation

Asthenosphere

SUBDUCTION ZONE: *This diagram shows what happens when thin oceanic crust is subducted under the thicker continental crust. The zone is characterized by deep ocean trenches, volcanic activity, and mountain building (orogeny).*

melt at the same time. The lighter and more volatile components melt first. This process is called "chemical fractionation." The lighter components then rise back toward the lithosphere, rather as a hydrogen balloon rises in air, or droplets of olive oil rise in water.

Where this rising magma finds a crack in the crust, it flows out on the surface. The result is a volcano—or, more accurately, chains of volcanoes, since the fractionation process is taking place all along the subduction zone. The volcanoes tend to be more or less evenly spaced (the volcanic islands of the Lesser Antilles in the Caribbean Sea, are a good example of this pattern) and may rise to towering height, as did Japan's Mount Fuji. These volcanoes may build up impressive strings of volcanic mountains, like those of Java and Sumatra.

(Thus far we have spoken of plate tectonics as if it were a completely ironclad theory with no shortcomings. In fact, there are more than a few holes in it. For example, many active volcanoes are nowhere near the borders of crustal plates. The Hawaiian Islands are a prominent example of this exception to Wegener's rules. There are numerous other spots—in Central Europe, to name one—where there have been huge eruptions in the distant past, far from the intersection of crustal blocks. Of course, this does not mean Wegener's theory is invalid; it merely means there are some things it does not explain. The mechanics of plate motion have yet to be worked out completely, though the plates do move as Wegener said they did. And geologists are starting to think that subduction zones are quite different from what Wegener described: rather than getting squeezed out of existence along subduction zones, there is reason to think the plates are stretched to death, and some geologists go so far as to say the subducted plates are not subducted at all! Overall, the theory of plate tectonics hangs together well. But there is still much fine tuning to be done on the theory, and it will probably change greatly in years to come, as we learn more about the earth's interior.)

The Dance of the Continents

The descent of crustal plates is not always a smooth process. As the plates rub together, they vibrate. The earth trembles, and the third characteristic event along the subduction zones is produced: earthquakes.

Very few of these earthquakes are destructive. For every quake that causes significant damage to property or takes lives, there are thousands of others that do no harm, and many that are never even felt. It is hard to predict, however, just how a crustal plate will behave while it is being subducted. It may generate lots of earthquakes close to the surface, or the plate may wait until it is miles underground to start rumbling. It may cause many devastating quakes, or only a few. As a rule, however, a descending crustal plate —signified by a deep trench nearby and a line of volcanoes —is a warning that severe quakes are at least a possibility.

Look at a map of earthquake foci, the points where quakes are centered, and a pattern will quickly emerge. The quakes tend to concentrate in a few areas of the globe. There is a high-risk quake area in the Mediterranean, where the African crustal plate is pushing northward into Europe and gradually squeezing the Mediterranean Sea out of existence in the process. This collision of plates explains why "earthquakes rock Italic ground," as one old English ballad had it. Another hot spot of quake activity is found in the Middle East, running through southern Iran. This was the location of the devastating Tabas earthquake of 1978, which shook whole towns into rubble and killed thousands of persons. The Middle East quake zone—which may also have been responsible for the fall of Jericho, as reported in the Old Testament—is almost adjacent to the Himalayan zone, where the collision of India with Asia has pushed up the world's highest mountains and also tortured the crust severely. There are a few other isolated areas of intense earthquake activity scattered around the Atlantic and Antarctic Oceans.

The most intense zone of quake activity, however, is the belt that Mallet delineated around the edge of the

Pacific Ocean: the Ring of Fire. A U.S. Coast and Geodetic Survey map of the world, published several years ago, shows the epicenters of some 30,000 earthquakes recorded between 1961 and 1967. The Ring is virtually black with dots marking where quakes have struck. No other part of the world has more seismic activity in such a small area.

A similar map can be made of the world's active volcanoes. At least 60 percent of them are concentrated in the Ring of Fire. From Parícutin in Mexico to Krakatoa in Indonesia, from Katmai and Bogoslov in Alaska to Wairakei in New Zealand, the Ring of Fire has encircled the Pacific Ocean with mountains that spit fire and ash, and even explode at times, with a violence matched only by the more spectacular works of nuclear engineers.

The map of quake foci may give the impression that only one plate is involved in this natural violence: the Pacific plate, colliding with its neighbors. The Pacific plate is indeed responsible for much of the earthquake and volcanic activity in the Ring of Fire. As the Pacific plate grinds toward the northwest, toward the coasts of Japan and Siberia and Alaska, it meets three other plates—the Indian, the Eurasian, and the North American—and creates deep subduction zones as the relatively thin and yielding crust under the Pacific Ocean is trampled under, one might say, by the thicker crustal plates that form the continents.

But the Pacific plate has a partner in violence: the Nazca plate, just west of South America. Here the Nazca plate, sliding westward and away from a mid-ocean ridge that runs through the Galápagos Islands, collides head on into South America, which is being pushed eastward by a similar ridge in the mid-Atlantic. This encounter has created the Andes Mountains, the rugged backbone of South America, where the Incas created their magnificent civilization, and where Charles Darwin worked to unravel the mystery of how species originate.

Darwin was frightened badly by an earthquake in Chile in 1835, when he visited South America during his cruise on H.M.S. *Beagle*. He had joined a shore party to look for specimens for his collection, when suddenly the ground began to move under him. He found it impossible to stand, and he had no choice but to lie down and wait for the earth to stop shaking.* He was uninjured, but a nearby town was destroyed by the tremor. Later he wrote, in his journal of the *Beagle*'s voyage:

> A bad earthquake at once destroys our oldest associations; the earth, the very emblem of solidity, has moved beneath our feet like a thin crust over a fluid; one second of time has created in the mind a strange idea of insecurity, which hours of reflection would not have produced.

The continents will continue sliding about the globe, destroying old associations and creating new ones. If a University of Chicago study is correct, Baja California will, over the next 50 million years, slide northward to about where San Francisco is now. The Mediterranean will become a long, narrow lake, and Gibraltar may be pushed right into the coast of Morocco. The Persian Gulf will be squeezed into a puddle as the Arabian Peninsula works its way northward toward Asia. Australia may collide with Japan or even Siberia.

Whether or not our descendants will be around to see that vastly changed world, it is impossible to say. But so far we have been an extraordinarily lucky species; and if our luck holds, we may be following the motions of the continents long after glacial creep has carried Alfred Wegener's body down to the shore and sent him drifting out to sea in an iceberg.

---

* The tremor was a relatively small one as Chilean quakes go: some 5,000 persons died in the earthquake and the tsunami that followed it.

V

"Darkness and Hell"

JUST ACROSS the North Pole from Wegener's resting place lies the Gulf of Alaska. This is perhaps the least hospitable part of the Pacific Ocean: a cold sea littered with ice and tossed frequently by gales that agitate the sea until there is no clear boundary between ocean and air.

Bordered by glaciers, remnants of the thick ice sheet that covered the land only a few thousand years ago, the Gulf of Alaska is one of the richest commercial fishing grounds in the world. One and a half billion dollars' worth of fish will come out of the gulf in a typical year. Especially prized are the Alaskan king crabs, giant crustaceans with sweet flesh and, in some, a six-foot leg span. A boat that goes out after king crabs may return with $150,000 worth of crab meat in its hold. Some boats make their crewmen rich. Some don't. Some never return at all. They sail out into the tempestuous gulf and vanish forever, their hulls smashed and decks ripped open by the storms that lash the southern coast of Alaska. A 100-foot-long boat, even a well-constructed one with the best navigational equipment, may be no match for the occasional freak wave, a towering mass of water pushed up where several wave systems happen to intersect. One in every seven waves: that is the traditional rule for telling when a monster wave will appear, but the rule is honored more in the breach than the observance. One never knows when a freak wave will appear to bury a boat under countless tons of water. These waves have been estimated at heights of 75, 80, even 100 feet on occasion. If such a thing were possible, an office building could be hidden in the troughs between these waves and no one would ever find it. When a freak wave strikes, it may simply push a ship under, and keep on pushing until the hull lies on the sea bottom, and the only physical evidences of the sinking are a few bits of wood, cork, and other light material that will eventually wash up on the shores of the Alaska Panhandle or the Aleutians.

The Aleutians are named for the native Aleuts, a people of Mongolian descent who are thought to have moved into North America from Asia during the last ice age. Sea level was lower then, for much of the ocean water was locked up in the glaciers that moved relentlessly down across the continents. The present-day Bering Strait, a narrow and shallow strip of water between Alaska and Siberia, did not exist. Instead, there was a land bridge between North America and Asia. Many things besides humans moved across this bridge—the mammoths and mastodons of North America, for example—and they were stranded in the Americas when the ice age ended and sea level rose, creating the Bering Strait and cutting off North America from Asia.

Some of the Mongolian-related peoples who crossed this land bridge moved far into southern parts of North America. They became the Indian tribes so prominent in American history: the Sioux, the Iroquois, the Cherokee, and others. But some of the migrants from Asia remained in the Far North, and among them were the Aleuts.

The principal industries of the Aleuts were hunting, fishing, and whaling. Long before Ishmael set out from New Bedford on his round-the-world voyage, the Aleuts were putting out to sea, in their own small but sturdy boats, in pursuit of whales. The Aleut whaleboats differed only in detail from those the *Pequod* lowered to chase Moby Dick. Both were small, narrow craft designed to present a minimum surface to the sea, so as to reduce friction and ensure a swift ride.

The men who sat in those whaleboats were short and stocky, with black hair and Oriental features. Arctic climate did much to shape the Eskimo physique. A small and chunky person conserves body heat better than does a taller, thinner person. Conserving heat was a condition of survival in the Far North, and natural selection worked in favor of short, stocky bodies.*

For thousands of years, the Aleuts seem to have had a reasonably peaceful civilization, with only occasional squabbles among themselves. They were accomplished artisans and, like the seafaring peoples of New England, developed the art of scrimshaw, or carving whale bones and teeth in decorative patterns. Some of these carved items were usually included in the tombs of dead hunters. The Aleuts followed the Egyptian practice of mummifying and entombing their dead, although such an honor was normally reserved for chieftains, highly successful hunters, and other distinguished citizens. Less honored persons were cremated. Sealed caves full of mummified Aleuts were found along the southern coast of Alaska when white men reached Alaska—caves that had remained unopened because the Aleuts believed that frightful curses awaited anyone who disturbed these preserved communi-

* Much the same thing has happened in other climates. The characteristic sharp nose of certain Middle Eastern peoples, for example, is an adaptation to dry desert air. The long nose increases the surface area of nasal membranes and thus moistens the dry air thoroughly before it reaches the lungs.

ties of the dead. The mummies date from before the Russian occupation of Alaska in the eighteenth century; after the Russians invaded and settled Alaska, "pagan" practices like mummifying were discouraged by the Russian Orthodox Church.

The Russian occupation of Alaska is a story of greed and brutality almost unparalleled in the history of the New World. It began when Czar Peter the Great, who received his education in Western Europe (and then whipped his teachers on the field of battle, using the very lessons they had taught him), was looking for ways to expand his domain, that vast "prison of nations" known as the Russian Empire.

Peter knew that expansion to the west would be difficult. His enemies there were much too well armed and too numerous. The east, however, was another matter. Russians had taken over vast eastern territories without much opposition; in fact, Russian soldiers chased the Khan of Sibir, for whom Siberia is named, all over the map before at last subduing him. So Peter reasoned that there might be better prizes farther to the east, in areas yet unexplored.

What excited Peter especially was the thought that Siberia and North America might be joined by land. If so, he might be able to send Russian troops overland into North America and carve out a Russian domain before the nations of Western Europe grabbed all the continent for themselves.

The prospect was intriguing, and Peter's curiosity was piqued even further by stories brought back to him by his Cossack tax collectors in Siberia. The Siberian tribes, Peter learned, told stories of a people called Aleuts who lived on a chain of icy islands far to the east of Siberia. If the Aleuts really existed, the Czar decided, they might have something of interest for him. Perhaps furs. Perhaps gold. Who could tell what might lie in those vast domains in the Far North of America?

There was only one way to find out. So in 1724 the Czar

sent an expedition to Alaska under the leadership of Danish explorer Vitus Bering. Bering's expedition sailed north along the Pacific coast of Siberia and established that there was no land bridge between Asia and North America. The Russian government, however, wanted to know more about this cold corner of the world and its inhabitants. So Bering was sent out again, and in 1741 his ship approached the coast of Alaska. He was the first white man to see the Alaskan shore.

This was the last voyage of Bering's life. It was a hideous experience for everyone on board; bad weather, cold, and scurvy tormented the men, and the expedition ended in disaster on a barren arctic island.

Bering's ship, the *St. Peter*, was returning to Russia when land was sighted. Bering mistook it for Siberia. But it was actually an island in the strait, and the ship was driven onto its rocky shore by the wind and tide. Bering died there, according to one of the survivors, under the bleak gray skies, on December 8, 1741. The island was named for Vitus Bering.

The survivors of Bering's expedition brought back news that delighted Peter the Great. There were indeed riches to be found in Alaska, particularly furs. While stranded on the island, a naturalist on the expedition made detailed observations of the seals, sea lions, and other marine mammals that lived in the waters. The men also brought back pelts as evidence.

Furs meant wealth, and soon a horde of rapacious fur hunters, the *promishlenkyi,* swarmed toward Siberia and Alaska in search of riches. The hunters' arrival doomed the Aleut way of life.

The Russians, though nominally Christians, were notably free of conscience when there was a ruble to be made. They decided that if the Aleuts stood in the way of their profits, then the Aleuts would have to be annihilated.

Annihilated they almost were, in a genocidal war even

more ferocious than that waged by whites against the native tribes in the western United States. Russian law of the late 1700s did not recognize crimes against humanity, and even if it had, the nearest law enforcement agencies were in Siberia, hundreds of miles away from the hunters. So the Russians were free to decimate the native population of southern Alaska.

Their brutality went far beyond what was needed to subdue the people. A Russian named Soloviev is still remembered in this part of the world for his crimes against the Aleuts. Once he decided to test the penetrating power of a rifle bullet. He tied several Aleuts together, front to back, then pressed the barrel against the chest of the first Aleut in line, and fired. He is said to have tested guns frequently.

Hunting and killing Aleuts appears to have been something of a sport among the Russians—a diversion from killing seals. The *promishlenkyi* sailed up and down the 3,000-mile-long southern coast of Alaska, turning Aleut villages into charnel houses wherever they went. The raids became even more savage after the Aleuts staged a brief rebellion, an uprising crushed so cruelly and efficiently that the Aleuts never resisted the Russian conquerors again.

Gradually, however, conditions improved for the Aleuts. Part of the credit should go to the Russian Orthodox Church, which treated the native Alaskans far more kindly than any other body of Russians had, and established schools to raise the Aleuts' level of literacy and learning. Unfortunately for the Aleuts, this brief period of relative peace came to an end in 1867, when, to raise money, the Russian government made a controversial deal with the United States.

Russia, then as now, had monetary problems and needed foreign cash. One way to raise it was to sell some of Russia's extensive real estate in North America. The most logical buyer for Alaska was the United States, which was in an expansionist phase of history and was grabbing any parts of the continent that were not yet nailed down by someone else. So the Russians let it be known that they would sell Alaska to the United States for the right price.

Enter William Henry Seward, U.S. Secretary of State for President Andrew Johnson. Gray-haired and craggy, with bushy eyebrows and a thin inverted V of a mouth, Seward looked like a caricature of a Methodist deacon, or a clean-shaven Father Time. He was actually one of the most far-sighted men ever to hold the post of Secretary of State, and almost single-handedly he added to the United States a territory bigger than Texas and California combined.

Seward had had his eye on the northwestern corner of the continent for years. In 1860, he predicted that Russia's settlements along the Alaskan coast would one day become "monuments of the civilization of the United States in the northwest." Now, seven years later, he had a chance to make his prophecy come true.

Haste was essential. Congress was about to adjourn, and Seward knew he had to act fast if a treaty of cession was to reach Congress in time to be considered. Seward met with his Russian counterpart, Minister Edouard de Stoeckl, at the State Department on March 29, 1867, and the Russians and the Americans worked until four the following morning to draft the treaty.

Congress had reservations about the proposed purchase. "Walrussia," one legislator called Alaska. "Seward's Icebox," someone else dubbed it. "Seward's Frozen Investment." "Seward's Folly." But eventually the legislators were persuaded, and in 1867 Congress approved $7.2 million for the purchase of Alaska.

Seven million dollars may seem a trifling sum to us today, accustomed as we are to seeing government budget figures in the billions and trillions. The former Department of Health, Education, and Welfare spent seven million dollars every two and a half days. In the 1860s, however, government spending was only a tiny fraction of what it is now,* and \$7.2 million represented a huge and seemingly risky investment.

The newspaper cartoonists had a field day with Seward and his treaty. One drawing showed Seward as a naïve little boy being conned out of his toys by a smooth-talking Czar. In another cartoon, an Eskimo in parka and snowshoes, harpoon in hand, shows up at the White House. Seward greets him: "My dear Mr. Kamchatka, won't you dine with me? My tallow candles are the finest, and my whale's blubber . . ." President Johnson, clearly uneasy, looks on in silence.

Alaska changed hands formally in a ceremony at Sitka, the Russian capital of Alaska, on October 18, 1867. Evidently the wife of the Russian Governor of Alaska, Princess Maksutova, had been practicing for the occasion. Right on cue, she swooned dramatically as the Imperial Russian flag was lowered and the Stars and Stripes were raised in its place.

The United States, on the whole, followed a policy of benign neglect toward Alaska until the 1890s. Then the discovery of gold opened a whole new era in Alaskan history and vindicated Seward's view that Alaska would be a priceless addition to American territory.†

The mineral deposits of Alaska—gold, silver, copper, and so forth—have repaid the original purchase price of Alaska thousands of times over. A mine in Alaska yielded \$300 million in copper before it closed in the 1930s. The deposits are there because the southern coast of Alaska is a subduction zone. The Pacific crustal plate is slipping un-

---

* There were times during the 1860s when the whole federal treasury contained no more than \$100,000.

† One of those who rushed to Alaska in the grip of gold fever was author Jack London. His reputation to the contrary, London knew very little about the Far North, and even less about prospecting. Once he burst into an assayer's office carrying a bag of what he thought was gold. It turned out to be mica, a common mineral not remotely related to gold. London also collected a vast amount of inaccurate information about the arctic, some of which turned up in his stories.

derneath the advancing North American plate, and molten material has been oozing upward from the melting Pacific plate to form rich deposits of metal ores.

The colliding plates have also made this coastline one of the most active, seismically and volcanically, in the world. The Aleutians themselves are a long string of volcanoes, and from time to time one of the volcanoes along the Alaskan coast does something violent, as one did on June 6, 1912. That date stands out like a beacon in the history of vulcanology. It was the day Mount Katmai went off.

Katmai is located near Kodiak Island, where the Alaska Peninsula (the western tail of the state) meets the mainland. This is the haunt of the towering Alaskan brown bears, the largest land-based carnivores on earth, who may weigh almost 2,000 pounds as adults and stand nine feet high on their hind legs. Occasionally one may see their tracks, the diameter of dinner plates, on beaches along the southern Alaska coast. Bears grow big there, and so do volcanoes. Mount Katmai stood 7,500 feet high in the first months of 1912. It had the characteristic cone shape of a volcano and was shrouded in glaciers. A massive mound of ice and cold lava, Katmai was one of several volcanic peaks: Snowy Mountain and Kukak Volcano to the northeast, Knife Peak Volcano to the north, and other volcanoes to the west and south. Mount Katmai, at the heart of this cluster, began to murmur some days before the eruption.

Katmai village, a few miles south of the volcano, was shaken by earthquakes on June 2. The quakes intensified on June 4 and 5. No one seemed unduly alarmed, however, for earthquakes were a common feature of life near Katmai, rather as summer thunderstorms are in the Deep South. What the volcano was doing in this period is unknown. Since Katmai was hidden from view by clouds, no one reported seeing emissions of steam or ash during these days, but a peculiar dark cloud was seen hanging over the mountain on June 5. Nobody was prepared, then, for what happened shortly after noon on June 6.

A thick ash cloud issued from Mount Katmai that plunged the area into total darkness for two and a half days. Volcanic ash began to fall on Juneau shortly thereafter—750 miles to the southeast. The Yukon Valley, about 1,000 miles north of Katmai, was also dusted by ashfalls. And even after the ash fell out of the air, other components of the cloud remained airborne, including sulfur oxides, which combined with moisture in the air to produce a mist of sulfuric acid—the acid used in car batteries. Soon the residents around Katmai found the acid drifting into their eyes, their lungs, their homes. As rain precipitated out of the air, an acid solution fell out of the sky on anyone unfortunate enough to be underneath. It even ruined articles hanging on clotheslines in Vancouver, British Columbia, 1,500 miles away.

Tremendous explosions could be heard from the volcano at 1:00 P.M. on June 6. The blast was heard over a radius of 800 miles from the volcano (though, inexplicably, no one noted it at Kodiak, a mere hundred miles away). Ash began raining down heavily on Kodiak Island and the waters around it. One of the ships unlucky enough to be in those waters was the U.S. Coast Guard cutter *Manning,* located about 100 miles southwest of the volcano, when the eruption occurred. Even though the explosion was inaudible on Kodiak, everyone could see the ash cloud plainly as it approached from Katmai around four in the afternoon on June 6. Gray ash started falling a few minutes later. Then a spectacular display of lightning broke out in the clouds above the *Manning,* and darkness enveloped Kodiak Island.

Captain K. W. Perry of the *Manning,* from his vantage point in Kodiak's harbor, watched uneasily as the ash piled up on the decks of his vessel and the sea around it. In some of the waters surrounding Kodiak Island, the ash was already so thick on the sea that there were ash rafts capable of supporting a man's weight. Visibility fell to less than a hundred feet.

Out of the darkness around the *Manning* came roars and deep rumbles, like a chorus of Kodiak bears amplified a thousand times. Thunder boomed from the clouds. The distant crash of avalanches on the land could be heard, and there was the faint crackle of St. Elmo's fire—static electricity—in the air as the eruption charged the atmosphere with ions. From time to time, the stench of sulfur drifted over the water toward the *Manning,* and Captain Perry and his crew wondered if they might soon share the fate of Pompeii. But the men of the *Manning* had no chance to sit and worry, for they were fighting a constant battle against the ash building up on the cutter's decks and superstructure. The ship's fire hoses were turned on to wash it away, and the rest of the crew fell to work with shovels, trying desperately to keep ahead of the accumulating mass.

The crew of the *Manning* got little sleep that night, Captain Perry reported. They were not even sure when the night ended and the day began, for dawn was hidden behind the black cloud from Katmai. Soon the ashfall began to diminish, and light seeped through the cloud—an eerie red light, colored by the fine material in the air, which blocked shorter wavelengths and allowed only the long red and orange ones to penetrate.

Around the *Manning* a vast sheet of ash rode on the water. The ship itself was intact and undamaged, however, and Captain Perry ordered the cutter to be made ready to take on refugees from the communities on shore. But the captain took no chances with the volcano; as soon as the ship had picked up some 500 persons from the surrounding area, he ordered it back to the outer harbor, from which an escape could be made easily to the open sea if Katmai erupted again.

Shortly after the refugees from Kodiak came aboard, a fine gray ash like dirty snow began falling again. But it accumulated to only an inch or so, and was dealt with easily by the *Manning*'s men.

On June 9, three days after the initial eruption, the

Manning put its guests back ashore. Yet the cutter's duty was not over, for ash had contaminated the water supply on shore, and the cutter remained briefly to supply water for the island people.

The *Manning*'s experience was calm indeed compared to that of another ship near Katmai at the time, the steamship *Dora*. At one o'clock on the afternoon of June 6, as the ship was approaching the strait to the north of Kodiak Island, Captain McMullen of the *Dora* saw a thick plume of what appeared to be smoke, rising from the shore west of the ship's position—probably, the captain thought, coming from Katmai Volcano. The plume rose and spread out rapidly over the land and sea. By 3 P.M., the cloud caught up with the *Dora* and shrouded the ship in ash and gloom so dense that bright electric lights could not relieve the darkness. The crew had to move along by touch as fine gray ash swirled about them like smoke, and even though the windows of the pilot house were shut, the ash filtered through. At one point the air was so full of ash that the helmsman had trouble seeing the compass in front of him. The cold air became cool, then warm, then hot. Below decks the *Dora* must have presented a truly infernal scene: a hot, dark set of cabins and corridors, filled with swirling ash and sulfurous gases. The dust entered everything. It filled the men's noses, their throats, their lungs. And, as the clerk said later in a newspaper article, when the ash got into one's eye, it was like "a dash of acid." He said he saw birds, overcome by the ash and fumes from Katmai, fall screaming out of the sky and land on the *Dora*'s decks.

Perhaps we still live in an age of miracles, because no one was killed in the eruption of Katmai. However, the fear of death fell icily on a small band of natives who were on a fishing expedition and were caught in their camp 30 miles from Katmai when the volcano erupted. The ash piled up around them to almost twice a man's height. There was no distinction between day and night, and the frightened fishermen burned their lamps twenty-four hours a day. There was no water, or at least none uncontaminated by ash. "Here are darkness and hell," one of the fishermen wrote, "thunder and noise."

No sooner had the rumbles from Katmai died away than the National Geographic Society put together an expedition to study the eruption's effects. They reached Katmai one month after it had erupted. Only part of the original mountain was there: Katmai had lost its summit. Where a towering peak had once stood, covered with white ice and cloaked in clouds, there was now a caldera big enough to swallow a city. The vast basin was three miles wide and half a mile deep. The sides of the caldera plunged almost straight down to the floor, on which a small lake had formed from the melted ice of glaciers.

One and a half cubic miles of Katmai's peak had vanished in the eruption. And that was puzzling, because the ashfalls from Katmai, heavy as they were in places (they crushed buildings in Kodiak), accounted for only a small fraction of that volume of rock. Where did the rest of the peak go?

Geologists at the site saw only one plausible answer. Katmai must have met the same fate as had Mount Mazama in Oregon thousands of years earlier: the peak had had the props pulled out from under it, so to speak, and collapsed. (Had the summit of Mount Katmai exploded —that is, been blown up and outward by pressure from below—then the easy-to-identify dark lavas that made up the mountain would have been clearly noticeable as dark chunks amid the generally light-colored ash from the volcano. No such dark pieces were spotted.)

A volcano died that day in Alaska, but a new one was formed. Called Novarupta, it was the vent through which magma had been drained away from under Katmai, some six miles away. Novarupta vomited a colossal ash flow during the eruption. Incandescent vapor and ash swept down from the mouth of Novarupta like the cloud that descended on St. Pierre from Mount Pelée in the Caribbean ten years earlier. But the *nuée ardente* (the "fiery cloud") from Mount Pelée was little more than a polite burp compared to the fiery tide from Novarupta. A glowing stream of ash and gas roared outward from the volcano and covered more than 40 square miles with a searing blanket of tephra hundreds of feet deep. The resulting fire storm burned forests for miles around the ash flow.

In a way, Katmai's remote location was a blessing. The eruption would probably have been one of the greatest natural catastrophes of all time had the volcano been located near a large city. Katmai's remoteness also made study of the eruption difficult, however, and so it was several years before one of the volcano's most spectacular offspring was found.

Robert Griggs, leader of a National Geographic Society expedition to Katmai, was climbing through Katmai Pass one day in 1916 when he noticed a puff of steam wafting skyward from the other side of a small rise. He and several of his companions climbed the rise and were astonished at what they saw: a whole valley full of steaming fumaroles, or vents from which hot vapors were seeping up from underground. Shortly thereafter, President Woodrow Wilson proclaimed the valley a national monument: the Valley of Ten Thousand Smokes.

This plain of fumaroles was probably laid down in the early afternoon of June 6, after Katmai's explosive eruption at one o'clock. A huge ash flow rolled down into the valley, burying anything and everything in its path. It moved with hurricane velocity, knocking down trees at the far end of the valley. Other trees were carbonized where they stood by the terrific heat of the flow, a heat so intense that it actually welded fragments of ash together.

Most of the vapor rising from the Valley of Ten Thousand Smokes was steam. A small part, perhaps 1 or 2 percent, consisted of hydrogen sulfide, hydrochloric acid, and other unpleasant compounds. These chemicals were deposited in the original ash flow and then began working their way toward the surface. The steam, on the other hand, probably resulted from rainfall and snow that seeped down into the still-hot ashes, then rose back to the surface as vapor. (The pressure of the vapor was surprising. Members of one early expedition to the site tried cooking breakfast in the steam from a fumarole—and found the blast of vapor would blow the pan right out of their hands unless they held it tightly.)

Katmai has stirred occasionally since the 1912 eruption. There were very minor outbursts from the volcano in the 1920s and 1950s, and in 1968 an eruption cast ash over an area 60 miles in radius.

For the moment, at least, Katmai is not a worry. But the 1912 eruption was sudden, and there were no early warnings. It is always possible that Katmai's next eruption will take Alaska completely by surprise; and as Alaska's population increases, so does the chance that Katmai's next outburst will take lives as well as damage property.

Volcanoes are not the only violent phenomena stirred up by the collision of crustal plates along the southern shores of Alaska. This area is also the site of many powerful earthquakes; and Alaska's frightening quake potential created an international controversy in 1970, when the U.S. Atomic Energy Commission announced the plan it had for a small and obscure Aleutian island called Amchitka.

VI

Cannikin

T H E W O R D "Godforsaken" might have been coined to describe Amchitka Island. A barren splinter of rock in the Aleutian Islands, 75 square miles in area and inhabited by birds, grasses, lichens, and sea lions, Amchitka lies between the Bering Sea and the Pacific Ocean, not far from the island where Vitus Bering was shipwrecked and died. Summer on Amchitka is little more than a break in the clouds, and winter is a months-long ordeal of mist, gloom, snow, and a humid chill that seeps through even the thickest clothing and drains away body heat as effectively as a dip in ice water.

Amchitka has seldom been important to anyone, except perhaps the native Alaskans. There was a brief flurry of military activity on Amchitka during World War II as U.S. armed forces mobilized in the Aleutians to counter a possible Japanese invasion of North America. The Aleutians turned out to be only a minor arena in the Pacific war, however, and the U.S. soldiers departed after the armistice in 1945, leaving behind them thousands of tons of military debris: oil drums, aircraft parts, cans, bottles, and more than 2,000 metal Quonset huts which still littered the landscape 25 years later. In warmer climates, the junk would have rusted away or been covered by vegetation; but in the Arctic, where everything from rusting to plant germination proceeds at an incredibly slow rate, the marks of war remain and probably will be visible even a century from now.*

Amchitka is so remote and so small and so poor in resources that the United States had very little use for it—until the age of atomic warfare. Then, because of problems with bomb tests, Amchitka's isolation itself became a valuable commodity.

Atomic weapons are difficult to test safely. If they are exploded in the atmosphere, fission products are released directly into the environment. These radioactive materials settle down through the atmosphere and onto the land and water. There the radioactive contaminants may enter the food chain, which culminates in human beings.

Radioactive fallout, for example, may land on a pasture and be eaten by a cow. The cow ingests the fallout and passes it along in its milk to humans. If the fallout contains strontium 90 or some other isotope that mimics calcium in human biochemistry, then radioactive material may lodge in the bones and bombard the surrounding tissues with radiation. The result may be leukemia or some other disease caused by radiation. Other elements may be concentrated in different organs: radioactive iodine in the thyroid gland, for instance. And with every nuclear bomb test in the atmosphere, the number of persons likely to get some radiation-related disease increases, because more fallout is released into the atmosphere.

---

* Arctic climate makes the ecosystems there peculiarly susceptible to damage by humans. Tractor-tread impressions in the tundra, for example, may be visible two or even five decades after they were made.

The possible effects of atmospheric testing on health alarmed many scientists and public-health authorities around the world in the late 1950s and early 1960s. Finally public pressure to halt atmospheric testing became so great that in 1962 the United States and the Soviet Union signed an agreement to halt the testing of nuclear weapons in the atmosphere. (The treaty was drawn up shortly after a test over the Pacific set off a frightening display of light in the sky over Hawaii: the sky turned pink and green and finally a ghastly blood-red. This terrifying spectacle only added to the public clamor to stop the atmospheric testing of nuclear weapons.) Except for a few incidents involving nonsignatories to the treaty, such as France and China, the agreement appears to have remained unbroken.

The atmospheric test ban, however, created a problem for the military. It had been easy to test bombs in the open air. Just build a tower for a bomb in the desert, or send the bomb up by balloon, and set it off: cheap and simple. Where else could one test a bomb? Undersea tests would be almost as bad as atmospheric tests, if not worse; the explosion would send up vast quantities of radioactive water and pollute marine ecosystems with radioactivity, not to mention setting off possibly devastating tsunamis.

When tests in the air and sea were ruled out, only one place was left; underground tests on land. Bombs could be set off in cavities far underground, after being lowered down through shafts drilled through thousands of feet of rock. Subterranean blasts would be more expensive and involved than tests in the open air, but much safer. If the shaft was drilled deep enough, fission products would be contained in a melt puddle at the bottom of the underground cavity created by the blast. No radioactivity would escape to foul the environment. Underground testing seemed clean and, from an ecologist's standpoint, relatively safe.

So after the test-ban treaty was signed, testing moved underground. But the armed forces and the civilians at

the Atomic Energy Commission soon learned that underground explosions, while usually clean, were not completely free from unpleasant side effects.

One of those effects was earthquake activity. Some underground explosions in Nevada were strong enough to
shake buildings perceptibly in Las Vegas and nearby communities, and civic leaders protested to the government
that they had enough troubles without being rocked by
man-made earthquakes as well.

The federal government then started looking for an
underground test site far from any large population centers, where bombs could be set off without fear of shaking
skyscrapers.

The search revealed a seemingly perfect spot: Amchitka
Island, an isolated member of the Aleutian chain near the
international date line. In 1966, the Atomic Energy Commission designated Amchitka a test site for nuclear weapons, and three years later a one-megaton nuclear device
code named Milrow was detonated under Amchitka.

The choice of Amchitka, however, gave geologists reason for worry. Amchitka is situated in the Ring of Fire,
near the epicenters of numerous past earthquakes. There
in the subduction zone where Alaska meets the Pacific
plate, one might say the crust has a "hair trigger": even a
small disturbance, geologists feared, might be sufficient to
set off a destructive earthquake. Only a few days before
the Milrow test, the White House Office of Science and
Technology released a sobering report about the possible
effects of nuclear testing in this shaky corner of the Ring of
Fire. The report said that underground tests in Nevada, a
state much less active seismically than southern Alaska,
had caused flurries of small but substantial earthquakes.
What might happen in the Aleutians? The White House
report concluded that the consequences of underground
tests of nuclear weapons in the seismically active Aleutians
"could be extremely serious."

Milrow went ahead on schedule, despite the ominous

warning. And after the last rumbles had died away, it was clear no serious damage had been done. There was no quake. Scientists were able to land on the island shortly after the explosion for studies of the blast's effects. According to a report published in the *Geological Society of America Bulletin,* Amchitka had weathered the explosion well. Outside the immediate area of the explosion, there was very little vertical movement of the ground—less than five inches in most spots. Much greater displacements had been measured at test sites in Nevada. In short, Amchitka seemed capable of withstanding more underground tests, because the island seemed seismically inactive and generally solid as a rock. Bigger bombs, the geologists predicted, would cause no more harm than Milrow—that is, "practically none."

The Atomic Energy Commission was happy with that appraisal, because it had plans to test a device several times more powerful than Milrow at Amchitka. This test was code-named Cannikin.

A five-megaton nuclear device, Cannikin was part of America's plans for an anti-ballistic missile (ABM) system to protect United States cities against Soviet missiles in the event of war. The Soviet Union was said to have deployed an ABM system around Moscow, and naturally the United States was interested in acquiring such a system as well.

Opinion was divided among scientists. Some thought ABMs would work. Others thought no ABM system, however big and sophisticated, could prevent the Soviets from delivering at least one or two warheads to a chosen target; and one warhead would be enough to wipe out a city. This difference of opinion encouraged the Department of Defense to investigate ABM technology.

U.S. ABM plans called for a two-layered anti-missile defense. The first line of defense against incoming missiles from the Soviet Union would be the Spartan missile. Spartan was designed to intercept and destroy hostile missiles several hundred miles out in space. Rather than hitting the missiles directly, however, Spartan was intended to zap them with a destructive barrage of x-rays from the explosion of its nuclear warhead. The x-rays from Spartan were supposed to cause "thermomechanical shock" in the heat-resistant nose cones of the enemy missiles. The fierce assault of x-rays would heat up the nose cone and make it break up or evaporate. Then the missile and its nuclear payload would burn up or disintegrate harmlessly in the atmosphere during re-entry.

If any missiles should get past Spartan, then the second part of the American ABM system—a smaller rocket, called Sprint—would take over. Sprint was shaped like an elongated ice-cream cone and was aptly named, for it traveled many times faster than the eye could follow. One second the sky over a Sprint launcher would be perfectly clear. A fraction of a second later, there would be a trail of smoke reaching upward as far as the eye could see. One never saw the missile. Sprint could stop an incoming missile from exploding but could not prevent radioactive fallout from showering down on nearby cities. Sprint was the last-ditch ABM defense.

America had the technology to build the rockets. But would their all-important warheads fire as planned? There seemed little reason to proceed with the ABM program unless there were some assurance the warheads worked. And so the Department of Defense and the Atomic Energy Commission decided to test the Spartan five-megaton warhead at Amchitka.

Cannikin was more than just a repeat of Milrow. Its explosion would generate a sizeable earthquake at the test site. And "earthquake" is a highly potent word in southern Alaska, where one of the most disastrous quakes in history took place on Good Friday of 1964.

At 5:26 P.M. on March 27, 1964, the ground under Anchorage began to undulate like a carpet being shaken. A few miles to the east, at a point about midway between

Anchorage and Valdez, two blocks of the earth's crust had begun sliding past each other along the Denlai Fault. In less time than it takes for a commercial break on radio or television, the earth shuddered. When the quake ceased, much of Anchorage was gone. The main street had been broken up vertically into a long string of small cliffs. Anchorage alone suffered some $275 million in damage. The airport control tower was destroyed and the controller on duty was killed in its collapse. On balance, however, Anchorage was lucky. Even more devastating than the tremor itself was what it created in the waters around the quake's epicenter: a seismic sea wave.

The tsunami rippled out from the quake site as the tremor uplifted the land and displaced water. The wave raced away from the epicenter at express-train speed. In deep water, it posed no danger; it was so long and comparatively shallow that it was all but imperceptible in waters well offshore. Near the land, however, the tsunami began to "feel bottom." The water piled up in the shallows, and the wave rose into a mass several stories tall.

Breakers three stories high slammed into Seward, a bustling port city with a large fuel storage depot near the railroad tracks along the waterfront. Topped by flaming oil, the tsunami picked up massive boxcars and locomotives and carried them along as if they weighed ounces instead of tons. After the tsunami had passed, the rail lines were gone, either carried away or buried in silt, and the fuel storage tanks lay scattered like upset pill bottles, their contents afire. The waterfront simply vanished under the impact of the wave.

At Kodiak, the same community devastated earlier in the century by Katmai's eruption, history repeated itself, but with a slight difference. When Katmai erupted, the town was buried in ash. When the tsunami from the Good Friday quake arrived, Kodiak was buried in water. Picking up fishing vessels from the harbor, the wave hurled them inland over the tops of houses and buildings. Flood-waters drowned the downtown section and wiped out the local crab industry: boats, canneries—practically every-thing—disappeared. Almost half the Kodiak fishing fleet was demolished, and surviving boats were damaged badly by the debris picked up and hurled against their hulls. According to eyewitness reports, a general store near the waterfront was lifted off its foundation, carried out into the harbor, swept back toward land again, rushed back toward the sea once more, and finally settled almost at its original location.

Seward, Valdez, Kodiak, Anchorage—all the communi-ties along the southern Alaskan coast were rocked or shat-tered or flooded by the earthquake and its resulting sea wave. (The wave damaged coastal cities as far away as Crescent City, California, where it came ashore as a tower-ing breaker that piled trucks atop one another like shoe-boxes.) The Good Friday earthquake was the most powerful ever to strike North America, and the second most powerful ever recorded to that date. The energy released by the tremor was estimated later as roughly equivalent to 200,000 megatons of TNT. Two hundred thousand megatons works out to about 1,000 tons of TNT for every man, woman, and child in the United States. The Alaska quake released some 4,000 times as much en-ergy as the largest nuclear device ever exploded, and several hundred times more energy than the sum of all atomic weapons exploded up to 1964. Damage was estimated at a third of a billion dollars and eventually rose to almost a billion. More than 100 persons were either killed or simply vanished in the earthquake and the tsunami.

The words "Good Friday" had a tragic meaning after the Alaskan earthquake of 1964; and when news of the planned test at Amchitka Island leaked out, the people of southern Alaska were suddenly reminded of the shat-tered main street of Anchorage, the flaming wall of water at Seward, the fishing boats sunk or smashed at Kodiak.

Would the mini-quake from Cannikin serve as a trigger for a repeat of the Good Friday catastrophe?

Alaskans feared it might. Their spokesman in Washington, Senator Mike Gravel (Democrat-Alaska), who had opposed testing on Amchitka for years, warned that the AEC had no way of knowing what the effects of Cannikin —the most powerful nuclear device ever exploded underground to that date—would be. Alaskans were not reassured by statements from the AEC and the U.S. Geological Survey to the effect that Amchitka Island was geologically stable and had endured the Milrow test relatively unscathed. Nor did the people ease their opposition to the planned test when the Council on Environmental Quality, in April, 1971, tried to reassure them that the long-term effects of Cannikin on the environment would be "minimal"; for what seems minimal to Americans in the lower forty-eight states might seem disastrous to Alaskans who had the bomb going off in their very backyard.

As publicity grew around the planned test, some disturbing information about Cannikin came to light:

The Spartan warhead to be tested at Amchitka was said to be obsolete. If the warhead was outdated, then there seemed to be no reason to proceed. The AEC's insistence on carrying out the test only made many Americans wonder if the federal government, having spent millions of dollars on preparations for Cannikin, was determined to go ahead with the test merely to avoid losing face.

The Nixon administration itself seemed divided on the isue of Cannikin. The Environmental Protection Agency (EPA), while it did not come out specifically in opposition to Cannikin, was rumored to be highly critical of the test, and would not allow its report of possible resulting dangers to be classified "top secret."

The head of the Council on Environmental Quality was quoted in *Newsweek* as saying the blast from Cannikin might set off a series of increasingly powerful tremors, building up to a severe earthquake. He was also quoted as saying such a quake could generate a tsunami that would imperil cities and towns all around the rim of the Pacific Ocean.

Several dozen U.S. Senators were alarmed by the planned test and made every effort to discourage the Nixon administration from going ahead with it. Thirty-five Senators sent a petition to President Nixon asking him to call a halt. Much the same request came from a dozen world-famous scientists, including Dr. Linus Pauling and Dr. George Wald, who asked that the proposed test be postponed so that Congress could debate its merits and drawbacks.

But the Nixon administration persevered in plans for the Amchitka blast. And as newspaper cartoonists depicted mad scientists setting bombs in Alaska and President Nixon being surprised by an Alaskan whale rising up in anger, the little Aleutian island was prepared to receive the bomb.

Cannikin would explode more than a mile underground. To be exact, the shaft containing the warhead was 5,875 feet deep. The shaft was no ordinary hole in the ground, either. A conventional drill bit for oil or gas wells is only six or eight inches in diameter. The drill bit used on Amchitka was ten feet wide. Sinister black, its face was studded with more than a dozen bright-orange cutting elements called "burrs." The burrs looked like beer barrels covered with spikes. The whole assembly weighed as much as several automobiles. Altogether, the drill removed more than 450,000 cubic feet of rock from the island's heart.

The scene on Amchitka's surface was much like that above an exploratory oil well. A cluster of prefabricated buildings surrounded the site. A steel tower marked the spot where the warhead was lowered into the deep pit drilled for it. At first glance, there was nothing to indicate that the energy of ten billion pounds of TNT would soon be released in a tightly contained fireball far under the surface.

Conditions underground during such a test are hard to imagine, because all our traditional concepts of matter and energy break down completely in the inferno of a nuclear explosion. For a split second, the earth under Amchitka would be hotter than the surface of the sun. Neutrons at the core of the fireball would form a gas as dense as steel. Conditions under Amchitka would be unlike anything else in the known universe, except perhaps reactions in the hearts of stars. This was the fury the U.S. government planned to unleash under Amchitka, almost within shouting distance of a deep offshore subduction zone and several potentially dangerous fault lines. Alaskans were scared, and so were other nations around the Pacific basin.

Canadians were particularly opposed to the test. Their Pacific shore stood exposed to any tsunamis that might be generated if a major quake did result from the Cannikin test. The thought of a tsunami like the one at Seward in 1964, slamming into coastal cities such as Vancouver, was almost too awful to contemplate; and so the Amchitka explosition set off a preliminary explosion of protests in Canada. Anti-American demonstrations erupted all along the border. In Windsor, Ontario, young demonstrators barricaded the bridge to Detroit with lumber, blocking traffic for hours. One Canadian group warned that if Cannikin was exploded as planned, several dozen American businesses would be bombed in retaliation. Less drastic protesters planned to charter a boat, sail it to Amchitka, and lie just offshore at the planned moment of explosion, in hopes of stopping or delaying the test.

Other nations were worried as well. Japan, located right in the path of any tsunamis that might be generated by the Amchitka blast, delivered a strong protest to Washington and asked that the test be scrubbed. Peru and Sweden did the same. But the United States remained adamant: Cannikin would go off on schedule.

(One nation remained silent through the Cannikin controversy: the Soviet Union. Though the U.S.S.R.'s eastern shores stood to be hit hard by any seismic sea waves from earth tremors in the Aleutians, the Soviets made no formal objection to the test. Moscow knew such an objection would be pure hypocrisy, as Russia had its own program of underground nuclear tests under way; and if the international effort to stop Cannikin succeeded, then similar pressure might someday be applied to the Soviets.)

As the controversy raged over Cannikin, preparations went ahead on schedule at the test site in Alaska. The warhead was lowered into place, and the shaft was sealed with some 5,600 tons of sand and gravel. The shaft was wired from top to bottom. A hundred thick cables radiated out from the test site, like the arms of some exotic sea creature. These cables would carry data about the explosion to instruments on the surface, in the split second before the heat and blast from Cannikin destroyed the underground sensors.

Far underground in the cavity drilled for Cannikin was a television camera. It sent back a strange image of the nuclear warhead, a conical, finned device suspended from the roof of the cavity. It looked like a giant cake decorator. It also contained 250 times more explosive power than the atomic bomb that obliterated Hiroshima. On command from an observation post 23 miles away, Cannikin would explode and release its five megatons of energy—about enough to destroy Manhattan and its adjacent boroughs—within the space of a suburban living room.

The thought of 250 Hiroshimas going off under their state, in an area long notorious for earthquakes, gave Alaskans and opponents of nuclear testing the determination of tigers to fight Cannikin down to the final second before the switch was thrown. But the AEC remained firm in its support for Cannikin.

All through the weeks before the test date, the AEC

reiterated the argument that the warhead should be tested if the Spartan system was to be built. The commission backed up its position with some convincing facts. For one thing, there was no record of a tsunami ever being generated by an earthquake in the *western* Aleutians, where Cannikin was to be tested. The devastating tsunamis of recent years, such as that from the 1964 Good Friday quake, had originated in the eastern part of the southern Alaska coast. Moreover, the Soviet Union had, in previous months, carried out at least two subterranean bomb tests roughly equal in yield to Cannikin, without serious results.

In short, there was no historical evidence to indicate Cannikin might lead to disaster. But there is always a first time; and the government's effort to reassure the public of Cannikin's safety failed to convince many Americans—and other peoples around the Pacific basin—that the test was a wise idea.

Cannikin's opponents took heart when a group of thirty-three Congressmen began legal action to force the Nixon administration to put all its cards on the table. Reportedly, seven federal agencies, including the State Department and the Office of Science and Technology, were against the Amchitka test, while only two agencies—the AEC and the Department of Defense—were in favor of it. The undersecretaries of these agencies had put their views into a report on Cannikin, and the Congressmen wanted that report released. Cannikin's foes hoped this tactic would delay the test for several months, until some of the mystery surrounding it could be dispelled.

But the test could not be stopped by paperwork. The President of the United States was the only person who could order Cannikin canceled or postponed, unless the U.S. Supreme Court ordered it halted.

The court battle over Cannikin continued right down to the wire. Test date: November 6, 1971. As Canadians shouted opposition to the test in public demonstrations, and protesters marched near the White House with signs warning of quakes and tsunamis, the Supreme Court was called into special session—on only a few hours' notice—to hear an appeal from a lower court concerning Cannikin. The Court was warned by the Nixon administration that any delay of more than a few hours would jeopardize the success of the test. The Justices had ninety minutes to deliberate. Their verdict: go ahead. The vote was four to three in favor of the test. Environmentalists had failed, by only one vote, to halt Cannikin.

Five thousand miles away in the western Aleutians, the Spartan warhead lay waiting more than a mile underground. A few miles away from Amchitka, technicians sat at their consoles ready to send out the signal that would release the fury of ten billion pounds of TNT.

At last the signal flashed out over wires to the bomb.

It took less than a millionth of a second. Neutrons hit plutonium atoms inside the warhead and set off a fission reaction. Hydrogen in the "heavy water"—deuterium—also inside the warhead began fusing under the unthinkable heat and pressure of the fission explosion. Fusion released still more energy, starting a whole new atomic explosion, all in less than a millionth of a second.

The ground above the test site heaved skyward. A fan-shaped cloud of rock fragments and water burst up from ground zero (the technical term for the bomb's location) and fell back slowly toward the island.

Amchitka rocked under the multi-megaton force of the bomb. Cannikin had created an artificial earthquake of magnitude 7 on the Richter scale.

Shock waves from the blast rippled outward from the test site, through the earth's crust, along the fault lines of the southern Alaska coast. Tremendous potential energy is stored along those faults. A bit of that energy had been released in 1964, and dealt the communities there a blow from which they were, in 1971, only just recovering. All around the Pacific basin, observers waited tensely, watching for signs of the tremors and tsunamis they feared might follow Cannikin.

The hours following the explosion were tense ones for Cannikin's opponents. There was always, it seemed, the chance that the nightmare they envisioned would come true, and the relatively gentle jolt from Cannikin would set off a delayed reaction, an ever-increasing series of tremors as the crustal plates started sliding and grinding against one another along the fault lines that rim the Gulf of Alaska. But those fears were never realized.

Cannikin caused no quakes other than that from the explosion itself. No tsunamis raced out from Amchitka to batter Pacific shores. Cannikin was a success. The only physical damage was to the island itself. A few sea lions and birds died. That was all.

But damage of a different kind was done at Amchitka. The federal government acquired a reputation for bull-headed persistence in the face of widespread public protest. U.S.-Canadian relations, then at a low point because of the Vietnam War and Canadian resentment of America's "economic imperialism," were pushed even lower by the Cannikin test. Allies of the U.S. began to wonder if the government would risk natural disaster, in its own territory and abroad, solely in the interest of engrossing its war machine.

The public has a short memory, and in a few months the controversy over Cannikin was all but forgotten. But the possible link between underground nuclear testing and earthquakes returned to the headlines a few years later, following a killer earthquake that struck Tabas, Iran, in 1978.

The earthquake occurred in September and killed some 25,000 persons. There was nothing to set this quake apart from hundreds of others in the history of Iran . . . or so it seemed at first. But it soon became clear that there was something odd about it.

For one thing, seismologists are usually admitted to the

area of such a quake after the event, to assess the damage. This time, however, quake experts were denied permission to visit. Were there things at Tabas that they were not supposed to see?

Something else was unusual about the earthquake. A few hours before the quake leveled Tabas, the Soviet Union had tested a nuclear device underground, about 1,500 miles away, near the city of Semipalatinsk in Siberia.

Russia's bomb test was unusually powerful. The bomb exploded at Semipalatinsk yielded about ten megatons, twice as much as the Cannikin test of 1971. It was also a shallow test as underground explosions go—about a mile down.

This extraordinarily big and rather shallow explosion set earthquake experts in the United States and Europe to thinking. Was there some connection between this abnormal explosion and the earthquake that hit Iran almost immediately afterward?

The Iranian quake was itself highly abnormal. It was shallow, like the Semipalatinsk test. The epicenter was about 10 miles below the surface at Tabas—much nearer the surface than usual. Moreover, the Tabas quake differed from most natural earthquakes in that there were no apparent aftershocks, the little tremors that follow the main event in a day or two. The British magazine *New Scientist* (October 12, 1978) suggested "it is possible" that the Tabas quake was the result of "a nuclear test . . . gone awry," and cited a German seismologist who reportedly announced some connection between the Soviet test and the Tabas tremor.

Let us suppose, for the sake of argument, that nuclear bomb tests may set off earthquakes inadvertently in seismically active areas. Might bombs then be used to set off quakes deliberately?

That was the premise of a 1978 story by British-American writer Alistair MacLean. In his novel *Goodbye California*, MacLean describes a plot by terrorists to touch off seismic disturbances along California's San Andreas Fault, using nuclear devices planted underground. The terrorists' plot is foiled at the last moment by a California highway patrol officer and his son.

Such ideas make interesting reading. But how feasible are they in practice?

From time to time, stories appear in the press about geophysical warfare, a new concept of fighting in which the natural environment would be turned to military purposes. Many fiction writers (and a few scientists) have dreamed up scenarios of future wars fought with guided hurricanes and artificial earthquakes as well as guns and bombs.

Perhaps there will be an earthquake machine someday, and it may even be used to shake down a few cities in wartime. For the moment, however, geophysical warfare in general seems little more than a pipe dream, for a variety of reasons.

First, the target would have to be in a seismically active area, preferably along a fault where strain has been building up for decades and a major quake seems imminent. Some large cities meet this condition. Tokyo and Los Angeles are prominent examples.

Second, the attacker would have to have some way to set off a quake. Nuclear bombs might work. Set them in shallow holes along the fault line, and touch them all off at once. Then sit back and watch the resulting earthquake level a few cities. In theory, this technique might multiply the destructive power of a few bombs a hundredfold.

But what if the attempt failed?

The chance of success in such a scheme would seem to be very small, because seismology is still an infant science and many things about earthquakes are still a mystery to us, including their "triggers." How much energy would one have to inject along the San Andreas Fault to cause a quake capable of leveling San Francisco? No one knows, or seems willing to hazard a guess. Possibly a well-placed bomb would do it, or possibly it would require as much megatonnage as a full-scale nuclear assault. In the latter event, an enemy would do better to aim his bombs at the city itself, and at least be assured of some result.

Also, the nations of the world have a good reason *not* to indulge in this new and still highly speculative kind of warfare, if it ever becomes practical.

The advantage of geophysical warfare—its ability to masquerade as a natural disaster, and save the attacker from retaliation—is also its drawback. For if a geophysical assault can mimic a natural disaster, then a natural earthquake (or whatever) might be mistaken for a deliberate attack, and thus set off a conflict of unimaginable proportions.

Fortunately, that kind of warfare is fantasy, at least for now; and with luck it will remain so until our civilization can find an alternative to war for settling differences among nations.

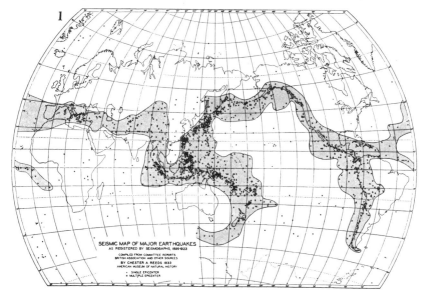

A seismic map of the world.

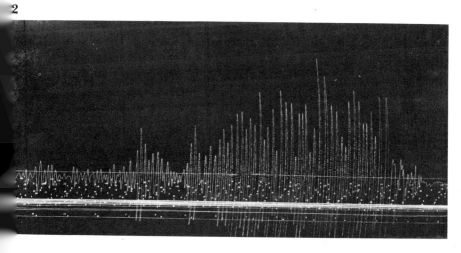

A seismic record of the 1939 earthquake in northern Japan.

Damage to City Hall caused by the San Francisco earthquake, 1906.

A devastated San Francisco after the earthquake.

A view looking south along the San Andreas Fault, Elkhorn Scarp, California.

Martinique eruption cloud.

Shattered but unburned trees after Mount Pelée eruption.

Alaska earthquake. March 27, 1964. Collapse of 4th Avenue near C Street, Anchorage, due to landslide caused by the earthquake.

Major plume erupting from summit crater of Mount St. Helens volcano, Washington, taken at about 11:30 A.M., May 18, 1980. In background, steam and ash clouds are being blown to the northeast. In foreground, white linear features are logging roads, dark patches are mature trees.

A series of satellite photographs showing the eruption of Mount St. Helens on May 18, 1980.

8:45 A.M. PDT
Eruption + 0 Hrs 6 Min

10:15 A.M. PDT
Eruption + 1 Hr. 36 Min

1:15 P.M. PDT
Eruption + 4 Hrs 36 Min

4:15 P.M. PDT
Eruption + 7 Hrs. 36 Min

A rise of liquid lava more than 30 feet high.

VII

Izanami's Children

EARLY ON THE MORNING of December 7, 1941, a bomb from a Japanese warplane fell down the funnel of an American battleship, the U.S.S. *Arizona,* in Pearl Harbor, Hawaii. Gutted by the bomb, the *Arizona* settled onto the bottom of the harbor, trapping inside her hull several hundred men. There they still lie. Atop the submerged wreck of the *Arizona* is a sleek white memorial where visitors can look out at the warship's hulk, just visible beneath the surface. Among the visitors are many Japanese. Some of them cry. Others watch impassively. One wonders whether any of the visitors know the *Arizona* was bombed and sunk because plates of the earth's crust happened to meet in a particular way.

At the far western edge of the Pacific Ocean lie the islands of Japan. The Japanese have an interesting legend of how their land was created. In the beginning, Japan did not exist. There was chaos, a formless, swirling mass of vapor. In the midst of the vapor stood a bridge, and on the bridge stood two deities, the god Izanagi and the goddess Izanami.

Watching the confused mass of vapor before them, Izanagi and Izanami decided to bring order to it. Izanagi touched the mists with his spear and made them condense into some cousin of sial. The globules fell to the waters far below, forming the only dry land on earth. The god and goddess were delighted with their handiwork and descended for a close inspection.

As they circled the islands, Izanami and Izanagi appear to have taken a good look at one another for the first time, and they were pleased with what they saw. When the goddess laid eyes on the god, she praised him for his masculine beauty. (The names Izanagi and Izanami mean, repsectively, "attractive man" and "attractive woman.") Izanagi might have run to her arms then and there, but he was a male chauvinist and thought it inappropriate for a female to initiate a courtship. Therefore he made another circuit of the island and, when he saw Izanami again, got in the first word this time: *What a beautiful woman!*

At first the god and goddess had trouble consummating their marriage, because they had no knowledge of sex and procreation. They learned by watching wild animals. Eventually they started conceiving and bearing children, and after some early blunders (somehow Izanagi gave birth to their first child), they succeeded in turning out a long line of offspring: the islands of Japan.

Childbirth seems to have been as risky for gods as for humans, because Izanami was incinerated accidentally while giving birth to a fire god. Thereafter her husband had to reactivate his womb and carry on without her. Soon Izanagi graduated from spawning islands to creating new gods. He may have regretted that decision, because his son Susanu turned out to be a sex maniac and a delinquent. He raped his sister Amaterasu, the sun goddess, and this immoral union gave rise to the long string of Japanese emperors. But our principal concern here is not the crimes of Susanu. More interesting from a geologist's point of view are the first children of Izanagi and Izanami: the islands of the Japanese archipelago.

The islands of Japan follow a gentle arc from the cold seas off Siberia in the north to the near-tropical waters off the Philippines. Altogether, Japan is about the size of California. It has many other things in common with California as well, including volcanoes and a high incidence of earthquakes because of the Ring of Fire. The Ring follows the curve of the Japanese archipelago for the nation's whole length, and has touched almost every aspect of life in Japan—the people, their history and culture—in one way or another.

Even the legend of Izanagi and Izanami may be read as a metaphor of Japan's geological history. The islands of Japan were pushed up by the collision of the Pacific and Eurasian crustal plates. This meeting corresponds roughly to the meeting of the god and goddess. Just as Izanami was forced to submit to Izanagi during their courtship, the thinner Pacific plate has been overridden and subducted under the thicker continental plate to the west. The "children" of this collision, the volcanoes of the Japanese archipelago, have scorched large areas of Japan from time to time, much as Izanami was burned up while giving birth to a god of fire. And a person with an active imagination might see in the depredations of Susanu a metaphor for the islands' long history of devastating earthquakes.

Essentially, the history of Japan is a drama played on a stage set by the Ring of Fire. Indeed, there are countless examples of how the Ring has affected Japanese history. For instance, when Japan started its expansion in eastern Asia in the 1930s, in order to form a "Greater East Asia Co-Prosperity Sphere" (the euphemism for a new Japanese empire), one of Japan's goals was what Hitler called

Lebensraum—living space for the Japanese people. Japan had a high population density, and it was only natural that the Japanese should look to neighboring countries for room to expand. The Ring of Fire was partly to blame for the overcrowding of Japan: the collision of the two crustal plates had made Japan a narrow and rugged chain of mountains, in many parts of which the land was too high or too steep for settlement.

The natural resources of neighboring nations also attracted the Japanese, and here again the Ring of Fire was largely responsible. Agricultural land, which China and other nearby countries had in abundance, was scarce in Japan because of the mountainous terrain; and even when every square inch of arable land was utilized, the Japanese islands still had a shortage of cropland for feeding their huge population.

Then there were mineral resources to be exploited, especially in southeast Asia. The subduction zone along the coast of Indonesia, for example, had concentrated tin and other valuable metals the Japanese needed to keep their imperial war machine running. More importantly, there was oil in this part of Asia: another gift from the Ring of Fire, which had created conditions suitable for petroleum formation where the crustal plates ground together.

The Japanese knew that if they were to have a free hand in eastern Asia, the United States Navy would have to be crippled or eliminated as a power in the Pacific. So a carrier strike force was sent east from Japan to knock out the U.S. Navy in its Pacific base at Pearl Harbor. The Japanese ships were able to sneak up on Hawaii without the Americans detecting them. And early on Sunday morning, December 7, 1941, Japanese planes flew in low and dropped their bombs on the aircraft lined up unprotected at Hickam Field and on the large warships moored along Battleship Row. One of the bombs hit the *Arizona*, and the battleship sank in water covered with two feet of fuel oil. The destruction of the U.S. fleet at Pearl Harbor was, in a sense, just a long-delayed reaction to the collision of the Asian crustal plate with the Pacific plate and the Indian plate: a collision that helped to create the incentives that lured Japan to war.

Japan has suffered greatly from its position along the Ring of Fire. Earthquakes hit the islands frequently; and Japan, being an island nation, is often struck by tsunamis from those same tremors. Vulcanism is also a hazard here. The volcano Asama erupted in 1783 with such violence that the finely divided ash it cast into the upper atmosphere, 20 miles or more above the surface, caused a haze to cover the northern latitudes for the next year, chilling the earth measurably.

One of the worst natural disasters to strike Japan was the great Kwanto earthquake of September 1, 1923. Measured at 8.2 on the Richter scale of earthquake intensity, the quake occurred on the eastern coast of Japan near Tokyo and Yokohama. The shocks were minor at first, and the hundreds of thousands of persons who felt the initial tremors thought: Just another earthquake. (A perceptible quake occurs somewhere in Japan almost every day.)

This was, however, anything but just another earthquake. Before the Kwanto quake was over, more than half a million homes would be destroyed, and some 143,000 persons would lie dead—killed not by collapsing buildings so much as a fire touched off by the tremors.

Two things combined to make Japanese cities highly susceptible to fires. The first was the widespread use of charcoal braziers—*hibachis*—to cook food. The second was the construction of buildings. Many of the homes in Japan were flimsy firetraps by Western standards. Wood-framed, they made extensive use of lightweight and highly flammable materials such as paper. There was a good reason for this construction; it was less expensive than brick or stone and, if shaken down in an earthquake or destroyed in some other way, could be rebuilt relatively cheaply and easily. The wood frames were also more flexible and thus more likely to survive earthquakes than a less resilient stone or brick building was. So this method of construction—developed, ironically, in response to the unstable earth under the Ring of Fire—was widely employed, and would prove fatal to a multitude of people after the Kwanto earthquake.

The earthquake began about ninety seconds before noon. It was a Saturday, and Tokyo and Yokohama were full of activity: shoppers in the business district, ships entering and leaving the harbor, mothers tending children at home and preparing to cook the noon meal. Probably no one felt the very first tremors; but they registered as marks on seismograph paper at Tokyo University. Geologists looked at the machine and watched in horror as the marks grew in size. The earthquake had started small but was growing to mammoth proportions; soon vibrations were felt plainly all over the two cities.

Like a struck gong, the earth under Tokyo began to oscillate as two plates of the crust ground slowly past each other. At first the shocks were concentrated near the northern end of Sagami Bay, just east of the quake-prone Izu Peninsula and a few miles south of Tokyo Bay. But the epicenter of the quake moved northeastward—the worst possible direction, for it brought the earthquake directly into Tokyo.

Most of the flexible wood-frame buildings in Tokyo could withstand a moderate earthquake. But very few buildings, flexible or not, can withstand the power of an earthquake that measures 8.2 on the Richter scale—about the same magnitude as the San Francisco earthquake of 1906.

At first the floors shook underfoot. Then the thin internal walls of houses began to shake and sway. Large and supposedly quake-resistant buildings fell apart like wet cookies, and a fire consumed much of the urban area shortly after the tremor. Trees whipped back and forth, and bamboo groves near the edge of the city were agitated so violently by the ground motions that they splintered with loud crackling, rattling sounds.

When the tremor was over, and the last rumble had died away, other sounds were heard. There were screams from men, women, and children trapped and crushed half to death under the wreckage of their homes.* There was the thump and crack of still-falling masonry as buildings continued to shed bricks and ornamental stonework. And there was the crackle of flames as coals from upset braziers touched the wreckage of homes and set off countless fires all over the Kwanto area.

To add to everything else, there was a stiff wind blowing from a typhoon offshore, whipping small individual fires into one huge holocaust. In a short time all of Tokyo and Yokohama, from the waterfront to the inland suburbs, was aflame.

In the rural areas, residents were trying to escape their homes and reach what seemed relative safety outside. Often their progress was hindered by the bamboo thickets that were cutting themselves into sharp-edged fragments as they churned back and forth. To walk upright into such a thicket was suicide; a bamboo fragment can slash a person to ribbons as effectively as a sword (one reason the samurai, if they could not afford metal swords, used to make their weapons out of knife-edged bamboo). Near the ground, however, there was very little motion, so one got through the bamboo by crawling on the ground while razor-sharp shards swayed back and forth just overhead.

The waterfront buildings were built mainly of wood, and went up like kindling. Men and women, their escape cut off by the spread of the fire, jumped into the water

---

* As in many other severe earthquakes, the number of fatalities in the Kwanto quake was disproportionately high in certain age groups. The very young and the very old suffered the most casualties; they were the most likely to be indoors where buildings could fall on them.

in the hope that ships would rescue them. Some ships did. Others had too many problems of their own to worry about refugees from shore. The wind was picking up flaming bits of wood and paper and dropping them on the ships, creating a terrifying fire hazard. The ships' crews went to work with hoses, rakes, and even their bare hands to keep their vessels free of the sparks and fiery fragments from shore. Some eyewitnesses said the water in the bay was *boiling*, even though the fire on shore probably lacked the heat to vaporize water more than a few feet from land. This phenomenon has been observed many times during earthquakes along the Pacific shore, even when there was no combustion on land. In a later chapter, we will take a close look at the "boiling" sea that often accompanies large quakes, and see how it may be a clue to the cause of earthquakes and tsunamis—as well as a potentially tremendous energy source for the future.

The Boso Peninsula, east of Tokyo, suffered less damage than the city, but only because the peninsula was less densely populated. Half a dozen towns there were destroyed almost completely by the tremor. The Kanagawa Prefecture to the north was also hit severely. The town of Simasoga was flattened. In the entire area shaken by the earthquake—the Tokyo-Yokohama metropolitan area and its surrounding prefectures and peninsulas—between 550,000 and 650,000 homes were destroyed, and, as stated, some 143,000 persons were killed.

What made the Tokyo-Yokohama earthquake and fire so much more devastating than the San Francisco quake several years earlier? The tremors were about equal in intensity; and while the Japanese cities were more densely populated than San Francisco, that difference alone cannot account for the vast disparity in casualties.

Perhaps the attitude of the Japanese themselves had much to do with it. Westerners in Tokyo and Yokohama at the time of the earthquake were astonished at how little the Japanese did to fight the fire and save themselves.

Henry Kinney, a magazine editor, looked on in disbelief as men stared blankly while the fire consumed their homes, and, in some cases, their friends and families as well. It would have been easy for them to stop some of the fires, Kinney wrote later in an article for the *Atlantic,* or at least retreat to safer locations. But their attitude was *shikataganai:* "You can't fight it," or "What will be will be." This fatalism probably cost hundreds, if not thousands, of lives.

Though the Japanese were unwilling to fight the fire, they devoted much energy to finding a scapegoat for it: the Korean minority in Japan. Japanese had (and still have) an almost universal prejudice against Koreans, who occupy much the same position in Japanese society that Jews did in Europe until very recently. Koreans are said to be rich and devious, and to control many highly profitable businesses, legal and illegal. No matter if they look poor, or middle-class, their appearance is just show, intended to conceal the fact that they are making vast profits at the expense of the simple, honest Japanese. That, at least, was the widespread belief in Japan at the time of the Kwanto earthquake; and so it was easy for the Japanese to transfer the blame for the magnitude of the disaster from themselves to the Koreans. Several thousand Koreans—whose only "crime" was to have been in Japan at the time of the tremor—were gathered up by vigilante groups and subjected to kangaroo trials. The charges were arson and looting. The outcome of the so-called trials was never in doubt, and the Koreans were executed to the cheers of the public. Undoubtedly the government could have stopped this atrocity had it wished; but officials gave their sanction to the vigilantes, and Korean heads rolled in the days after the earthquake.

To Japan's old enemy Russia, the earthquake was a source of pleasure, for Russia was still smarting from the beating it took from Japan in the 1904–1905 Russo-Japanese War. The Russian fleet had been wiped out in a battle with the Japanese Navy, under the command of the brilliant Admiral Togo. When Russian mathematician Alexei Nikolaevich Krylov heard the news of the Kwanto earthquake, he announced (with tongue firmly in cheek) that he had used the quake to calculate the distance from the earth to the throne of God. Russia's prayers, he said, had started out from the earth in 1905, traveling at the speed of light. Eighteen years later, the earthquake shook Japan as God's judgment on Japan traveled back at the same speed. Dividing that delay in half, Krylov figured it was precisely nine light-years to God's seat.

Things had been going badly for Japan long before the Kwanto earthquake. The government was widely viewed as corrupt and bumbling, and an economic depression was settling on the country. The people were unhappy and grumbled constantly about their ineffective leaders; political assassinations were almost commonplace. It was a difficult and maddening time for the Japanese. And on top of it all came the earthquake.

The government, which probably was as inept and corrupt as the people believed it to be, tried its best to deal with the aftereffects of the earthquake, setting up shelters for the homeless, providing food and water and medical attention. But the destruction caused by the tremor was so great that even the richest and most efficient government would have had trouble meeting the challenge. As a result, the situation went from bad to worse. The government lost much of what little respect the people still had for it, and Japan's economic condition was made still worse by the destruction of two of its major commercial centers.

When order breaks down in a country, it is often restored by an autocratic government. That is precisely the kind of government Japan got shortly after the 1923 earthquake, when Japan came under the rule of its warlords.

At the same time, Japan, battered and hungry, recognized that nearby countries had plenty of the resources Japan needed, especially agricultural products from China, which Japan had coveted for years. Japan therefore decided to build up its military strength in preparation for seizing foreign territory . . . and a few years later, the bombs were falling on Pearl Harbor.

It is an exaggeration to say that the 1923 earthquake *caused* World War II in the Pacific, of course. But the Kwanto quake is certainly one of the things that pushed Japan from peace to war, and led to a global conflict that brought irrevocable change to society and politics all over the world.

Individual earthquakes seldom have such a severe effect on life in Japan. The Japanese people have learned to coexist with the quaking earth, since there is very little they can do to make it less active; and this attitude of resignation may have contributed toward the fatalism one finds in Japanese philosophy—a philosophy that was much in evidence after the Kwanto earthquake.

How will the Japanese behave in the next big quake? The world may soon find out, because there is reason to think the area around Tokyo is due for a severe shaking in the near future.

The Japanese call it "the Tokai quake." Tokai is a section of the Shizuoka Prefecture, which surrounds Suruga Bay about 90 miles south of Tokyo, near Mount Fuji. This section of Japan is subject to frequent destructive tremors. One such quake, which occurred early in 1978, measured 7.0 on the Richter scale—fully a tenth as strong as the Kwanto quake of 1923—and did $20 million in damage. Two dozen persons were killed. The quake's proximity to Tokyo disturbed geologists and civil-defense authorities; had the tremor occurred just a bit farther north, a large part of Tokyo would have been destroyed.

Seismologists base their belief in an imminent Tokai quake on a theory of earthquake prediction known as the "gap method." One of the most promising approaches to earthquake prediction, the gap method uses the record of past earthquakes to indicate where future tremors are likely.

Earthquakes are centered at specific locations along a fault. One day, a quake may strike at point A. A year later, another tremor is noted at point B, 100 miles away. Point C, 50 miles farther along the fault, is shaken the following year. Since the strain along the fault has been released by the earthquakes at those points, they are unlikely to shake again for a long time to come. The points to worry about, then, are *in between* these quake sites—that is, the gaps in the quake map. In the gaps, strain may be building up to the critical point, so that a quake is not far off.

The gap method has been used with notable success in Latin America. In 1979, geologists made an accurate prediction of a Mexican quake, using the gap technique. What about future quakes?

They were the subject of a meeting in New York in May, 1980, of earthquake specialists from all over the world. The prognosis was disturbing.

One ominously quiet area along the Ring of Fire is, as just mentioned, the Tokai gap, midway between Tokyo and Osaka, where many seismologists think a superquake is due almost anytime. This area is one long string of residential and industrial properties, and the results of a major quake there may be compared to a San Francisco-scale tremor striking the Northeast industrial corridor of the United States, between Boston and New York.

The United States has reason to worry, too. There are two suspicious gaps in the earthquake map of the Aleutian Islands: one near the root of the Alaska Panhandle, roughly midway between Juneau and Anchorage, and the other at the tip of the Alaska Peninsula, about where the Aleutians begin. This is sobering news indeed for the people of southern Alaska, many of whom still have vivid memories of the destruction in Anchorage and the massive tsunami that followed the Good Friday earthquake of 1964.

We may be uncertain exactly when and where the next severe quakes will strike along the Ring of Fire, but gradually our prediction methods are improving, and someday we may be able to predict earthquakes—time, place, and intensity—with much greater accuracy than is possible today. Whether we will want to do so is another matter. As a later chapter will show, earthquake prediction may be a cure almost as bad as the disease.

When the Japanese armed forces swarmed southward toward the islands of the Malay archipelago during World War II, they saw all around them the results of vulcanism: towering cone-shaped mountains, their summits frosted with ice.

Much less conspicuous was a little ring of islands in the strait between Java and Sumatra. Lang, Verlaten, and Rakata, the maps called them. Rakata's inner face was peculiarly steep. It looked as if something had sliced the island in half and lifted a chunk away. That is exactly what happened one day in 1883, when an ascending column of magma met an obstruction and proceeded to make an obscure island called Krakatoa one of the most famous volcanoes in history.

VIII

The Safety Valve

"*DURING THE CLOSING DAYS* of the month of August, 1883, the telegraph cable from Batavia carried to Singapore, and thence to every corner of the civilized world, the news of a terrible subterranean convulsion—one which in its destructive effects to life and property, and in the startling character of the world-wide effects to which it gave rise, is perhaps without a parallel in historic times."

Thus begins an important and frightening document in the history of science: the British Royal Society's 1888 report on the explosion of the volcanic island Krakatoa in the Dutch East Indies five years earlier. The 500-page book tells, in understated prose that makes the story all the more chilling, how an undistinguished volcano in the Sunda Strait between Java and Sumatra blasted itself into history one day in 1883 and made the word "Krakatoa" a synonym for disaster for generations to come.

The Sunda Strait connects the South China Sea with the Indian Ocean. This shallow stretch of water, less than 600 feet deep in many places, is one of the most important sea lanes of the world. Much of the commerce of the British Empire passed through this strait, on its way to and from the ports of Djakarta and Singapore. The Japanese had looked enviously at the waters of the Dutch East Indies before World War II, and in 1942 sent two battle fleets south under the command of Admirals Ozawa and Takahashi to seize the Indies for Japan. Not far from the Sundra Strait, Dutch Rear Admiral Karel Doorman, commanding a patchwork flotilla of warships from several nations, made his brave but doomed effort to push back the Japanese and keep the Indies in Dutch hands. Outnumbered and outgunned, the Admiral went down with his flagship and five other ships under his command. Japan held the islands for only three years and was forced to return them to the Netherlands in 1945.

The Sunda Strait and the islands around it are perhaps the most intense focus of volcanic activity in the world. Java, an island about the size of England, has some 35 volcanoes, more than half of which have erupted in the last three centuries. Some are active almost continuously. The island is riddled with hot springs and geysers, boiling evidence of the constant tumult underground. Much the same conditions prevail on the island of Sumatra, just west of Java, and on the smaller islands of Bali, Lombok, Timor, and Flores, to the east. Flores has at least 16 volcanoes squeezed into an area no bigger than Connecticut; six of the volcanoes are clustered as tightly as bowling pins, near the eastern tip of the island.

A sea-floor map shows the reason for this hot spot of vulcanism. Here, along the Java Trench just to the south of Java and Sumatra, the Indian Ocean crustal plate is being subducted under a southeastern tongue of the Eurasian plate. The lighter components of the Indian plate are melted as the plate descends, and seep back to the surface through fissures in the overlying rock. The result is the Indies' impressive chain of volcanoes, some of them more than 12,000 feet high.

The path of the descending plate may be traced easily on a chart of earthquake foci. Southwest of Java and Sumatra, where the plate has just begun its trip underground, quakes are centered near the surface. On the other side of the islands, under the Java Sea, quakes originate much deeper underground as the subducted plate "groans its last" before being melted and reabsorbed into the mantle.

Two fissures intersect in the Sunda Strait, and at their conjunction is Krakatoa. The Krakatoa of today is only a fragment of the island that stood here prior to 1883.

A century ago, Krakatoa was a volcanic island several square miles in area. It was shaped roughly like an eggplant, with the stem pointing northwest toward Sumatra. There were three volcanic cones on Krakatoa: Rakata, the tallest (2,623 feet), at the southern end of the island; Perboewatan, a small cone (about 300 feet), at the northern end; and Danan, an intermediate cone (1,400 feet), in between.

Close around Krakatoa were several smaller islands. Verlaten Island, a curved splinter of rock about two miles long and half a mile wide on average, lay roughly one mile northwest of Krakatoa. Lang Island, slightly larger than Verlaten, stood about half a mile to the northeast of Krakatoa. The fourth member of the group, Polish Hat (it was shaped more or less like a three-cornered hat of the kind worn in colonial days), was an insignificant pile of volcanic debris in the Krakatoa Channel between Krakatoa and Lang Island. The whole complex of islands was no more than six miles in diameter.

To a casual observer, the Krakatoa group looked like just another cluster of small islands. The peculiar curve of Verlaten and the close spacing of the islands, however, indicated to geologists that this had been the site of a terrific eruption and explosion thousands of years earlier.

We cannot reconstruct the history of Krakatoa precisely, because much of the geological evidence of its past has been destroyed in eruptions. Geologists can tell, however, that there was once a towering volcano on this site— perhaps more than two miles high—that was destroyed in a colossal eruption millennia ago.

One day, long before historical records of eruptions were kept, this proto-Krakatoa rumbled to life. Earthquakes shook the land, and finally the top of the mountain expelled a miles-high cloud of ash and steam. Chunks of volcanic rock—solidified lava and pieces of rock torn from the throat of the mountain itself—rained down onto the land and water for perhaps 100 miles or more around the volcano. But the eruption was so intense that it could not last for long.

An earthshaking series of explosions took place. Much of the summit was blasted upward and pulverized. What remained of the volcanic cone then collapsed, leaving what geologists call a "basal wreck," the shattered bowllike stump of the destroyed volcano.

The jagged rim of the basal wreck became the islands surrounding Krakatoa, Verlaten Island and Lang Island. The position of the islands followed the curve of the basal wreck and gave geologists a clue to the size of the volcano that once loomed above this part of the East Indies.

The explosion of the former Krakatoa must have been truly a world-shaking event, because the mountain is thought to have been some 25 miles wide at the base and more than 80 miles in circumference, about half the size of Rhode Island. It would take a nuclear explosion in the megaton range to shatter such a huge peak completely, and something equivalent seems to have happened here many years ago.

From the ruins of that volcano rose a new Krakatoa, as magma continued to seep up from underground. This younger volcano was known as Rakata, meaning "crab," to the Javanese, most likely because of shellfish to be found in its waters. The Dutch mispronounced the name as "Krakatau," and the word found its way into English as Krakatoa. (There is another and more appealing story of how Krakatoa got its name. A visiting foreign dignitary is said to have been passing through the strait one day and asked his boatman the name of the volcanic island. The boatman's reply in Javanese, "I don't know," sounded something like "Krakatau," and the visitor took that sentence to be the volcano's name.)

There were many visitors to these islands in the ten centuries or so before Krakatoa's eruption in 1883. Traders from the Middle East arrived in the 1200s and introduced the Islamic religion. Islamic beliefs and traditions were fused with the existing Hindu culture of the islands, and Mohammed and Vishnu learned to coexist in the islands near Krakatoa.

Europeans, notably Marco Polo, began arriving around the year 1300; and with the expansion of European sea power in the centuries that followed, it was only a matter of time before the islands of the East Indies became European possessions.

While other Eupropean powers were busy carving out overseas empires for themselves elsewhere in the world, the Dutch moved into the Indies. Beginning in the late sixteenth century, the Dutch replaced the former government of the islands with one of their own. To their credit, the Dutch were less brutal than many other colonial powers in history, perhaps because they were wise enough to see that no great force was needed to take over these islands. It was just a matter of "persuading" the local authorities—sometimes at gunpoint—to cooperate with them in exploiting the Indies. The traditional system of government was left intact. The native nobility kept their jobs and titles, and life went on much as before, except that the nobility was controlled from behind the scenes by resident Dutch bosses.

This tropical empire was relatively gentle as empires go. It was, of course, organized to make a few persons rich at the expense of many others, but the average person in the Dutch East Indies seemed reasonably content with Dutch rule. Probably the Dutch did a better job of governing the people than the people could have done for themselves. And if the natives of the Indies had any thoughts about rebellion and independence from the colonial yoke, they kept such thoughts to themselves. (This is not to say that the Dutch empire in the East Indies was a paradise; many workers were exploited brutally by local native authorities, with the tacit approval of their Dutch overlords. But on the whole, Dutch domains in the Indies were infinitely more pleasant places to live in than, for example, some of the overseas lands conquered by Japan in its expansionist period during the 1930s and 1940s.)

The islands were every European's idea of tropical beauty. They supported lush forests (which grew out of soil made up partly of ashes deposited by past eruptions of Krakatoa and other nearby volcanoes) full of edible fruits and of bamboo, the principal building material of the islands. Perhaps the most attractive place near the Sunda Strait, at least to Europeans, was Anjer, one of the largest local ports, situated on the Javanese shore almost within swimming distance of Krakatoa. One visitor to Anjer shortly before the eruption of 1883 described the port as "exceedingly pretty," a town of clean white buildings with red tile roofs, surrounded by a dense growth of tropical fruit trees and some 20 smaller villages. The other local towns along the coast were tied to Anjer by a post road, and none of them was more than a couple of hours' journey by boat from Telok Belong, the other major port, on the shore of Sumatra within sight of Rakata's summit.

Though the volcano and its neighboring islands were covered with beautiful tropical vegetation ("affording a wonderful relief to eyes long accustomed to the monotony of a waste of waters," one report on the island declared),

Krakatoa was uninhabited. Perhaps because it was said to be a haven for pirates, and also because of its reputation for volcanic violence, residents of nearby islands visited Krakatoa only to fish in its waters and occasionally gather fruit and timber from the forests.

Europeans likewise found little to interest them on Krakatoa. They sounded the waters around the island meticulously for the purpose of navigation, but never bothered to survey its interior systematically, nor even to make an accurate chart of its shoreline. Sailors considered Krakatoa little more than an obstruction in the strait, and generally Krakatoa was treated as just another bit of local scenery.

Although local legends said the volcano had rumbled to life occasionally in the past, and there were ominous prophecies of still more eruptions to come, no written records of Krakatoa's eruptions were kept until Europeans settled the East Indies.

Even those records are sketchy, up to Queen Victoria's day. The mountain erupted briefly in 1680, but there are only fragmentary accounts of the incident, and it seems to have done no signicant damage. Forests were burned away but grew back in the next few decades.

Krakatoa remained comparatively quiet for the following two centuries, and the 1680 eruption became only a dim memory. Then a series of earthquakes in 1880 reminded residents of the area that Krakatoa was not dead. A quake on September 1 damaged a lighthouse nearby and was felt 1,000 miles away in Australia.

The next rumblings came in 1883. On the morning of May 20, sounds like naval gunfire offshore were heard in Batavia (now Djakarta), about 100 miles from Krakatoa. An earthquake rattled windows all over the area for several hours, and the crew of a mail boat steaming through the strait noticed the compass needle gyrating wildly. No one knew the source of the quake until the following day, when Krakatoa spat out a jet of steam and sent ash drifting onto Butzenbourg and neighboring towns.

Already Krakatoa was showing signs that this eruption would be unusual. In most eruptions, smoke and steam emerge from the summit of a volcano or from smaller, "parasitic" cones on its flanks; but the master of a ship passing near Krakatoa saw vapor billowing out from around the base of the volcano, much as steam hisses out from around the rim of a teapot lid when water is boiling inside under high pressure. The steam jets from Krakatoa indicated something might be plugging up the main chimney of the volcano and forcing gases to build up inside.

However, this escape of steam and smoke seemed not to cause alarm. It was business as usual at Batavia and Butzenbourg.

Before long, though, it was clear this would be a spectacular eruption. Bright bursts of light, possibly from superheated gas escaping, accompanied loud explosions and the release of smoke and ash; lightning sparked in the plume that rose above Krakatoa.

Something besides ash began to fall from the sky. Chunks of pumice rained down on the land and onto the decks of ships nearby. On May 23, a vessel sailing near Krakatoa found thick layers of the rock fragments floating on the sea.

Ships at sea had a splendid vew of the plume from the eruption. The captain of the German ship *Elisabeth* estimated its height at about seven miles, considerably higher than the four- to five-mile-high plume from a recent eruption of Vesuvius. On May 22, the captain of another vessel noticed that the smoke and vapor came not from the summit of Krakatoa, but definitely from around the base of the volcano, as had been reported earlier. Flashes of light, each followed by an explosion, were accompanied by showers of pumice and ash which fell as far as 300 miles away. A light ashfall was reported at Timor, more than 1,000 miles from Krakatoa, but may

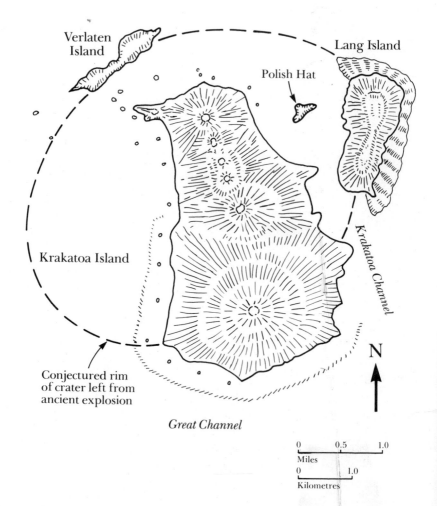

Verlaten
Island

Lang Island

Polish Hat

Krakatoa Channel

Krakatoa Island

N

Conjectured rim
of crater left from
ancient explosion

Great Channel

| 0 | 0.5 | 1.0 |
Miles
| 0 | 1.0 |
Kilometres

KRAKATOA ISLAND AND SURROUNDING ISLANDS: *This diagram, modified from British Admiralty charts, shows the volcanic island and its neighboring islands as they appeared before the explosion of 1883. The shorelines of the islands as pictured here are approximate, since no official survey was ever made of Krakatoa before its destruction. Sumatra and Java (not pictured here) are to the upper left and lower right, respectively.*

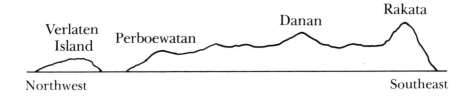

Verlaten Island   Perboewatan   Danan   Rakata

Northwest   Southeast

Verlaten Island   Rakata

Northwest   Southeast

BEFORE AND AFTER: *These two drawings show the profile of Krakatoa before (top) and after (bottom) the explosions of August 1883. Note that the peaks of Danan and Perboewatan were destroyed totally, and only part of Rakata, at the southern end of the island, survived.*

have come from another source.

The area around Krakatoa might have been evacuated if the quakes and explosions had continued unabated. But the volcano soon settled into relative calm, and it appeared the worst was over. This short pause in the eruption gave a few intrepid men in Batavia the chance to visit Krakatoa and see firsthand the effects of the eruption. It would be the last time anyone set foot on the island—and lived to tell about it—before its last convulsions.

A steamer left Batavia on May 26 with an exploration party on board. That night, as the ship approached the island, the men heard several loud explosions. It seemed reasonably safe to proceed for the moment, however, and the steamer continued on course for Krakatoa, arriving there on the morning of Sunday, May 27.

A ghostly sight awaited the visitors to the island. Krakatoa appeared shrouded in snow—finely ground volcanic glass. The "snowfall" covered parts of the adjacent islands as well. The rain of pumice had stripped trees of their leaves and branches and left only trunks standing.

Oddly, some trees on Rakata, the tallest peak, were almost unharmed. Why had they, seemingly the most vulnerable trees on the island, been spared?

Rakata, it turned out, was not in eruption. All the activity had come from little Perboewatan, the 300-foot cone at the northern end of the island. Perboewatan was still erupting, and Jules Verne could hardly have conceived a more melodramatic scene. Explosions shook the island every ten minutes or so, and each blast bared the red-hot lava in the volcano's throat, casting an eerie light on the clouds overhead.

The island seems to have resembled a World War I battlefield. Stifling fumes were pouring from the volcano, and explosions sent chunks of pumice—some of them three feet wide—whizzing in all directions at the velocity of rifle bullets. (Some bits of pumice, the Royal Society report noted five years later, were cast into the upper atmosphere, caught by high-altitude winds, and carried in the direction opposite to winds at the surface. The noise of the eruption was deafening at close range, and it was said afterward that the din made a rifle blast sound like the popping of a champagne cork by comparison.

Even in the face of these hazards, several climbers started up the sides of Perboewatan for a look at the caldera. The slope was fairly gentle, but ankle-deep pumice made climbing difficult. At last the climbers reached the summit and looked down into Perboewatan.

The caldera was more than half a mile wide. Evidently it had been enlarged greatly by the explosions. Its walls sloped down to a flat floor, some 500 yards across, covered with a thin dark crust of solid rock that hid the molten lava below. A hole about 150 feet wide, in the center of the floor, belched steam with ear-shattering noise.

Deafened by the racket and half roasted by the heat, the exploration party retreated after collecting a few rock specimens for study. A photographer on the ship lying offshore took a photograph of the eruption at this stage. A dark mushroom cloud, like that of a nuclear explosion, rises diagonally above Krakatoa, and a veil of ash falls from the cloud toward the ground.

There were no casualties on that visit to Krakatoa, but, as noted, it was the last such excursion. When Captain Ferzenaar, a cartographer, tried to land on Krakatoa for a survey on August 11, the thick cloud of dust and vapor prevented him from going ashore. Where the clouds parted, he saw that the once-lush forests had been destroyed completely; only a few scorched tree trunks were visible.

Through July and most of August, the eruption continued. There were earthshaking detonations, and mild tremors kept rocking the strait, but in time the locals seem to have gotten used to the spectacle and taken it in stride. In any event, there was no mass exodus from the area. Possibly those who wished to leave found it hard to do so because of the difficulty of navigation.

Crumbly volcanic rock lay deep on the sea for hundreds of miles around the volcano. Captain Johnson of the ship *Idomene* noted in his logbook for August 11, "Passed through large fields of pumice." A week later, Captain Thomas of the bark *West Australia,* in the Indian Ocean about a thousand miles west of Krakatoa, recorded seeing "a great amount of lava today." The next day he mentions "large quantities of pumice," some pieces a yard in diameter.

As volcanic rock rained nonstop from the sky, explosions kept booming out over the water from Krakatoa. On the morning of Sunday, August 26, the bark *William H. Besse* was about thirty miles east of the island when all on board heard a series of "terrific reports" like "the discharge of heavy artillery." Krakatoa was blowing up.

All through the summer, the volcanic island had been transforming itself into a giant bomb. A set of peculiar circumstances—probably the same as had destroyed the previous volcano here, ages before—had let gases build up to tremendous pressures inside the island, until even the weight of the overlying rocks could contain the blast no longer.

Krakatoa blew up because cool sea water came in contact with the magma at the volcano's heart. It is widely believed that the water was simply turned to steam, which built up pressure until, so to speak, the boiler burst. Actually, it seems more likely that the gas pressure came not from steam but from gases bubbling out of the molten rock itself.

That was the conclusion of Professor J. W. Judd of the Royal Society's Krakatoa committee. Water and other volatile materials, Judd pointed out, may be dissolved in molten rock far below the earth's surface. These components may make up 15 percent of some magmas. While the molten rock is under intense pressure far underground, the water and other volatile substances stay in solution because the pressure is so great that the dissolved gases have no room to fizz out of solution.

Near the surface that awful pressure is relieved as the magma expands and seeps into crevices all through the crustal rocks. With the pressure off, the gases come out of solution, just as a canned soda bubbles when one pulls the tab. The rock may solidify as the bubbles form, and the result is pumice or scoria.

What if those gases escaped from the rock, however, but could not escape from the volcano? Judd imagined that was what happened at Krakatoa because of sea water seeping into the magma chamber.

The inrushing water would have cooled down molten rock near the surface and literally dampened the force of the eruption there. But this damper was applied *only at the surface.* Below, the molten rock was still releasing gases from solution, but the gases were unable to escape because the cooled rock above them blocked their upward path.

The effect, Judd said, was the same as "fastening down the safety valve of a steam boiler, while the fires below were maintained in full activity." Pressure built up and had nowhere to go until the volcano blew apart.

Krakatoa exploded in a series of staggering detonations on the 26th and 27th of August.

At 1 P.M. on the 26th, loud explosions were heard at Batavia and Butzenbourg, 100 miles from Krakatoa.

At 2 P.M., Captain Thompson of the ship *Medea,* about 75 miles E.N.E. of Krakatoa, saw a column of smoke and vapor shoot up from the strait to an altitude estimated at more than 15 miles.

By 5 P.M., the explosions could be heard all over the island of Java.

No one in Batavia slept that night. The noise was compared to that of nearby cannon and was, by itself, strong enough to tilt pictures on the walls.

Captain Watson of the British ship *Charles Bal* had

perhaps the best view of Krakatoa's last convulsion. On Sunday afternoon, the 26th, the ship was only ten miles south of Krakatoa. Watson saw the island covered with roiling black smoke. Besides the deafening explosions, he heard a strange crackling sound that may have been caused by chunks of pumice colliding in midair. The cataclysm scared Watson so badly that he decided to shorten sail and beat around the island to the east rather than approach further. Around 5 P.M., large hot pieces of pumice started thudding down on the *Charles Bal*'s deck.

On board the *Sir Robert Sale,* Captain Wooldridge looked toward Krakatoa at sunset and noticed the island had "a most terrible appearance." A "dense mass of clouds" blackened the sky, and in the darkness Wooldridge saw "fierce flashes of lightning." He described the cloud directly above the island as "an immense pine-tree with the stem and branches formed from volcanic lightning." He smelled sulfur on the wind.

Captain Watson, on the *Charles Bal,* saw an equally spectacular display of fireworks that night. "Chains of fire" shot skyward from the volcano, Watson said, while "balls of white fire"—probably lava—rolled down the flanks of the island. The smell of sulfur was all but over-powering, and Krakatoa showered the ship with a cinder-like fallout. Soundings were made, and the lead came up hot from a depth of 180 feet. The individual blasts from the island merged into one almost continuous explosion from midnight until four in the morning, and Krakatoa must have looked like a colossal strobe light: the sky, Watson said, was "one second intense blackness, the next a blaze of fire."

The eruption charged the air with electricity, and soon the lightning was joined by another eerie electrical phe-nomenon on the ships themselves: St. Elmo's fire. This was no doubt the "pinky flame" Watson observed in the rigging of his ship that night.

Watson's crew appear to have kept their heads during

this weird display. Not all the ships' crews were so calm. The glowing plumes of static terrified the Asian crew of the steamer *Loudon,* in the Bay of Lampong some 50 miles northwest of Krakatoa. Fearing a "spirit" would destroy the ship, the men climbed the rigging and tried to beat out the "flames" with their bare hands.

Captain Wooldridge, on the *Sale,* watched the eruption from about 40 miles away. Late in the afternoon of the 26th, he had seen the cloud around the island as "an immense wall with bursts of forked lightning . . . like large serpents rushing through the air." That night the wall of cloud turned into a "blood-red curtain," yellow at the edges, illuminated by the lightning. Captain Sampson of the bark *Norham Castle,* close to the *Sale*'s position, saw "flickering flames" behind the cloud, and halos of static in the rigging of his ship. The flames were either lightning or possibly flashes of light from the glowing lava itself as explosions blew away the thin layer of cooled rock over the lava and lit up the overhanging clouds with an eldritch orange glow.

St. Elmo's fire was not the only thing covering the ships' rigging that night. Moisture in the tropical air combined with the fine dust from Krakatoa to produce a rain of mud which stuck to decks, spars, and rigging. This extra weight above decks theatened to make the ships top-heavy, or "crank," and more likely than usual to capsize. Climbing aloft to scrape off the mud, however, was to risk death from electrocution: lightning struck the mainmast of the *Loudon* at least five times during the night. The mud accumulated on the *Loudon*'s deck at the rate of half an inch per minute.

The morning dawned clear at Batavia, but between 7 and 10 A.M. the cloud from Krakatoa moved in. By 10:15 lamps were required to see indoors, and a few minutes later a watery mud-rain began falling. The rain gave way just before noon to a fall of small lumps of dust cemented together by moisture. Around 1 P.M., the rain of dust tapered off, and stopped at around three o'clock. The cloud cut off sunlight up to 150 miles away from Krakatoa, though dust did not fall everywhere.

As the lumps of dust fell on Batavia, Krakatoa was blasting itself to pieces. There were four huge explosions on the morning of the 27th, starting at 5:30 and ending just before eleven o'clock. While no one seems to have seen those explosions through the pall of smoke and ash that surrounded Krakatoa, the effects of the blasts were felt almost immediately on the *Sale*, which was bombarded with chunks of rock. At the same time, mud-rain fell again on the *Sale*, the *Charles Bal*, and the *Norham Castle*. Their crews, who had had to risk death by lightning the previous night while scraping muck off the decks, now had to brave falling boulders as they tried to clean the heavy mud off their vessels.

The noise of the explosions spread out over the Indies. A Lloyd's agent at Batavia reported that "in the early morning the reports and concussions were simply deafening." The captain of the ship *Sea Witch*, 500 miles away at Surabaya, heard the explosions so distinctly that there seemed no way they could have come from Krakatoa. Officials at Singapore, 522 miles from Krakatoa, thought the sounds came from a ship firing its guns as a distress call, and two rescue ships were sent out to see what the trouble was. Government officials at Macassar and Timor —970 and 1,350 miles from the volcano, respectively—also thought the sounds came from a ship in distress, and sent out boats to investigate. Tribesmen at St. Lucia Bay in Borneo thought they were under attack by Dutch troops and fled in panic. Even phone communications were disrupted; the telephone office at Singapore reported that until midafternoon on the 27th, conversation "was utterly impossible" on the line to Ishore. "On raising the tubes a perfect roar, as of a waterfall, was heard, and by raising one's voice the clerk at the other end heard the voice, but not one single sentence was understood." The police chief at Rodriguez, an Indian Ocean island some 3,000 miles away from Krakatoa, heard rumbles as of "heavy guns" firing far away. Never before or since in history have sounds been heard so far away from their point of origin without the use of electronic communications.

It was Wednesday, the 29th, three days after the last series of explosions began, before the *Loudon* was able to get under way. The ship moved slowly through thick rafts of pumice between the Bay of Lampong and Krakatoa. What the sailors of the *Loudon* saw at Krakatoa had no precedent in history.

The northern half of Krakatoa had vanished. Where Perboewatan and Danan had stood, there was only water. Rakata had been sliced in two vertically—all 2,623 feet of it—by the explosions. The whole stratigraphic history of the volcano lay exposed, layer on layer of tuff (volcanic detritus) and lava, from the nearly horizontal strata on the bottom—deposited when the volcano was young—to the steeply angled beds near the summit. It was like looking at a giant piece of stage scenery from the rear, which the audience is not supposed to see.

Krakatoa was, in fact, a piece of scenery in a drama staged in a worldwide theater, with a cast of millions; and the destruction of Krakatoa itself, the greatest natural explosion in history, was only a curtain raiser. What followed in the next few days would make the death of Krakatoa seem almost insignificant.

IX

Aftermath

THE HARBORMASTER at Colombo, Ceylon (now Sri Lanka), had never seen anything like it. Ships in the harbor were whirling about at their anchorages like weathervanes in a changing breeze.

The cause of the ships' strange motion was the seismic sea wave, the tsunami, created by the explosion of Krakatoa. When the volcano exploded, part of the energy of the blast was transferred to the surrounding water. A wave rippled out from the volcano, and the force of that wave would be felt all over the world—most destructively, by the luckless communities along the shores of the Sunda Strait.

A few minutes after the explosion of Krakatoa, the wave reached the *Loudon*. Still shaken from the electrical pyrotechnics set up by the eruption, the officers and crew of the *Loudon* must have been hoping the worst was over. That hope was shattered, as were the nearby towns along the coast, when the tsunami from Krakatoa arrived.

The men of the *Loudon* saw a huge wave rising out of the sea, rushing toward themselves and the shore. Hastily, the ship was turned bow on to the approaching wave. The captain knew that a ship's only chance of surviving such a wave was to meet it directly and perhaps ride up over it in relative safety. A ship parallel to the wave would be capsized and sunk.

Loudon survived. Just as the ship had finished turning to meet the wave, the tsunami struck.

As the wave front lifted it like a bathtub toy, the ship jumped upward, rose to the crest of the wave, hung poised for a moment, stern out of water, and then slid with sickening velocity down the back slope of the wave.

That dizzying ride over, the sailors turned their attention toward the shore. The wave that had come so close to sinking their ship, was now moving relentlessly toward the coast and the city of Telok Betong.

In a few seconds, the water rolled over Telok Betong and annihilated it totally. Shops, homes, docks, warehouses, churches—everything was wiped out in this huge upheaval of the sea. Three more waves followed. Had the *Loudon* been closer in, it would probably have been picked up by the tsunami and smashed onto the shore.

The same scene was repeated all along the coasts of Java and Sumatra near the Sunda Strait. When the tsunami struck Tjaringin on the Javanese shore, only one tree in the town survived. The wave picked up several huge lumps of coral from offshore and carried them seven miles inland. The nearby town of Penimbang, 10 miles from the sea, was submerged completely. The marketplace at Karang Antoe was full of shoppers and merchants when the wave arrived. Three hundred corpses, most of them women, were counted there after the tsunami had passed.

More than 2,000 persons at Anjer and Batavia were killed by the wave. Fifteen hundred more were killed at Bantam. Several entire islands vanished. So many of its victims were obliterated that we will probably never know exactly how many persons died in the tsunami from Krakatoa. Estimates range between 30,000 and 80,000, but these are little more than guesses. Most persons who died from the Krakatoa wave vanished as if they had never been born.

In some places, only a few yards and seconds separated life from death. The lighthouse at Second Point, a few miles southeast of Krakatoa on the Java shore, was struck by lightning shortly before the tsunami arrived. The lightning electrocuted several convicts who were working below, tethered together with iron chains that carried the lethal shock from one man to another. Their bodies were not yet cold when the lighthouse keeper saw the wave approaching, and scrambled for the only remotely safe spot he could find: the top of the lighthouse. He and the lighthouse survived.

The keeper of another lighthouse along the strait, some miles away at Fourth Point, was less fortunate. He survived the tsunami but saw his lighthouse cast down and destroyed, his wife and child carried away and drowned.

The sea was not the only thing convulsed by Krakatoa's eruption. The earth itself let loose its pent-up fury, as if encouraged by the bold display at Krakatoa. Papandayang and several other volcanoes on Java roared to life and sent hot mud and lava flows rushing down their slopes, and several dozen square miles of the Javanese coast subsided abruptly and disappeared under the sea.

The most striking effect of Krakatoa's eruption, however, had to do with the air. Long after the sound of Krakatoa's death had stopped echoing across the water, bits of the volcano itself were still in the air; their presence would have a small but measurable impact on world climate in the following year.

Much of the material put into the atmosphere by Krakatoa was exceedingly fine. The volcano had acted rather like a giant grindstone during its eruption. Bits of pumice were ground together by the turbulent air currents in and above the maw of Krakatoa, and reduced quickly to a powder like confectioner's sugar. This fine solid material was lifted easily into the upper air, in huge amounts, by the convection currents rising from Krakatoa. The powdery pumice took a long time to settle out of the air at that altitude, where there are no periodic storms to wash the air; and as the particles from Krakatoa began spreading around the earth, wafted along by the jet stream, they intercepted incoming sunlight. The result: less sunlight reached the ground, and temperatures began to fall in the months after Krakatoa exploded. The growing season was a week shorter than usual in Great Britain that year. Mean annual temperature worldwide fell about .5 to 1 degree Fahrenheit during the year 1884—not a huge change by everyday standards, but enough to cause a chillier than usual winter. In fact, world climate cooled perceptibly all through the late 1880s and part of the following decade as well. Some climate experts attribute this change, at least in part, to the dust from Krakatoa.

The idea that volcanic eruptions may change climate is centuries old. In 1784, Benjamin Franklin noted that the year 1783 had been unusually cool, and that sunlight reaching the ground seemed somehow diffused. He remarked that when the sun's rays "were collected in the focus of a burning glass, they would scarcely kindle brown paper."

Franklin also reported that a "dry fog" hung over the land during the summer of 1783, and that this fog appeared to be cutting off some of the incoming sunlight. But what could have caused this strange phenomenon?

Franklin suspected a volcanic eruption. He proposed that the "vast quantity of smoke" ejected from the volcano Skaptar Jökul in Iceland had created the cloud, blocked part of the incoming solar radiation, and given the northern latitudes a colder than usual year.

Most likely Franklin was right. The probable cause of

the chill in 1783 was volcanic ash high in the atmosphere. Skaptar Jökul, however, in all likelihood could not have put out enough particulate matter by itself to have such an impact on climate. The Icelandic volcano appears to have had a partner in climate change: the volcano Asama in Japan, which erupted about the same time, with much greater force.

A century and a half after Franklin published his speculations about volcanoes and climate, a U.S. Weather Bureau study of temperature as a function of solar radiation showed an interesting correlation between the Krakatoa eruption and temperature change. The study showed that immediately after Krakatoa's eruption in 1883, the total heat received from sunshine dropped to about 88 percent of the normal figure, a reduction of 12 percent from normal, and more than 16 percent from the previous year. Mere coincidence? That seems unlikely when one studies the graph of temperature variations over the next few decades.

There were several intense volcanic eruptions, among them Bogoslov Volcano in Alaska, in 1889. Insolation dropped 4 percent the following year. The change was even more marked in 1902 when, immediately after the eruptions of Mount Pelée and La Soufrière, the temperature measurements fell precipitously, from 101 to 88 percent of normal. The Katmai eruption in Alaska in 1912 had still greater effect. From a reading of 101 or so in 1911, the temperature reading dropped to 84 percent in a few months.

The physics of this process can be very complicated. The dust particles in the air, for one thing, do not merely block out sunlight as one does when pulling a window shade. The particles also *scatter* sunlight, so that the total amount of solar radiation reaching the ground may be greater than one might expect after a volcano has pulverized several cubic miles of rock and shot them into the air. As a rule, however, more rock flour in the upper atmosphere means less sunlight reaching the ground, and consequently lower temperatures.

The drop in temperature is not felt equally everywhere, of course. In the tropics, where sunlight is abundant and a loss of 1 percent or so may be negligible, one may not notice any serious effects from an eruption. In the higher latitudes, however, a drop in insolation can be serious, because the incident angle of light is lower in the regions nearer the poles and sunlight is harder to come by.

To illustrate, let us see what happened after an eruption before and considerably more violent than Krakatoa: that of the volcano Tambora in the Dutch East Indies in 1815.

Tambora, some 13,000 feet high, loomed above the island of Sumbawa near Java. It was inactive in the early days of European settlement and was generally thought to be extinct, until the mountain began to throw up small ash showers in 1814. But no one seemed alarmed about these minor eruptions, and so the residents of the area were unprepared for the tremors which shook the island on the night of April 5, 1815, heralding an eruption of truly earthshaking magnitude.

Explosions rumbled out from the volcano's throat. British troops in the vicinity of Tambora went on alert. Their commander heard the thunderous noise offshore and feared an invasion from sea might be imminent. The true source of the noise became apparent, however, when the cloud of ash and smoke from Tambora spread out over the surrounding area for 300 miles, turning day into night and burying the islands in Tambora's immediate vicinity under layers of ash.

Sir Thomas Stamford Raffles, the British soldier and adventurer who founded Singapore, was serving as military governor of Java at the time and thus had a ringside seat for the spectacle. Several different accounts of the eruption are attributed to him, but the following excerpt conveys as well as any the essence of what he saw:

Almost everyone is familiar with the intermitting convulsions of Etna and Vesuvius . . . but the most extraordinary of them can bear no comparison, in point of duration and force, with that of Tomboro. This eruption extended perceptible evidences of its existence . . . to a circumference of a thousand statute miles from its centre, by tremulous motions and the report of explosions; while within the range of its more immediate activity, embracing a space of three hundred miles around it, it produced the most astonishing effects, and excited the most alarming apprehensions. On Java . . . the sky was overcast at noonday with clouds of ashes; the sun was enveloped in an atmosphere whose palpable density he* was unable to penetrate; showers of ashes covered the houses, the streets, and the fields to a depth of several inches; and amid the darkness explosions were heard at intervals, like the report of artillery or the noise of distant thunder. So fully did the resemblance of the noises to the report of cannon impress the minds of some officers, that from an apprehension of pirates on the coast vessels were dispatched to afford relief. . . .

The eruption began on April 5, and was most violent from the 11th to the 12th, and did not quite cease until July. . . . The first detonations, which were heard in Sumatra, a distance of 931 miles, were taken for discharges of artillery. Three columns of flame rose to an immense height, and the whole surface of the mountain soon appeared covered with incandescent lava which extended to enormous distances; stones as large as the head fell in a circle several miles in diameter, and the fragments dispersed in the air caused total darkness. . . . The . . . abundance of ashes expelled was such that in Java, at a distance of 310 miles, they caused complete darkness in midday and covered the ground and roofs with a stratum several feet thick. The region in the vicinity of the

---

* It was common practice in nineteenth-century Britain to refer to celestial objects, sometimes even those with feminine names like Venus, as masculine.

volcano was entirely devastated, and 12,000 natives died.

The eruption reached its climax on the night of April 10–11. Raffles described this phase of the eruption as follows:

> The whole mountain appeared like a body of liquid fire, extending itself in every direction. The fire and columns of flame continued to rage with unabated fury, until the darkness caused by the quantity of falling matter obscured it about 8:00 P.M. . . . Between 9:00 and 10:00 P.M. ashes began to fall, and soon a violent whirlwind ensued which blew down nearly every house . . . carrying the roofs and light parts away with it.

Tambora, like Krakatoa, submerged nearby coastal areas under a tsunami, and lost most of its towering cone. After the eruption, Tambora, having lost an estimated 36 cubic miles of rock, stood almost a mile shorter than before. Much of that rock was spread around the surrounding countryside, but a fraction of the ejecta, the very finest material, was cast into the upper atmosphere and had the same effect that Krakatoa's dust veil had in 1883. Americans began to notice those effects, particularly in the chilly Northeastern states, about a year after Tambora blew its top.

It was difficult to gauge any chilling effect from Tambora's dust cloud that winter. Severe weather is the norm for New England in the winter, and the winter of 1815–16 shows no signs of having been much colder than expected. It seemed unusual, however, when winter weather lingered into early spring, then late spring, and then early summer. Indeed, the summer was so cool that year that 1816 became known as "the year without a summer" and "eighteen hundred and froze to death."

New England farmers were handicapped by the abnormally cool weather, because it delayed the planting of

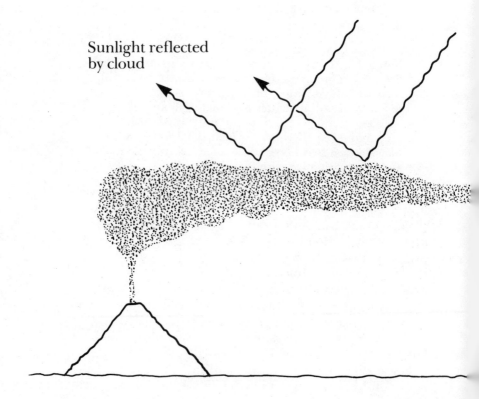

Sunlight reflected by cloud

HOW VOLCANOES CHILL THE EARTH: *The cloud of ash and smoke from a volcanic eruption intercepts incoming sunlight and reflects it back out into space. Thus insolation—the amount of solar energy reaching the earth's surface—is reduced, and temperatures fall.*

crops by some two weeks. Once planting was under way, it seemed the cool weather might be about to lift and a good —if shortened—growing season would begin. One day in June, the temperature reached 90 degrees. Only twenty-four hours later, however, the mercury fell below freezing, and frost formed on the crops. Three successive cold waves moved down into New England from Canada in the first part of June, dumping several inches of snow on the plants in the field.

Snow in summer: that was the bizarre sight New Englanders faced in 1816. When the land should have been covered by hot and humid air, it was blanketed by snow. "Christmas in July" was more than merely a figure of speech in the Northeast that year.

One might expect such weather to destroy food crops completely. In fact, the unusual weather seems to have improved the quality of some grains. Wheat and rye apparently thrived, and matured into fine heavy kernels, since they took longer than usual to ripen in the chilly weather. Root vegetables also are said to have done well that year because of the heavy precipitation brought down with the cold fronts. Corn was hard hit; it requires a certain amount of hot, humid, rainy weather to be successful. But otherwise the harvest that year was reasonably good, all things considered.

Other parts of the northern temperate zone were less fortunate. Eastern Canada experienced such a poor harvest that starvation became a significant cause of death among low-income families. France and Britain were plagued by crop failures, and in some parts of Europe the populace was reduced to eating rats, cats, dogs, and virtually anything else that would fit in a pot. The price of grain rose 400 percent in a few months in Switzerland, and Europe as a whole spent a hungry year until the harvest of 1817, when larders could be refilled.

The near-famine conditions in France created all manner of problems for the regime of King Louis XVIII, the conniving monarch who had, only a few months earlier, survived Napoleon Bonaparte's unsuccessful attempt to put himself back in power. The Napoleonic Wars had left France exhausted and bleeding, and the additional hardship of crop failures in 1816 was more than many Frenchmen could bear. Insurrections rose left and right as the French people, deciding they had suffered enough, took out their anger on the government. Grain was reportedly so scarce in many areas that farmers hesitated to take their produce to market for fear of being robbed and killed by hunger-crazed peasants along the way. Soldiers had to be called in to protect those farmers who did take their food to town, and sometimes the soldiers found themselves fighting pitched battles with thousands of starving men and women determined to reach the food on the wagons.

Canada and Europe needed grain desperately, and they turned to the relatively well-off Americans for help. American grain exporters complied. The huge food shipments overseas increased inflation in the United States, however, and American consumers were enraged to see the price of everything connected with grain rising sharply. (Here we see how history repeats itself. In the early 1970s, another change in climate wiped out much of the Soviet grain crop, and the hungry U.S.S.R. turned to the United States, its newfound partner in détente, for extra food. America complied with the Russians' request, but the grain deal to the Soviets was so poorly managed by the federal government that it cost the taxpayers millions of dollars in increased food prices. This "great grain robbery," as it was called, might have been avoided if U.S. officials had taken time to study the events of 1815 and 1816 before consummating the deal with the Soviets. To paraphrase the saying: those who are ignorant of history are likely to repeat it.)

A more pleasant result of Tambora's eruption was colorful skies. The dust that intercepted incoming sunlight and chilled the world in 1816 also made sunsets much more brilliant. The same thing happened after the eruption of Krakatoa. Sunsets were so brilliantly red in parts of New England after the Krakatoa disaster that fire companies spent hours chasing the sunset, thinking the light came from a burning city just over the horizon.

These displays in the sky were easy to explain. The fine ash in the upper atmosphere blocked short wavelengths of light and allowed only the long wavelengths, red and orange, to penetrate to the ground. This was the effect seen on a much smaller scale following the eruption of Katmai in Alaska by the crew of the U.S. Coast Guard cutter *Manning.*

If volcanic eruptions can cause the kinds of climatic changes described here, one wonders if they could have considerably more effects. Could a tremendous eruption or series of eruptions cool down the world enough to start an ice age?

Vulcanism has long been popular as a possible cause for the ice ages, those periods of glaciation that covered North America and Europe with sheets of ice miles thick. There are four major ice ages that we have charted in the Cenozoic, and it has been suggested that glaciation might be set off by a seemingly small drop in mean annual temperature worldwide: perhaps 6 or 7 degrees Fahrenheit. This cooling would mean more snow would fall, and less of it would melt. Snow remaining on the ground would increase the earth's "albedo"—its reflectivity—and bounce sunlight back out into space. That loss of heat from sunlight would, in turn, lower temperatures still more, generating more snowfall, a still higher albedo . . . and so on, indefinitely.

It is difficult to say how great a drop in temperature would be needed to set such a cycle in motion. Possibly it would take a much greater initial cooling to instigate an ice age. But the often quoted figure of 6 or 7 degrees

Fahrenheit is not too much more than the change attributed to volcanic eruptions in the last few centuries. A recent study pointed out that after one major eruption, or series of eruptions, the hemisphere is likely to cool off by a degree or so for the next year. One eruption can accomplish this. Krakatoa did. Now, what would happen if, for example, half the volcanoes in Indonesia opened up at the same time, and spewed out several hundred cubic miles of solid material? Such an event seems within the bounds of possibility, in view of what happened after the eruption of Tambora. An ice age might be the result.

Volcanoes are not, of course, the only accepted explanation for glaciation. The well-known Milankovitch hypothesis, put forth several decades ago by a Soviet climatologist, invokes irregularities—"wobbles"—in the earth's orbit and axis of rotation as the cause of ice ages. These wobbles affect the amount of sunlight reaching the earth's surface and result in periodic heating and cooling of the globe. Milankovitch's hypothesis has held up well in light of actual data, and many geologists and climate experts think the irregularities in the earth's orbit, as well as changes in the tilt of its axis, many indeed account for many long periods of glaciation.

/ We may be protected from such coolings, to some extent, by something our industrial civilization has been doing for the last century and a half: putting carbon dioxide into the atmosphere. Carbon dioxide released by the burning of fossil fuels, such as coal, oil, and so forth, has been building up steadily for decades, and recently climatologists have begun to think that the excess might have serious effects on the earth's climate. Carbon dioxide has an unusual property: it tends to trap heat in the atmosphere and prevent it from escaping into space. Sunlight can get in to warm the world, but heat cannot get out. This process is called the "greenhouse effect," and far from being a problem, it may turn out to be a blessing someday, if the carbon dioxide acts as a buffer

against the chilling effect of volcanic dust in the air. In the event of some future super-eruption, we may need all the carbon dioxide we can get.*

* Dr. Dewey MacLean of Virginia Polytechnic Institute set off a controversy among paleontologists some years ago when, in a 1978 article in *Science,* he proposed that the greenhouse effect might have destroyed the dinosaurs. MacLean's hypothesis of a "terminal Mesozoic greenhouse" is complicated, but can be summarized as follows. A buildup of carbon dioxide in the atmosphere, near the end of the dinosaurs' reign, may have doomed the dinosaurs by interfering with their sex lives. Higher temperatures created by the greenhouse effect made the dinosaurs less fertile (the sex organs of higher animals—including, presumably, dinosaurs—are very sensitive to heat and cold) and led eventually to their extinction as the dinosaurs lost the ability to reproduce.

X

Ripples in a Basin

IT WAS A FESTIVAL DAY in Sanriku, in
northern Japan, on June 15, 1896. Crowds along the sea-
shore were enjoying themselves, playing in the sea and
strolling along the sand, when, around seven in the evening, the ground shook slightly underfoot. No one was
alarmed at first. Quakes are not unusual in some parts of
Japan, and nothing seemed to set this quake apart from
most others . . . until the water started receding from the
shore. The sea moved out with an odd sucking, hissing
sound, faintly audible to those standing nearby.

It was not time for the tide to turn, nor had anyone
present ever seen the tide go out so quickly. What was happening? The answer came about an hour later.

First there was a rumbling noise like thunder far offshore. Then the source of the noise appeared: a wall of
water 100 feet high, rushing toward the land.

The people on the beach were trapped. They had no way to escape the colossal breaker that towered above them and broke with a force equivalent to that of a nuclear explosion.

Destruction was complete. The countless tons of water in the wave wiped the shoreline clean of life and property. What remained after the wave had passed was a pathetic jumble of wood, stone, silt, and sand—the sediment and debris picked up in the wave and hurled onto the shore.

Awful as the destruction was, it might have been worse. The fishing fleet was at sea when the wave, probably generated by a quake far beneath the sea, dashed itself on the shore at Sanriku. Curiously, the ships hadn't felt a thing as the wave passed them. When the ships returned to what had been their port, however, the sailors were greeted by the horrendous sight of human bodies—men, and women and children—floating on the waters, smashed almost beyond recognition by the force of the wave. More than 25,000 persons died that day at Sanriku, and perhaps 10,000 buildings were swept away.

The dead at Sanriku were the victims of a tsunami, the kind of wave that rippled out from Krakatoa after the volcano exploded in 1883. Tsunamis are one of the most dreaded phenomena in the Pacific and also one of the least understood. We are gradually learning more about these killer waves, but they remain an unpredictable and potentially catastrophic force of nature; their reputation for total destruction is well deserved.

Though we have no way of knowing how many tsunamis have swept the Pacific shores since history began, we estimate that the total is probably well into the thousands. Here are only a few of the better-known tsunamis in history.

Chile, 1575. An earthquake somewhere offshore generated a giant tsunami that slammed into the port of Valdivia and destroyed at least two Spanish galleons.

Chile, 1757. A series of giant tsunamis battered the town of Concepción, which had already been devastated by a major earthquake.

Krakatoa, 1883. The seismic sea wave from Krakatoa's eruption circled the world twice.

Hawaii, 1946. One of the most famous tsunamis of the twentieth century, this wave was generated by an earthquake in the Aleutian Islands. On April 1, 1946, residents of Hilo, Hawaii, were astonished to see the waters offshore rising into a 40-foot breaker. Taller than office buildings, the waves smashed into Hilo. More than 175 persons were killed, and the shore of Hilo Bay was pummeled and deluged by the tsunami. Damage eventually reached $25 million. The ocean's assault on Hawaii did more damage than the Japanese attack on Pearl Harbor had done a few years earlier. This disaster was one reason the nations around the Pacific set up an early-warning system for tsunamis several years later.

Chile, 1960. An earthquake that occurred simultaneously with volcanic eruptions shook the Chilean coast over a length of several hundred miles, killing 4,000 persons in Chile alone. The damage was carried across the Pacific by a tsunami that spread out from the Chilean coast and inundated shores as far away as New Zealand and the Philippines. Waves several stories high battered the shores of Japan. Altogether, the tsunami from the Chilean quake killed some 180 persons and caused an estimated $50 million in damage.

These dry figures, however, convey very little of the power and horror of a tsunami. For that, let us read the testimony of a man who saw a tsunami firsthand: Lieutenant J. G. Billings of the U.S.S. *Wateree,* a naval vessel that was caught in a tsunami while visiting the port of Arica, Peru, in 1868.

Billings was relaxing in the cabin with the *Wateree's* captain in the late afternoon, when the men felt the deck shudder under them. The vibration, Billings thought, was like that caused by an anchor chain rattling out through the hawsehole. But there had been no order to drop anchor, and Billings and the captain went out on deck to investigate.

The officers looked toward the shore and saw the land rippling like the sea. The hills, Billings thought, "seemed to be capsizing." The ground movement raised a cloud of dust over the land, and the cloud "swallowed up" the town.

> As the dust thinned out, we rubbed our eyes and stared, unable to believe what we saw: where a few seconds before there had stood a happy and prosperous city, busy, active, and full of life, we saw nothing but ruins. The . . . unhappy people caught under the wreckage of what had been their houses were struggling among the ruins, and everywhere shrieks, cries of pain, and calls for help tore the air.

The captain knew a tsunami was likely to follow the quake, and he ordered extra anchors dropped and everything on board made ready for the assault of a wave.

But the *Wateree*'s men had duties on shore as well as on board. When they saw survivors of the earthquake standing on the docks, calling for help to the sailors on their ships, the crew prepared to lower a boat to pick up the survivors and bring them on board before the tsunami reached shore.

The tsunami arrived, however, before the rescue could be made:

> We on board were organizing a body of men to be sent ashore . . . when all at once a hoarse murmuring noise made us look up; looking toward the land we saw, to our horror, that where a moment before there had been the jetty, all black with human beings, there was nothing: everything had been swallowed in a moment by the sudden rising of the sea, which the ship, floating upon it, had not noticed.

The *Wateree*'s nightmare was just beginning. Another earthquake occurred shortly after the jetty and its occupants disappeared in the wave. Once again the land rippled. This time, however, the sea had an even more terrifying experience in store for the ship and its occupants. The waters, Billings recalled later,

> . . . drew back from the land until we were stranded and the bottom of the sea was exposed, so that we saw what we had never seen before, fish struggling on the sea-bed and the monsters of the deep aground. The round-hulled ships rolled over on their sides, while our *Wateree* sat down upon her flat bottom; and when the sea came back, returning not as a wave but rather as a huge tide, it made our unhappy companions turn turtle, whereas the *Wateree* rose unhurt on the churning water. . . .
>
> The Peruvian ironclad *America* . . . was still afloat, and so was the American ship *Fredonia*. The *America*, who had tried to get out to sea with her engines at full speed before the withdrawal of the water, was nevertheless partially stranded, and her hull was stove in. Now the sea was carrying her at a great speed toward the shore, and . . . she seemed to be running to the assistance of the helpless *Fredonia*, which was being drawn toward the cliffs. . . . Captain Dyer of the *Fredonia*, believing this to be the case, ran aft and hailed the man of war, which was now no more than a few yards away, "Ahoy! You can do nothing for us; our bottom is smashed in. Save yourselves! Good-bye!" A moment later the *Fredonia* broke to pieces against the cliff, and not a man was saved, while a countercurrent miraculously took hold of the Peruvian ship and carried her in the other direction.

By now the sun was almost down, and in the last light the men of the *Wateree* saw a grisly scene on shore:

> The last rays of the sun were lighting up the Andes when we saw to our horror that the tombs in which

the former inhabitants had buried their dead, in the slope of the mountain, had opened, and in concentric ranks, as in an amphitheater, the mummies of natives dead and forgotten for centuries appeared on the surface. The nitre-impregnated soil had preserved them astonishingly, and the violent shocks . . . now uncovered a horrifying city of the dead.

By this time the crew of the *Wateree* were starting to think "the Day of Judgment had come," and the world was about to end in cataclysm at any moment. Judgment Day had not arrived, but nature had one last ordeal in store for the *Wateree*.

It had been dark for some time when the lookout hailed the deck and said that a breaking wave was coming. Staring into the night we made out a thin phosphorescent line which . . . seemed to be rising higher and higher in the air; its crest, topped by the baleful light of that phosphorescent glitter, showed frightful masses of black water below. Heralded by the thunder of hundreds of breakers all crashing together, the tidal wave [was] upon us. . . .

With a terrifying din, our ship was engulfed, buried under a half-liquid, half-solid mass of sand and water. We stayed under for a suffocating eternity; then, groaning in all her timbers, our solid old *Wateree* pushed her way to the surface, with her gasping crew still hanging onto the rails.

No men were killed or reported missing. Before the knowledge of that "miracle"—as Billings called it—could register on the men, however, they noticed the *Wateree* was no longer moving. When dawn came, they saw the reason why.

Wateree had been carried two miles inland by the tsunami. Because of her flat bottom, she had settled upright. Only an incredible chance had saved the ship from total destruction: she lay less than 200 feet from a sheer cliff, and if the wave had carried her just a bit farther, she would have been smashed to pieces.

Other ships in the harbor when the tsunami struck were less fortunate. Near the *Wateree* lay the remains of a British three-master. The anchor chain was wrapped several times around the hull, showing how the vessel had been rolled around its long axis, like a rolling pin, by the tsunami.

Gruesome evidence of the earthquake's power surrounded the *Wateree* on all sides. Billings saw the body of a woman seated on the body of a horse, "both having been swallowed by a crevasse as they were flying for their lives." Other bodies, crushed and mangled by the tsunami, lay in heaps along the outskirts of town where the wave had deposited them. Nothing remained of the town itself. "Where it had stood there stretched an even plain of sand. Except in the suburbs on the mountain slopes there was not a single house to show where Arica had been."

We are used to thinking of waves as moving masses of water. And near shore, where the breaker rises and rushes across the land in a flood of foam and water, waves are just that. But in the deep sea, the tsunami—in a sense—has little material existence. It is just a moving shock front of energy spreading out from the quake's epicenter. The molecules of water may oscillate a bit, but they remain stationary, on average, as the waves goes by. To illustrate, put a cork in a bathtub full of water and generate a mini-tsunami by splashing with your hand at one end of the tub. The wave passes by the cork, but the cork stays approximately in place. It may rise and fall a bit as the wave passes underneath, but its net horizontal motion is practically zero. So it is with a tsunami in the deep sea. There is no great rushing wall of water in mid-ocean where a tsunami marches by. A ship may ride over a huge tsunami without anyone on board noticing a thing. Ships at sea were untroubled by the tsunami from Krakatoa, for example, even though that wave annihilated shorelines in the vicinity of the volcano.

Only when the tsunami nears shore does it take on the familiar appearance of a wave. The reason for the change has a complicated mathematical explanation, but ultimately the reason is simply that the waves find themselves getting "kicked upstairs" by the rise in the sea floor.

As the waves approach the shore, and water becomes more shallow, they begin, as noted earlier, to "feel bottom." Then, as the waves run out of depth, they rise and take on the form we recognize as a breaker. Friction slows down the bottom portion of the wave, and the top portion falls forward and breaks, as waves do on the beach on a stormy day.

Shallow water has a dramatic effect on wave velocity. In mid-ocean, a tsunami may travel close to the speed of sound, 750 or 760 miles per hour. Friction with the bottom in shallow water may cut the wave's speed to only 50 or 60 miles per hour near the shore. This braking effect also causes the waves to crowd up on one another. In mid-ocean, there may be a hundred miles or more between crests of the tsunami waves. Near shore, the distance may be only a few thousand feet. So one wave may hammer the land, to be followed in only a few moments by another. This happened in Hawaii in 1946; after the first wave struck, others followed, adding to the destruction.

We know that tsunamis tend to travel in such "chains" or "trains," but the physics of wave trains at sea is still highly mysterious. In some way not well understood, the wave train appears to lay down energy at the front and pick it up again at the rear; the process is something like a rolling tank tread. But the study of waves is progressing rapidly, and new computer-based mathematical models of wave motion may soon unlock many of the mysteries of this familiar, yet strange phenomenon.

One interesting thing about tsunamis is that they may

explain many of our ancient myths and legends about floods. The most famous flood legend is, of course, that of Noah and the Ark. And if one examines the Biblical account closely, it bears a striking likeness to modern descriptions of tsunamis.

The story of the universal deluge is told in the book of Genesis and begins with God's decision, several generations after Adam and Eve were created, to destroy the human species for its sins. "The earth also was corrupt before God, and the earth was filled with violence. . . . And God said unto Noah, The end of all flesh is come before me; for the earth is filled with violence through them; and, behold, I will destroy them with the earth." (Gen. 6: 11, 13.)

God gives Noah instructions for building an ark—that is, a large vessel—of gopher wood, and explains the reason for the project: "I [will] bring a flood of waters upon the earth . . . everything that is in the earth shall die." (Gen. 6:17.) After the Ark is finished, God orders Noah to stock it with animals for repopulating the postdiluvian world. Then God announces: "For yet seven days, and I will cause it to rain upon the earth forty days and forty nights; and every living substance that I have made will I destroy from off the face of the earth." (Gen. 7:4.)

Right on schedule, the flood arrives:

> . . . all the fountains of the great deep [were] broken up, and the windows of heaven were opened. And the rain was upon the earth forty days and forty nights. . . . And the flood [continued] forty days upon the earth; and the waters increased, and bare up the ark, and it was lift up above the earth . . . and the ark went upon the face of the waters. And the waters prevailed exceedingly upon the earth; and all the high hills, that were under the whole heaven, were covered. Fifteen cubits upward did the waters prevail; and the mountains were covered. (Gen. 7:11–12, 17–20.)

The Biblical account says the waters covered the earth for about five months (Gen. 7:24). Gradually, the flood subsides: "The fountains . . . of the deep and the windows of heaven were stopped . . . and the waters returned from off the earth continually." (Gen. 8:1–3.) At last the Ark comes to rest on the mountains of Ararat, the waters drain away completely, and Noah and his family emerge from the Ark to begin the job of repopulating the earth.

Artists and motion-picture producers have had a field day with the Deluge. Michelangelo showed distraught men and women scrambling onto the few remaining bits of dry land as the Ark floated off majestically in the background; the waters look calm, as if they were merely accumulating slowly from the rain. Most illustrators and filmmakers have followed Michelangelo's example. The flood is almost invariably shown as starting with a rain; the rain becomes a tempest, and then a world-drowning deluge from the sky.

A careful reading of the Genesis text, however, shows that rain is not named as the sole cause of the flood. Instead, the narrator says that "the fountains of the great deep" were broken up. That image seems to indicate that the floodwaters came from the *sea*, not from the sky. Indeed, the opening of the "windows of heaven" is mentioned almost as an afterthought, and may refer to winds rather than torrential rains. Were the "fountains" that caused the flood in this legend actually the tsunami from an earthquake or volcanic eruption at sea?

One potential objection to that theory is the time the flood is said to have covered the land. Genesis says the waters lingered for months; and even if we assume the times given in this account are exaggerated by a factor of 10 or even 100 (it was common practice then to use large symbolic numbers to indicate that something took a long time), then the Noachian deluge, as reported in the Bible, lasted longer than tsunami waters would cover the land. The tsunamis that devastated southern Alaska after the

Good Friday quake of 1964 arrived and left in a matter of minutes, not days or weeks. Never has a tsunami been known to hang poised over the land for months on end, as Noah's flood is said to have done, before flowing back to the sea. Does this objection mean the tsunami theory of the flood is invalid?

Perhaps not. The Genesis story indicates the waters lifted the Ark over the mountains and finally brought it to rest in a mountainous region. If the wave did carry the Ark into an area of mountains and valleys, then floodwaters might have been trapped in those valleys and taken a long time to drain away. Conceivably, a vessel could have floated for weeks or months in the drowned valleys. And if the mountains were low, a very large tsunami might be able to lift a ship over them. Genesis says the Ark topped the mountains by 15 cubits (roughly 25 feet), and tsunamis have been known to reach more than 1,000 feet on the walls of fjords on the southern Alaska coast.

Here, of course, we are in the realm of speculation. But the legend of Noah and the Ark does bear an interesting likeness to what happens when a tsunami rushes over the land; and this explanation is especially attractive when one considers that the Mediterranean and its neighboring seas, where these legends originated, are frequently shaken by major earthquakes.

We are on firmer ground when we come to another story, that of Moses and the parting of the Red Sea. If one reads this story in a literal frame of mind, it does sound rather like the spectacle Cecil B. De Mille filmed for his picture *The Ten Commandments*. But the story may also be read in such a way as to describe the effects of a seismic sea wave.

This episode comes from the book of Exodus, the account of the Israelites' captivity in Egypt, the career of Moses, and the plagues God sends on the Egyptians to force them to release the Israelites. In the climactic scene of the book, the Israelites flee Egypt and set up camp on the shore of the Red Sea. Pharaoh is enraged to see part of his country's work force deserting Egypt, and gives chase with his army.

Trapped between the sea and an angry Pharaoh, the Israelites need a miracle, and God provides one. "But lift thou up thy rod, and stretch out thine hand over the sea, and divide it," God tells Moses, "and the children of Israel shall go on dry ground through the midst of the sea." (Exodus 14:16.)

Moses does as God orders. The waters part, and the Israelites march across the exposed sea bottom to the opposite shore.

Livid to see his slaves escaping, Pharaoh orders his horsemen and charioteers to follow them through the part in the waters. Pharaoh discovers, however, that chariots are not meant to be driven through mud and ooze. The author of Exodus reports: "The Lord . . . troubled the host of the Egyptians . . . that they drave them heavily." (Exodus 14: 24, 25.)

Then God orders Moses to stretch out his hand once again, to bring the waters back upon the Egyptians and drown them. Moses does as told. The waters rush back to their "wonted flow," and all the host of Pharaoh is drowned.

Could anything sound more like the account of a large tsunami? First the waters retreat, exposing the bed of the sea. The water then returns a few minutes later—long enough for one to walk across a narrow stretch of sea bottom—with devastating force, and crushes and drowns anyone in its path. The Exodus account of the Red Sea crossing might, with a few details changed, be a report of the Sanriku disaster.

Of particular interest is how Exodus describes the parted waters: ". . . a wall unto them on their right hand, and on their left." (Exodus 14: 29.) A wall of water: that is how approaching tsunamis are often described, and the words of Exodus lend still more weight to the hypothesis that the Red Sea was actually parted by a seismic sea wave.

The big question is, naturally, what generated the wave? The Exodus took place at about 1447 B.C., as best we can tell from Biblical chronology. This date happens to be very close to the estimated time when the volcano Santorin, also known as Thera, exploded in the Mediterranean. This violent eruption wiped out the Minoan civilization (archaeologists believe) and probably gave rise to the legend of Atlantis, the mythical continent that sank beneath the sea in a single day. If some archaeologists such as Angelos Galanopoulos and L. Sprague de Camp are correct, then the tsunami from the explosion may have inspired the Red Sea story in the Bible as well. If so, the parting of the sea would have had nothing at all to do with Moses' gestures at the seaside, but rather with the destruction of an island far to the north.

There are strong echoes of these stories in the myths and legends of peoples along the Ring of Fire. One story concerns the life and unhappy reign of Emperor Yahu, the ruler whose reign separates China's mythical past from its historical era.

Apparently Yahu had the bad luck to live in a time of great natural catastrophes, chief among them a colossal flood. China was reportedly overwhelmed by a tremendous wave that broke over the mountaintops and inundated the valleys, as the Emperor noted in his account of the disaster.

The floodwaters filled the valleys for the next several decades, and the Chinese tried to remove the waters by draining the land with canals. A government official named Kwan was put in charge of this seemingly hopeless task, but he was executed shortly thereafter when the Emperor thought the work was going too slowly. Kwan's son Yü took over from his late father and succeeded where Kwan had failed.

On the strength of this success, Yü was made emperor, and he founded his own dynasty. Was Yü thus made an emperor by a tsunami? It is tempting to think so, because some of the Chinese quakes within historical times have released enough energy to create huge tsunamis, perhaps capable of sweeping over low mountains.

Fortunately, no waves of that magnitude have occurred within recent times. A tsunami even four or five feet high can cause considerable damage, however, and, as noted previously the nations around the Pacific basin have organized a special warning system to notify coastal areas along the Pacific shore whenever a potentially destructive tsunami is heading their way.

The network was set up in 1948, shortly after the killer tsunami that hit Hilo, Hawaii. Since then the system has been steadily expanded and upgraded, until the network can flash warnings all around the Ring of Fire when a hazardous tsunami appears.

The nerve center of the network is a station in Honolulu, Hawaii, where the U.S. National Weather Service runs a tsunami information center. Whenever a quake occurs around the Pacific shore, seismologists notify the center, and observers at outposts along the coasts watch for signs of a seismic sea wave. If such a wave appears, or even seems likely to appear, then a warning goes out to countries all around the ocean. Data giving the speed of the wave and the estimated time of arrival at the areas in its path are relayed to give civil and military authorities time to get ready for a possible disaster.

All this sophisticated system can do, however, is warn. A tsunami is unstoppable. Once the wave ripples out from the site of a quake or eruption, all we can do is try to get out of its way. We can send astronauts to the moon, land robots on Mars and Venus, defeat epidemic disease, and crack the very chemical code of life itself; but with all our science and technology, we cannot stop a single ripple in a basin.

XI

Gold!

HIS NAME WAS Atahualpa. His people called him "Son of the Sun," and he presided over one of the greatest civilizations in history: the Inca Empire.

Atahualpa's domain stretched almost halfway down the Andes Mountains, from what is now Ecuador to a point just south of present-day Santiago, Chile. The empire was centered near the city we call Cuzco, Peru. Well-organized and served by a monumental set of stone-paved highways, the Inca Empire worshipped Atahualpa as its divine god-king. He had to work hard for that title, but enjoyed it for only a few months. Shortly after his installation as monarch of the Inca Empire, Atahualpa was killed and his empire destroyed. Ultimately, both perished because of something the Ring of Fire had deposited near the surface of their land.

The glory of the Incas has inspired many novels, plays, and motion pictures, many of which present a highly romanticized picture of the Inca Empire. To judge from these works, the Incas were a peaceful, contented, simple people, living happily under the benevolent rule of wise kings bedecked in feather costumes. About the only accurate part of this picture is the feathers. The Incas were not the innocent, happy pack of Noble Savages commonly depicted. They lived under a system that resembled modern Fascism in many ways, and their empire was assembled at the cost of countless human lives.

The Inca Empire started very small. At its beginning, around 1200, the empire consisted of a single valley surrounding Cuzco, about midway between modern Lima and La Paz. The original Inca monarch was Manco Capac, who set up a dynasty and gave himself the title Son of the Sun, which was passed down to his heirs and successors. He was also known simply as "the Inca."

The next several Incas did little to expand their realm. The ninth Inca, however, broke with tradition and made himself one of the greatest conquerors of all time. His name was Pachacuti, meaning "he who changes the world." He did precisely that, extending the borders of the Inca realm from a single valley to an area roughly the size of New England. His conquests began in 1438 and inspired his son Topa Inca, the second Inca emperor, to do still better. Topa Inca and his armies—who traveled on foot, because the llamas they used for pack animals were too small to carry a man—had extended the empire's borders vastly by 1493; it reached all the way from northern Ecuador to a river near what is now Santiago. The empire grew slightly thereafter, under the reign of the third emperor, Huayna Capac, until, by 1525, it was about the size of modern California.

The Incas did a good job of consolidating their empire. Every time some new land was conquered, the emperor sent his own provincial governor to live there. Sons of the local nobility were rounded up and taken to the empire's capital, either for sacrifice or to be educated in Inca ways and then sent home to act as administrators. It would be interesting to know what some of these captured youths thought as they saw Inca lords drinking out of cups made from the skulls of their slain foes.

The Incas were also master builders. Using only simple tools, an elementary knowledge of mathematics, and abundant manpower, the Incas built roadways and temples more impressive even than those of Imperial Rome. The Inca engineers, European visitors to Peru noted later, cut and aligned stones on the roadways so accurately that there was barely room to insert a piece of paper in the crevices. (Though the Incas had a magnificent road system, they did not develop the wheel for transportation. This fact has been publicized widely as a "mystery" of the Incas. Actually, there is no mystery. The roadways of the Inca empire had such steep gradients in places that wheeled vehicles would have been virtually useless on them. Much better for transport was the sure-footed—and self-repairing—llama.)

Huayna Capac, one of the last emperors, was a brutal conqueror who waged aggressive wars against the peoples of northern Ecuador and Colombia. One of his battles took so many lives that the lake where it occurred is still called Yaguarcocha (Lake of Blood). Even Huayna Capac, however, was surpassed in brutality by his son Atahualpa. The young warrior fought with the armies on the empire's northern frontier and won their respect, much as the young Julius Caesar had done centuries before him. What Atahualpa lacked was Caesar's clemency and sense of fair play. Atahualpa would use any means to secure his desired goals, and he had no mercy on defeated foes. He subjected his conquered enemies to the most humiliating and obscene punishments, such as eating human waste in public, before having them murdered.

While Atahualpa fought with the armies in the north, Huayna Capac was at home at his palace in Ecuador, fretting over strange and disturbing news from distant corners of the empire. Plagues were sweeping the provinces. Strange visions—including houses built on water!—had been seen. And there were stories of white-skinned, bearded men who had entered the empire and would conquer it, if the oracles spoke rightly. It turned out later that this information was entirely correct. If Atahualpa was worried, however, he did not show it. He was much more concerned about his rival for the throne, his half brother Huáscar.

Huáscar was named emperor after Huayna Capac died in 1525. Huáscar was Huayna Capac's legitimate son and rightful heir, and had every reason to command the entire empire. But Huayna Capac was partial to his illegitimate son Atahualpa, and gave the young warrior dominion over about 20 percent of the Inca Empire.

Atahualpa, however, was not a man to be satisfied with merely 20 percent of anything. He wanted the whole empire for himself, and he could back his claim with force of arms, thanks to the loyalty of the soldiers with whom he had served so long. So civil war broke out in the Inca Empire between the followers of Huáscar, the legitimate emperor, and the supporters of the usurper Atahualpa.

As emperor, Huáscar was able to put a huge army in the field against Atahualpa. But Atahualpa's men proved the better fighters, and they routed Huáscar's army in battle in Ecuador. Officially the number of dead was about 15,000, but the actual figure was probably much higher; Huáscar had good reason to downplay the body count.

Defeated in his first fight with Atahualpa, Huáscar put together another army . . . then another . . . then still another. He drained the manpower of the empire drastically in a frantic effort to halt Atahualpa's advance.

But the battle-hardened men under Atahualpa's command were not easily stopped by inexperienced peasant soldiers conscripted off the farm, and in the final battle of this awful conflict, Atahualpa's men hacked their way right up to Huáscar's bodyguard, cut the men down, and literally dethroned Huáscar. When Huáscar's men saw their emperor—who was, after all, considered a god and therefore invulnerable—heaved off his litter and pulled to the ground, they were terrified and fled in panic.

The Son of the Sun captured! It must have seemed like the end of the Inca world to many men on the battlefield near Cuzco that day; and in fact, the end of their empire was not far off. All the while Atahualpa had been fighting his way toward the throne of Peru, a monarch far across the ocean was planning an expedition that would soon topple Atahualpa as Atahualpa had dethroned his half brother.

The monarch was King Charles of Spain. Ever since the first European explorers had returned from the newly discovered Americas with tales of strange and wonderful sights and peoples there, rumors had circulated about the riches that were supposedly to be found. Abundant game. Vast uninhabited lands. And gold.

Gold. Atomic number 79, atomic weight 197, specific gravity 19.37, valence one or three; often found in veins of quartz or pyrite. Highly malleable, gold can be worked into almost any shape. A single gram of gold can be hammered out into a sheet 100 square feet in area. Gold is a fine conductor of electricity and will stand up to any but the strongest solvents. It is also the most coveted element in the periodic table, with the possible exceptions of uranium and plutonium.

Gold is not valued so highly because it is the rarest metal; astatine has that distinction. Gold is, in fact, surprisingly widespread. It even exists in sea water. A thousand tons of sea water will yield about a gram of gold—enough to make a paper clip. Gold is found in many other places, from stream beds to fossils, so rarity alone does not account for its value.

Neither is gold the most expensive metal. Iridium costs several times more per ounce than gold does. What makes gold so valuable is its mystique—a mystique that led Alexander the Great to fight wars for gold, King Solomon to mine the land of Ophir for gold, and the medieval alchemists to found the science of chemistry while looking for ways to turn lead into gold. Gold is the "royal metal," and its beauty and its many valuable uses, from jewelry to coating satellites, have made it the most eagerly sought commodity in the mineral kingdom.

One of its uses is coinage. It can either be made into coins or stored in the form of bullion to back paper currency. This use of gold is the reason King Charles, about the time Huayna Capac lay on his deathbed, was plotting a new conquest for Spain in the recently discovered lands far across the Western Ocean.

The Spaniards had, of course, no guarantee that riches existed in those distant lands. They had only rumors to guide them. But what rumors! Supposedly there was an empire in the western part of South America where gold was used as abundantly as wood or iron was used in Europe. Streets were said to be paved with gold, houses built of it, every person bedecked with it. Perhaps El Dorado, the fabled City of Gold, was there. Who could tell until Europeans actually went to the New World to investigate?

The chief investigator, in this instance, was a man named Francisco Pizarro. A tough, no-nonsense soldier, Pizarro signed a contract in 1526 for the conquest of Peru, the alleged land of gold. His troops numbered less than 200. He had 62 cavalrymen under his command, and some 100 foot soldiers. They had swords and a few guns. This tiny force intended to conquer an empire that none of them had ever seen.

Five years after Pizarro signed the contract, he and his men were marching through the heart of the Inca Empire, on their way to meet the Son of the Sun himself.

Pizarro had several things working in his favor. The first was surprise. No one in the Inca Empire had expected an invasion of this kind, from oddly garbed invaders who arrived in floating houses and wore metal suits instead of the Incas' traditional quilted armor (armor, incidentally, so efficient that the U.S. Army used it as the model for body protection for troops in World War II, four centuries after Pizarro landed in Peru). The Incas thought everyone outside their empire was a barbarian. No one expected the barbarians to come marching right up to the front door, as if they owned the place.

Also, the empire was too weak to repel an invasion. The civil war had killed a good portion of the men, and had devastated large areas of the countryside. Those Incas spared by the war were targets for plagues and pestilence that were ravaging the land at the time the Spaniards arrived—and, indeed, may have been spread inadvertently by the invaders themselves.

Perhaps the greatest single factor working in Pizarro's favor, however, was Atahualpa himself. Like many another tyrant who attains supreme power, the Son of the Sun had apparently begun to think himself more than human. Had he not dethroned his supposedly divine rival Huáscar? Did not the oracles of the empire say that Atahualpa was invincible? Had Atahualpa not left thousands of Huáscar's followers dead on the fields of battle, and still more of his supporters hanging from trees? What had the Son of the Sun to fear from these odd foreign visitors?

Atahualpa apparently forgot what the oracles had told his father: that white-skinned men with beards would conquer the Inca Empire. And if the oracles valued their heads, they were doubtless afraid to remind Atahualpa of that prophecy.

Atahualpa might have been heartened if he knew how scared Pizarro's men were. Some were so terrified by the carnage around them, the results of the civil war, that they lost bladder control. But the men feared Pizarro more than they feared the Incas, and were drawn on also by the legends of gold.

Pizarro arrived as Atahualpa, flushed with success, was on his way south from Ecuador to Cuzco, the imperial capital, to prepare for his installation as emperor. Atahualpa met the Spaniards at a resort called Cajamarca, about 600 miles north of Cuzco. Intrigued with his visitors, he sent presents to Pizarro and went to a hot spring to wait for the Spanish soldiers to see him.

The cunning Pizarro sent an interpreter and a small group of cavalrymen to invite the Emperor to dinner the following day. Atahualpa gave the Spaniards a friendly reception and told them they could stay in the town plaza. That was the first in a series of unbelievably stupid mistakes that would cost Atahualpa his throne and his life.

November 16, 1532: the Spaniards waited for Atahualpa. At sundown, the Inca paid his call on Pizarro.

Atahualpa made the error of walking into an enclosed courtyard—the perfect place for an ambush. Moreover, he and his party came unarmed. It is difficult to understand why such an experienced commander made such obvious errors in judgment, placing his own life and those of his retainers in deadly peril, unless he actually believed the words of his oracles, who said he was invincible.

If that was Atahualpa's belief, he abandoned it quickly.

Several hundred servants preceded Atahualpa. The Emperor was carried into the courtyard on a golden litter. Several thousand other Incas followed. Their songs sounded to the Spaniards like the cries of demons.

One man came forward to meet Atahualpa: a Dominican friar. He read briefly from a prayer book. Atahualpa took the book, glanced at it, and tossed it to the ground.

No sooner had the book fallen than shots thundered across the plaza. Pizarro's cavalrymen spurred their horses out of concealment around the edge of the plaza, and the infantrymen cut and stabbed their way through the crowd toward the Emperor.

Atahualpa's bodyguards—who, like the rest of the party, had come unarmed—fell like ninepins. The royal litter, suddenly unbalanced, tilted and threw Atahualpa out of his throne. The Spaniards captured the Son of the Sun and slaughtered the other Incas in the plaza. The Inca Empire had fallen.

Pizarro was victorious, and he had triumphed without losing a single man. The soothsayers' words to Atahualpa, the devastating effects of the empire's civil war, the plagues, the Incas' fear of cavalry, Atahualpa's stupidity—all these factors had combined to give Pizarro victory. A handful of Spaniards had conquered one of the greatest empires the Western Hemisphere had ever seen.

Atahualpa appears to have been a docile captive. A more courageous monarch would probably have died in the plaza that day with his subjects, trying to fight off the invaders. But Atahualpa, like Mussolini and many other tyrants in our own time, appears to have been short on physical and moral courage when he had to face an enemy alone, without the support of his armies. To save his own skin, Atahualpa cooperated with the Spaniards. He even took a Christian name, hoping it would please the invaders enough to make them spare his life.

The Inca monarch survived eight months after his capture, but only because the Spaniards thought him more valuable alive than dead. Pizarro held Atahualpa for ransom, and a heavy ransom it was.

The Spaniards demanded the Incas fill a room with treasure: once with gold, and twice with silver. The Incas complied.

And were able to comply because the Ring of Fire, which created the hot spring where Atahualpa had spent his last night as a free man, had also given the Inca Empire an abundant supply of certain metals—including gold.

One segment of the original supercontinent, Wegener's Pangaea, became the South American crustal plate. As that plate slid westward, it came into contact with the Pacific plate. South America, pushed on relentlessly by the spreading zone at the mid-Atlantic ridge, bumped and ground against the Pacific plate and thus generated the Andes.

Many things happened—and indeed are still happening

—along this tortured line of crustal rock. Volcanoes rose to towering heights. Earthquakes shook the land. Hot springs formed as the subterranean heat churned up by the colliding plates warmed water far underground and sent that water back to the surface at scalding temperatures. The hot water underground did much more, however, than generate thermal springs. It gave the Andes rich deposits of metal ores as well.

Look at a mineral resource map of South America and you will notice a dense concentration of mines along the Andes. Tin, molybdenum, tellurium, silver, gold, copper —all these valuable metals and more are concentrated in the Andes. And while the genesis of some of these ores is still something of a mystery, most geologists agree that the ores were laid down by "hydrothermal" processes.

Hot water deep underground carries a heavy load of dissolved minerals. Some thermal springs are so rich in dissolved solids that they are dangerous to sip, and even breathing the steam from them can be risky. In some places, the metals and other materials in solution precipitate out, because there is just no more room for them in the saturated water. This is how the ores of the Andes were created.

Here gold and tellurium were deposited. A few miles away, silver came out of solution. Copper is especially abundant in the Andes, as a low-ranking military officer discovered one day in Chile. He found a greenish rock and took it back to camp with him. The ore was assayed and found to be rich in copper. Today there is a world-famous mine at that spot, and it is named for that lucky officer— El Teniente, the lieutenant.

The metal that interested the Spaniards and drew them to Peru, however, was gold, and the Incas had it in abundance: not enough to pave the streets with, but enough to amass a huge treasure by European standards. The Incas mined the metal from "placer" deposits—where gold has been eroded away from its original source rock (known to miners as the "mother lode") and laid down in sediments. Just remove the sediments, by panning or sifting or whatever other process, and the gold remains. Placer deposits usually are easier to find than the mother lode, and may be much more profitable as well, because nature has already mined the gold through erosion, and concentrated it in the sands and gravels.

Gold may turn up in many forms in nature. It may occur as a metal. This form is called "native" gold, and may be seen as the small glittering chips a fortunate panner may still find in the gravel of stream beds in certain parts of the United States. Native gold may appear as massive nuggets weighing hundreds of pounds, or as delicate fernlike fronds of gold embedded in quartz or other crystalline rocks. Gold in the latter form is one of the most beautiful sights in nature.

More often, gold occurs in less elegant forms. It may join with tellurium to form tellurides, dirty-looking minerals which, at first glance, seem to have nothing in common with the shining gold of Atahualpa's realm. Gold may also form a thin coating over pyrites, the iron sulfides commonly known as "fool's gold" because they look so much like actual gold. (Pyrites fooled many a prospector in the days of the California gold rush. Specific gravity tests could be used to tell the look-alike minerals apart—gold is much heavier per unit volume than pyrite—but a quicker and simpler test was to heat the sample in a fire. Pyrite would give off sulfur oxides, with a characteristic smell of brimstone, while gold would remain unaffected.)

Sometimes gold turns up in strange forms and places: embedded in coal seams, for example. But it is found most often in areas of past or present volcanic activity, where hydrothermal activity is strongest; and so the Ring of Fire, which created precisely those conditions along the Pacific shore of South America, gave the Inca Empire enough gold to satisfy, at least temporarily, the Spaniards' greed. (According to Spanish accounts of the conquest of Peru, the

Incas were astonished at the Spaniards' lust for gold and asked if the Europeans *ate* the metal.)

During the eight months that Atahualpa lived after his capture, he enjoyed all the creature comforts befitting a Son of the Sun, and still exercised some power over his empire. He ordered his defeated rival Huáscar executed after forcing him to eat feces in public. But time was running out for Atahualpa, and his end was as ignoble as his brother's. As soon as the ransom for Atahualpa was paid, Pizarro had the Inca monarch garroted. The Spaniards melted down the masterpieces of the Inca goldsmiths into bullion and sent the gold back to Spain. No one knows where that treasure went eventually; any records of its fate were probably lost long ago. Bits of Atahualpa's gold may fill teeth today, or be used as radioactive isotopes in cancer research.

Atahualpa was killed in 1533. Pizarro outlived him by only a few years. He was murdered in 1541 by followers of a rival Spanish commander. Reportedly, Pizarro's last act was to trace a cross, in his own blood, on the floor where he fell.

The Inca civilization was dead by the time Pizarro was killed. For a time, Spain lived high on the gold and silver shipped back to Europe from the former Inca Empire. Perhaps the most famous discovery in the Spaniards' new colony was Cerro Rico, the "hill of silver," in Bolivia. Actually a mountain almost three miles high, it was shot through with veins of rich silver ore, some of them more than 12 feet thick. There was also tin in abundance. The Spaniards probably had no idea they were mining the worn-down nubbin of an ancient volcano. All that mattered to them was getting the silver out of the mountain, and this they did so efficiently that a torrent of silver flowed out of Cerro Rico and over the sea to Spain. According to contemporary reports, it was not unusual to see a dozen cartloads of silver from Cerro Rico waiting on South American docks for shipment to Europe. That silver, too, was a gift of the Ring of Fire, which had deposited the metal ores by hydrothermal activity and put the ores within easy reach of the surface.

In time, however, the Spaniards discovered that too much of a metal can poison an empire as it poisons the human body. The flood of cheap silver from the New World undermined Spain's economy and sent the nation into an economic nosedive from which it has yet to recover. So the Ring of Fire ultimately undid both the Inca Empire and the Spanish Empire that succeeded it; and the agent of their undoing was the mineral wealth of the Andes—which, in the end, destroyed everyone and everything it touched, as surely as an earthquake or a volcanic eruption.

XII

Fire in the Caribbees

THE RING OF FIRE, as noted earlier, does not cling strictly to the Pacific shore. The Ring makes occasional detours into continents and even other oceans, bringing earthquakes and volcanic activity with it. A case in point is the Caribbean Sea, where the Caribbean plate collides with the North American and South American crustal plates. This collision has raised a chain of islands, the Lesser Antilles, along the plate boundary.

The Lesser Antilles follow an arc some 500 miles long, from the Venezuelan coast near Trinidad in the south to a spot just east of Puerto Rico in the north. About midway along this arc as one follows it north, the Lesser Antilles split into two separate chains of islands. The outer and shorter chain is called the Limestone Caribbees. These are relatively old volcanic islands topped by carbonate rock deposits. The other chain of islands, the Volcanic Caribbees, lies a few miles west of the Limestone Caribbees and consists mostly of active volcanoes.

Few parts of the world have a more colorful history than the Lesser Antilles and the waters that surround them. Once the Lesser Antilles were the domain of the Arawak Indians, a basically peaceful people about whom we know little. Their culture was destroyed around the start of the fourteenth century when the Antilles were invaded by the Carib, a loose association of warrior tribes who lived originally in the Amazon basin and Guyana. Around the year 1300, the Carib, sensing easy pickings to the north, wiped out the Arawak in a series of invasions.

The Carib were known for ruthlessness and brutality, and ate the bodies of their victims; in fact, the word "cannibal" comes from the Spanish name for the Carib. Although they were formidable fighters on an individual basis, the Carib knew little of organized warfare and were so fiercely proud that they considered it degrading to take orders from a superior officer. These undisciplined warriors were thus easy prey for the well-trained and better-armed Spaniards, who took over the Lesser Antilles little more than two centuries after the Carib overran the peaceful Arawak.

The Spaniards themselves, however, fell prey in turn to pirates in the sixteenth and seventeenth centuries. The many small islands of the Caribbean Sea provided good anchorages and hiding places, and there were countless rich cargoes passing between Europe and Spain's American colonies. The Caribbean was thus a natural hunting ground for pirates, and perhaps the most famous of them was Edward Teach, the notorious Blackbeard. A man of great height and tremendous physical strength, Teach is said to have decorated his beard with pink ribbons and, on occasion, stuck lighted candles in his hat to terrify his opponents. He had a taste for practical jokes such as lighting pots of sulfur below decks, and he had a unique way of maintaining his authority. Once a visitor to Blackbeard's ship was dining in the captain's cabin with Teach and a member of the crew. Without warning, Teach blew out the candle on the table and fired his pistol in the dark, hitting the crewman in the leg. After recovering his composure, Blackbeard's visitor asked why he had fired. Blackbeard answered reasonably, "If I didn't do something like that now and then, my men would forget who I am!" But Blackbeard appears to have had few problems with scheming sailors on his ship, because he was careful to keep the men supplied liberally with rum. Blackbeard was killed in 1718 during a battle with a British warship off the barrier islands of North Carolina. It took twenty-five wounds to kill him. His head was brought back to Virginia on the end of a pole.

Perhaps the richest and most infamous city of the Caribbean in the latter seventeenth century was Port Royal, Jamaica. One could buy virtually anything in Port Royal if one had the money; the city was a sparkling emporium of wares from all the corners of the world—silks from the Orient, gold and silver artifacts from Spain's South American colonies, and every kind of rich food and strong drink one could imagine. A citizen of Port Royal described it in 1683 as "the Storehouse or Treasury of the West Indies . . . a continual Mart or Fair. . . ." The city's pious critics probably overstated the depths of its depravities, and in any event Port Royal made it clear by 1692 that the rapacious pirates had worn out their welcome there. Until then, the British authorities had encouraged pirates to drop anchor regularly at Port Royal, because the buccaneers spent much of their time attacking the ships of Britain's archenemy, Spain.

Port Royal grew steadily through the late 1600s. By 1692 there were several hundred buildings on the small spit of land that bordered the harbor. The residents ignored the Biblical injunction against building houses on sand, and they paid dearly for that error on the morning of June 7, 1692.

Unknown to the people of Port Royal, their wealthy

city stood near the boundary of the Caribbean plate and the North American plate. The two plates grind together as the North American plate moves westward. Earthquakes are one result. And shortly before noon that hot June day, a severe tremor struck Port Royal.

The earthquake turned the sandy soil along the waterfront into a near-liquid; the waterfront vanished into the sea. Thames Street and the shops along it slid into the churning water. Littleton's tavern disappeared, and with it the servants inside. The massive masonry walls of Fort James rocked and slid seaward. The King's Warehouse, a long wooden building running parallel to the waterfront, became driftwood in a matter of seconds.

One unknown but evidently rich man appears to have lost both his life and his costly watch in the disaster. The timepiece lay under water for more than two and a half centuries, until a team of marine archaeologists recovered it in 1959. Brass workings inside the watch were still undamaged by the salt water, but the hands were missing; presumably they were steel and had been dissolved in the sea. When an encrustation on the face of the watch was removed and subjected to x-ray photography, however, traces of the hands could still be seen. They indicated the watch had stopped at 11:43.

St. Paul's Church was destroyed in the earthquake, but its rector, Reverend Emmanuel Heath, had the good luck to be elsewhere when the tremor struck.

Heath took his duties as a clergyman seriously, and on the morning of June 7 he had been at the church reading prayers. He hoped this "shew of religion" would inspire some piety in the "ungodly debauched people" of Port Royal. After prayers, he proceeded to a place nearby where the acting governor of Jamaica, John White, met him and proposed they have some wine before their meal.

Just then, the earth began to tremble. Heath was alarmed at first. "Lord, sir, what is this?" he asked.

The governor seemed undisturbed. "It is an earthquake," he replied. "Be not afraid. It will soon be over."

White was correct. The tremor was brief. In those few moments, however, more than 60 percent of Port Royal slid into the sea, and 2,000 persons perished.

When the danger seemed past, Heath recovered his composure and went out to survey the damage. The appearance of a clergyman reassured the frightened people of the town that God had not deserted them after all, and Heath was almost smothered by the crowds of people who rushed up to him. Finally he persuaded his frightened flock to kneel down for prayers.

It was a hot day, and soon Heath was all but exhausted from praying aloud in the tropical heat. He must have had trouble concentrating on his prayers, because the ground beneath him was, he recalled later, "working all the while with new motions and tremblings, like the rolling of the sea."

Privateers looted the town that night, and Heath retired to the safety of a ship in the harbor, which was littered with the debris of ships destroyed in the tremor. The minister was disappointed to see how promptly the "lewd rogues" of Port Royal returned to their old habits of drinking and whoring, but he still hoped that "by this terrible judgment God will make them reform their lives, for there is not a more ungodly people on the face of the earth."

Heath's experience was illustrated later in a fanciful woodcut designed to edify sinners. In the center Reverend Heath can be seen kneeling in prayer with men and women arranged in a ring about him, arms upraised to heaven. All around, the "lewd rogues" are falling into cracks opened in the ground by the quake. One man, miraculously upright, is using a shovel to free someone trapped in a fissure up to his chest. A few feet away, a man trapped in a similar manner is having his face licked by a passing dog. The artist was innocent of perspective, and Reverend Heath, in the picture, is approximately the height of his church. In the years that followed, the Port Royal earthquake provided inspiration for many a sermon—sermons that may account for much of Port Royal's reputation as a city of sin. It is interesting to speculate on what the preachers would have said had they seen what happened just over the horizon from Jamaica in 1902. In one twenty-four-hour period, the Caribbean was rocked by two eruptions of staggering magnitude, either one of which would have been considered a once-in-a-century calamity.

The first eruption took place on St. Vincent, south of Jamaica. A pear-shaped island about 20 miles long and 10 miles wide at its broadest point, St. Vincent was known best—at least until 1902—as the site of the 1797 naval engagement that made Admiral Horatio Nelson's name a household word in Britain. Nelson's bravery and acumen at the battle of St. Vincent played a large part in the defeat of the Spanish fleet commanded by Admiral José de Córdoba. But Nelson was aided greatly by the fact that Spain's navy was in a state of disrepair at the time, and that the Spanish Admiral had barely enough men on hand to man his ships. Furthermore, the Spanish "sailors" were for the most part not sailors at all, but soldiers forced into duty on board and landsmen recruited by press gangs. The Spanish fleet was no match for the British, who besides having the advantages of a brilliant commander had the efficiency produced by long days of training at sea, in all kinds of weather. This battle proved that Britain really did rule the waves, and British sea power suffered no serious challenge for the next century.

St. Vincent is dominated by the volcanic peak of La Soufrière, at the northern end of the island. The name means "sulfur" or "brimstone"; the peak is 4,500 feet high. Dense tropical vegetation covers the island, and under that vegetation is a bewildering melange of volcanic material spewed out over the centuries by La Soufrière.

The vegetation is wiped out periodically in eruptions, one of which, in 1718, lasted three days and blackened the daytime sky with ash. Ash accumulated ankle-deep on St.

Christopher, 300 miles north of St. Vincent. This eruption destroyed the summit and left a caldera called the "old crater." Another crater was formed in the 1812 eruption, which once again hid the sun behind clouds of ash and smoke. As with other eruptions, the noise of this one was mistaken for naval gunfire offshore, at Barbados, and soldiers on the island prepared for a possible invasion by sea.

Things were quiet on St. Vincent for the next 89 years. Then the volcano began to stir in its sleep in the spring of 1901. Earthquakes shook the island and alarmed the residents greatly. But the tremors soon ceased, and the people of St. Vincent returned to their daily routines.

Quakes resumed about a year later, in April, 1902. By now it was clear to at least some persons on the island that La Soufrière was building up to some kind of violent event. When the mountain began issuing clouds of ash and steam, parts of the island were evacuated.

Only certain parts were evacuated, however, and here we see how strangely the human mind can behave. Most of the residents who left were from the leeward side of the volcano, where winds blew the clouds of ash and smoke directly overhead. By contrast, residents of the windward side had less trouble with ashfalls, and they refused to budge. This attitude was something like saying the leak at the stern of your rowboat need not worry you because you are sitting in the bow. More than a thousand deaths resulted.

The first puffs of steam emerged from La Soufrière early on the afternoon of May 6. More outbursts of vapor followed, and by the next morning the eruptions had merged into one continuous outpouring of gas. A lake inside the crater, heated almost to boiling, spilled out of its bed and cascaded down the mountainside as a river of hot mud, or *lahar*. The eruption grew steadily more violent and, on the afternoon of May 7, let loose a nightmare on the remaining residents of St. Vincent.

Out of the volcano burst a thick hot cloud of dust and

gases. Heavier than air, the cloud flowed downslope with the force of a gale. Glowing rocks were mixed in with the cloud, like ghastly lanterns in a fog.

This was the *"nuée ardente,"* the fiery cloud—one of the most terrifying phenomena of nature. Few names are more apt. The *nuée ardente* is a superheated mass of gas and clastic material, much like a dust or sand storm, but dozens of times hotter and more deadly. The cloud bakes, on the spot, any flesh it touches. Inhaling it is like breathing flame. It carbonizes wood and, in general, sterilizes a landscape almost as effectively as an atomic bomb. And if anyone caught by a *nuée ardente* should have the miraculous luck to escape being roasted alive, then the gases in the cloud—sulfur oxides, hydrogen sulfide, and the like—virtually guarantee death by asphyxiation. The *nuée ardente* is something like a napalm explosion and a gas attack rolled into one. It came rolling down the slopes of La Soufrière like an avalanche.

As it raced downhill, the water vapor in the cloud, beginning to cool slightly from contact with the air, condensed into mist. The result was a hot mud that clung to skin and scalded as would steam from a boiler. The ash and mud coated everything they touched: buildings caught in the cloud's path, trees knocked flat by the impact of the *nuée ardente,* and many of the 1,350 persons who stayed behind on St. Vincent after the eruptions began.

La Soufrière shared one thing with many other great natural disasters. There were some persons who passed through the middle of the cataclysm and came out unscathed. More than a hundred persons on St. Vincent avoided harm entirely by hiding in a rum cellar. When they emerged from the cellar, they found a landscape almost as desolate as the moon. The ashfalls had killed nearly all vegetation on the island. About 30 percent of St. Vincent was laid waste completely; it stood as bare and lifeless as when the island had first risen from the sea. For two more days the eruptions went on, making the island shudder under a continuous series of blasts.

At last La Soufrière fell silent. When the first survey team reached the crater after the eruption, they found that the volcano had lost 730 feet from its summit.

La Soufrière was still roaring when one of its neighbors in the Antilles awoke: Mount Pelée, on the island of Martinique, about a hundred miles to the north. And even though La Soufrière had roared long and loud, it was soon clear that she had merely been introducing the principal speaker: Mount Pelée.

"Pelée" means "peeled" or "bare" in French, and Mount Pelée's name is sometimes translated into English as Bald Mountain. Supposedly the mountain acquired its name from a patch of bare rock near the summit. Dr. Fred Bullard of the University of Texas, however, points out the similarity between the volcano's name and that of Pele, the Hawaiian volcano deity, and suggests the likeness may be more than just coincidence.

Mount Pelée occupies the northern tip of Martinique, one of the largest of the Volcanic Caribbees. Shaped like a mitten with a short thumb, Martinique stands about 40 miles long and 16 miles wide. The island is known primarily for two things: one is its rum, distilled from the abundant sugar cane; the other is the eruption of Mount Pelée in 1902, less than twenty-four hours after La Soufrière devastated St. Vincent.

The volcano, like La Soufrière, is complex in structure and seems to shift its center of eruption often. Parts of the peak are destroyed in violent eruptions; then the same eruptions build the peak back up again. In the years just before 1902, however, no one seemed afraid of the volcano or its caldera. There was a lake in the half-mile-long caldera, and it was a popular spot for picnics. It had a tranquil name: L'Étang des Palmistes (Palm Lake). There was another lake in the caldera as well, L'Étang Sec (Dry Lake), and a small fumarole, the only outward sign of the powerful forces at work beneath the mountain.

One entered the caldera, for picnics or whatever other reason, through a gap in the southwest side. This gap looked out over St. Pierre, the bustling commercial city on the island's western shore about six miles from the volcano's summit. A *nuée ardente* could cover that distance in the time it takes to fry an egg.

At that time, St. Pierre was the trading center of Martinique and one of the most important commercial cities of the Caribbean. Surrounded by lush tropical scenery and blessed with a good harbor, Martinique was a thin arc of homes, offices, and shops, about a mile long and a fourth as wide. There was a beach to seaward and a high hill on the landward side of the city. The one main street ran the length of the city and was crossed by shorter streets running from the sea to the hill behind St. Pierre. From above, the city looked much like any other well-to-do community in the Caribbean. There was a hospital, and a modest cathedral. Stores sold the local newspaper, *Les Colonies,* as well as a wide variety of manufactured goods, from cloth to canned foods. Under the red roofs of the city, there was a small ocean of rum, the liquor of choice in the Caribbean, stored in bottles and barrels. St. Pierre was a bustling, energetic little city, not unlike the seaports of New England in their heyday, a few decades earlier. Over it all loomed Pelée.

The nightmare began on April 2, 1902. (About the same time, quakes resumed on La Soufrière after a one-year hiatus.) A schoolteacher noticed new fumaroles were appearing in the upper valley of a river that ran down from the top of the mountain. Three weeks later, a stench of sulfur could be smelled over St. Pierre. There was a light fall of ash, and several mild but perceptible earthquakes shook the plates and silverware in the city's kitchens.

Then, on April 25, the floor of the caldera exploded. An ash cloud shot up from the summit of Mount Pelée, and rocks rained down on the mountain's slopes. A few brave individuals climbed to the rim of the caldera and reported that a cinder cone about the size of a house had formed there. The cone was steaming, and bubbling audibly.

More ash descended on St. Pierre. It was light-colored fine ash like that from Mount St. Helens, and the ashfalls gave St. Pierre the same snowbound appearance as Yakima, Washington, would have 78 years later. The ash blew and drifted, and it kept falling. Soon roads were impassable. Moreover, the ash was posing a hazard to health. Inhaled, the fine powder could interfere with breathing or even asphyxiate, for there were toxic gases trapped in the ash. When released from the ashfalls, those gases killed small animals; birds, their songs over, lay dead in the ashes where they had fallen.

Mount Pelée covered the city with darkness from its cloud. The sun could be seen, but only as a dim disk one could look at directly without hurting one's eyes. St. Pierre was a silent city as well: the ash deadened the sounds of footsteps and carriages, and its porous surface absorbed even the sound of voices. "The rain of ash is endless," said the local newspaper on May 3. The gray dust got into everything: shoes, clothing, furniture. The people of St. Pierre walked about the streets only when necessary, and when they walked, small clouds of fine ash swirled up about their legs. St. Pierre could be described in three words: gloom, grit, and silence.

If the city was quiet, however, the mountain was not. The sound of explosions rolled down from the caldera and set the townspeople's nerves on edge. Floods of hot mud and muddy water surged downhill from the summit and engulfed a sugar mill just north of St. Pierre. Several dozen workers were buried alive in the scalding mud, their tombstone the mill's chimney projecting above the lahar.

The disaster at the sugar mill was the final straw for the people of St. Pierre. They began evacuating the city, though with no clear purpose or sense of order. Logically, they should have tried to get as far away as possible. Instead, they remained on the island but sought high ground.

Apparently they feared more avalanches of mud, or perhaps a tsunami caused by the ever-increasing earth tremors, but clearly they had no idea of the real danger that faced them, and they paid for that ignorance with their lives.

The eruption grew in intensity on May 6, and the following day it seemed as if the Apocalypse had arrived. Lightning flashed in the dark cloud that poured from the volcano, though the sound of thunder was all but lost in the roar of the mountain. At the same time, heavy rains fell on the mountain, turning the ash into mud and sending it rushing in huge rivers down the valleys on the volcano.

At that moment, when heaven seemed to have turned its back on St. Pierre, the people huddled in the darkness at the foot of Mount Pelée needed hope more than anything else. And hope arrived in news from St. Vincent, their southern neighbor. La Soufrière had just erupted, a few hours ahead of Mount Pelée. Perhaps the outburst on St. Vincent would drain away some of the hot gases from under Mount Pelée, and the eruption would soon subside.

On the following morning, it appeared La Soufrière had done exactly that. The dark clouds of ash were gone, and the plume rising from the caldera of Mount Pelée was clean white steam. The worst, it seemed, was over.

But Captain G. T. Muggah of the British steamer *Roramira* was not convinced. His ship had been at sea during the eruption, and entered the harbor at St. Pierre early on the morning of May 8, decks coated with ash from the volcano. Standing on the bridge, he eyed the mountain suspiciously. There was still a thick column of steam issuing from the summit, indicating Mount Pelée was not yet ready to lie down. Captain Muggah told a passenger that he was not going to stay in St. Pierre an hour more than necessary.

An hour was all he had. At 6:50 A.M., the *Roramira* had just tied up alongside the seventeen other craft in the harbor. At 7:50 A.M., Mount Pelée exploded.

"Exploded" may be too strong a word. The mountain remained intact. But a series of detonations boomed out from the volcano and a mammoth black plume of smoke crowned with lightning rose from the summit. At the same moment, a ground-hugging *nuée ardente* flowed out of the volcano and down the mountain's slopes—a pitch-black cloud studded, some witnesses said, with flames. (Possibly the flames came from wood and other flammable material that ignited as the cloud touched it.) Clocks in St. Pierre read 7:52 A.M. St. Pierre had only seconds to live.

The cloud swept toward St. Pierre at a speed estimated later at 100 miles per hour, creating the effect of a powerful windstorm combined with the heat of a furnace. In a few seconds trees were stripped of leaves and branches and their trunks turned to charcoal. Many were unrooted and flung for hundreds of feet by the force of the blast. Walls several feet thick were knocked down as though they were picket fences. A three-ton statue was lifted from its pedestal and carried 50 feet through the air. Virtually every house in the city lost its roof to the fiery blast from Mount Pelée.

Broken open by the fierce wind, the houses filled quickly with the toxic gases from the cloud. If one did not die of the heat, then one was gassed to death. Not until chlorine was released on the battlefields of Europe during World War I could there have been a more horrible way to die.

The city was full of flammable material, and soon it added the heat of its own combustion to that of the *nuée ardente*. The resulting fire storm was so intensely hot that vessels could not have approached the shore to look for survivors.

In any event, none of the ships in the harbor were in condition to help the people on shore. The British steamship *Roddam* had its anchor chain snapped by the force of the blast, and *Roddam* wasted no time in fleeing to nearby St. Lucia. A dozen men on board were dead on arrival. Ten others were hospitalized with burns.

When the *nuée ardente* burst from Mount Pelée, the

passengers of the *Roramira* were preparing for breakfast. Suddenly a steward shouted to them, "The volcano is coming!"

A few seconds later, the shock wave hit the ship. The *Roramira* was lifted out of the water, then settled back into the sea. Passengers, unable to keep their feet, fell on the deck and were bashed against bulkheads and furniture. The blast shattered portholes and skylights, and steaming-hot mud from the cloud poured into the cabins and corridors. The noise of the volcano was deafening. The ship's purser described it later as like "a thousand cannon."

When the blast struck the *Roramira*, the purser ran to his cabin and wrapped himself in his bedclothes for insulation. A few seconds earlier, he had seen the black cloud roll over St. Pierre. There had been crowds of people on the docks, looking for some way to escape the onrushing cloud. When the cloud had passed, there was no one left on the landings. Some may have jumped into the water in hopes of escaping the *nuée ardente*, but they were probably cooked alive. The cloud from Mount Pelée heated the waters almost to boiling.

Many of the *Roramira*'s crew—28 out of a total of 47—survived the disaster. Captain Muggah was killed. So were all but two of the passengers, a young girl and her nurse. But, though the *Roramira* was severely damaged, much of her superstructure carried away, and the boats as well, at least she remained afloat. All other ships in the harbor except for the *Roddam* were capsized by the blast and sunk.

The cloud dissipated in a few minutes. Had it hung over the landscape much longer, no one in St. Pierre would have survived. Even so, there were only two survivors from the city.

One was a dockworker named Auguste Ciparis. He was in an underground jail when the cloud descended on St. Pierre; and although his cell was windowless and had only a small opening in the door, enough superheated gas seeped in through that opening to burn him seriously. He was rescued three days later, on Sunday—only then were the ashes cool enough for rescue parties to enter St. Pierre. His screams drew the attention of the rescuers, and he was taken from his cell to have his burns treated. At the time, the burns were so extensive that he seemed likely to die of them; but he recovered and later went into the entertainment business.

The other survivor was a young cobbler named León Compère-Léandre. He was trapped in his home at the time of the catastrophe, and burned on the legs, but was able to walk several miles to a nearby town after he recovered from the intial shock.

St. Pierre was no more. The first men to visit the ruins after the disaster saw a scene of complete desolation. From an elevation, one could see down into the gutted interiors of roofless homes and offices, stores and churches. The scene looked like a vast, broken honeycomb. Iron had melted in the heat from the cloud. Wood had turned to charcoal. Except for the two survivors, no one on land had lived through the *nuée*'s descent. There would be no more calamities quite like this one until the age of atomic warfare.

The May eruption of Mount Pelée destroyed about eight square miles of the island. Another large eruption, on August 30, added slightly to the zone of destruction. Still another eruption took place in December. The most impressive thing to rise from the volcano after the May 8 eruption was a huge mass of solidified lava. It appeared in the caldera around mid-October and surged upward like paste being extruded from a cylinder. By the first of December, the mighty tower of rock had risen to a height of 80 stories. Though technically known as a "spine" or "lava dome," the huge monolith was dubbed the Tower of Pelée.

At its greatest height, the Tower of Pelée loomed more than 1,000 feet above the surrounding caldera. A picture of the mountain taken in March, 1903, shows the Tower of Pelée in the distance like some huge memorial to the dead at St. Pierre, the ruins of which appear in the foreground.

The tower was brittle near its peak, however, and about a year after the eruption that destroyed St. Pierre, another eruption shook down about 200 feet of loose rock from the tower's top. The monolith kept on falling apart all the rest of the year. By the end of 1903, it was only a nub of rock surrounded by the debris of its own destruction.

Mount Pelée slept briefly, then awoke again in 1929. The eruption was less intense than that of 1902, but lasted more than three years. This time, residents of the island took no chances. They evacuated St. Pierre and other towns on the island, and no one died. (Thirty thousand persons had been killed in St. Pierre alone on that day in 1902.) La Soufrière slumbered a bit longer than Mount Pelée before rumbling back to life for a few weeks in 1971, 1972, and 1976. Fortunately, these eruptions were minor. Whether or not the next one will be minor, and when it may happen, no one knows. There is still fire under the Caribbees, and eruptions of the Caribbean volcanoes follow no clear pattern.

One danger, however, has been removed in the last few decades: ignorance. We know now that the volcanoes of the Caribbean Sea are still active—and potentially lethal. The lessons of 1902 guarantee there will be no repetition of the disaster at St. Pierre if the mountains give us any warning at all. Those lessons probably need not have been learned at the cost of two cities and thousands of lives; but the burned city teaches best.

XIII

Earthquake City

C A P T A I N Gaspar de Portolá is remembered primarily for a mistake he made in the autumn of 1769.

Portolá, commanding a party of some 50 Spaniards, was sent north from San Diego to explore Monterey Bay. His instructions for finding the bay were so vague, however, and the description given him so inaccurate, that he and his company marched right past Monterey without recognizing it.

The Spaniards continued on toward the north and, on the afternoon of November 4, 1769, found themselves standing on what is now called Sweeney Ridge, overlooking San Francisco Bay.

The huge natural harbor impressed the Spaniards greatly. The diarist of the expedition, Father Juan Crespi, commented later that "not only the navy of our Most Catholic Majesty, but those of all Europe could take shelter in it."

His Most Catholic Majesty held title to San Francisco Bay for only half a century. Mexico won its independence and took control of most of California, including San Francisco, until the territory passed to United States control in 1848.

By the late 1800s, San Francisco had grown from a single crude trading outpost to a cosmopolitan city of steep hills and a society so uninhibited that Rudyard Kipling described San Francisco as "a mad city inhabited for the most part by perfectly insane people." New England writer Richard Henry Dana, author of *Two Years Before the Mast,* put it more tactfully: "The customs of California," he said, "are free."

Dana visited San Francisco twice, with 24 years between his visits. He first saw the bay as a young crew member of the brig *Pilgrim,* out of Boston, in 1834. The *Pilgrim* sailed into the harbor on Friday, December 4. Dana described the bay later as "magnificent . . . containing several good harbors, great depth of water, and surrounded by a fertile and finely wooded country" where deer were found in abundance. The weather was surprisingly cold for California; Dana and his fellow sailors were surprised to find frost on the ground one morning, and they almost froze their bare feet while splashing around in the surf.

Dana found the "magnificent bay" in sharp contrast to some of its visitors, Russian sailors wintering there on board their brig. The "brutish faces" of the Russians offended the aristocratic Dana, as did the fact that the Russians apparently "dealt in nothing but grease. They lived upon grease, ate it, drank it, slept in the midst of it. . . . The grease seemed actually coming through their pores, and out into their hair, and on their faces." Dana speculated that this oily coating helped Russians survive their bitter winters.

The Russians must have been only a minor blot on the landscape, however, for Dana was entranced with the "large and beautifully wooded islands" of the bay area and added: "If California ever becomes a prosperous country, this bay will be the center of its prosperity."

That prophecy came true in less than three decades. When Dana revisited San Francisco in 1858, he found a community far advanced in size and sophistication over the small trading post which had been almost the only human habitation there 24 years earlier. Dana described his reactions:

> When I awoke in the morning, and looked from my windows over the city of San Francisco, with its storehouses, towers, and steeples; its court-houses, theaters, and hospitals; its daily journals; its well-filled learned professions; its fortresses and light-houses; its wharves and harbor, with their thousand-ton clipper ships, more in number than London or Liverpool sheltered that day, itself one of the capitals of the American Republic, and the sole emporium of a new world, the awakened Pacific . . . when I saw all these things, and reflected on what I once was and saw here, and what now surrounded me, I could scarcely keep my hold on reality at all, or the genuineness of anything, and seemed to myself like one who had moved in "worlds not realized."

Reality and fantasy still seem hard to separate in San Francisco at times, because San Franciscans tolerate and even encourage the unusual in all its forms. There are very few other cities in America where one can buy, from coin-operated vending machines on the street, a homosexual newspaper or a guide to local nude beaches.

San Franciscans even have their own peculiar way of using the English language. Optimism is "positive consciousness." "Space" may mean anything from cubic measure to a thirst for beer. And all the familiar buzzwords of the "new consciousness," from "laid back" to "mellow," originated somewhere around the bay.

This is a city of free thinkers, and many of the fads and crusades of the last several decades began in or near

San Francisco. The Beat Generation first showed its bearded face in San Francisco basements. The Berkeley Free Speech movement of 1965 foreshadowed the campus upheavals of the late sixties, and the "great San Francisco acid wave" marked the beginning of America's psychedelic counterculture. For a few months, the bay was the nucleus of the youth rebellion, and entrepreneurs tried to make a quick dollar by organizing bus tours to see the "hippie havens" in San Francisco's Haight-Ashbury district. (The hippies soon tired of seeing busloads of short-haired tourists rolling by and gaping at the "freaks"; flower children retaliated by running alongside the buses and holding up mirrors to the passengers' windows, so that the only "freaks" the tourists saw were themselves.)

The days of the youth revolution are long gone; the only reminder of that turbulent time is the occasional bright splash of psychedelic paint one sees on the houses along Haight Street, once the mecca of the counterculture. But the memories of the sixties are still vivid here; and even persons who have never visited San Francisco are likely to have strong memories of the city: especially of its earthquake.

The earthquake of 1906 is probably the single most famous event in San Francisco's history, and possibly the most famous earthquake of all time. The culprit in this earthquake, which caused the death of some 700 persons and gave San Francisco the nickname "earthquake city," was a long crack in the earth's crust known as the San Andreas Fault.

The San Andreas Fault is only a short ride from San Francisco by car or bus, and visitors to the city sometimes spend an hour or two trying to find it. In fact, the fault is hard to locate without the help of a geological map. Though Easterners come here expecting to find a gaping chasm in the earth, with sulfurous fumes and fire rising from it, what they actually find is an almost imperceptible change in the topography.

There is a slight offset in the shore at Mussel Rock in Pacifica, a wealthy southern suburb of San Francisco That offset marks the spot where the San Andreas Fault runs out to sea. Following the fault inland can be difficult if you are on the ground, because development has erased many of its traces. Here and there the fault shows up as a trench or rise. It runs along Skyline Boulevard in San Bruno as a nondescript ditch. The grass is dry and brown. A few bottles and cans litter the ground nearby. A cat prowls in the grass, looking for mice. This is the fearsome San Andreas Fault.

Within shouting distance of the fault is a junior college. Students here seem undisturbed about the presence of the San Andreas just a few hundred feet away. Ask them about it and they look slightly amused, as if this is a question they've heard countless times before from Eastern visitors.

"Oh, you should have been here for the earthquake a few months back," says a gum-chewing young woman in the bookstore. "I was in here when it happened. I looked back and saw the piles of books *swaaaaaaying. . . .*" She mimics the motion with her body. "That was a pretty good one," she concludes.

"No, I don't worry about getting hurt in an earthquake," another student says. "I do worry about my fish tank at home. I'm scared I'll come home someday and find my fish all over the floor."

San Franciscans tend to see their city's history of devastating earthquakes as nothing unusual. They point out that other cities in America are built on active faults. Boston, for example, has been shaken frequently over the last few hundred years. An earthquake in 1775 damaged houses all over eastern Massachusetts and knocked standing persons off their feet. Tremors continued all through the next century, including one that caused near-panic one Sunday morning and sent hundreds of proper Bostonians shouting into the street, many in their bedclothes and some completely naked, to escape being trapped in collapsing buildings. Charleston, South Carolina, was destroyed by an earthquake in 1883, and the most powerful earth tremor ever recorded in the lower forty-eight states occurred in the Mississippi Valley near what is now St. Louis, in the winter of 1811–12. There may be other active faults in the East, buried under hundreds or thousands of feet of sediment, of which we know nothing. One of those "hidden" faults rumbled to life briefly in 1974, when an earthquake shook New Jersey.

But California is still the most active state tectonically, and the reason has to do with the collision of the North American crustal plate with another plate—or, more accurately, several of them—over the last 60 million years.

The Cenozoic was just getting under way when the American plate came marching westward toward a mid-ocean ridge in the Pacific. There is no ridge off the California coast today, the continent having trampled it under. But 60 million years ago, the ridge existed, and between it and the continent to the east was a crustal plate now called the Farallon plate. A subduction zone was created along the western coast of North America as the continent approached, consuming the Farallon plate as it came. (The advance of North America had already broken off a chunk of the Farallon plate, and that chunk lay under the continent, slowly melting and generating vulcanism. This buried piece of the Farallon plate created a kind of furnace in the basement of western North America, and explains why geothermal activity and evidence of past vulcanism are found in places like Wyoming's Yellowstone Park, hundreds of miles from the Pacific trace of the Ring of Fire.)

As North America subducted more and more of the Farallon plate, earthquakes and volcanic activity increased along the Pacific shore. One can still see in the stratigraphic maps of California large deposits of volcanic rock that date from this period. Most of the rock laid down in this stage of California's history—the early and middle Cenozoic—was sedimentary, however, because much of what is now dry land, was under water. Only as we approach modern times, the Recent epoch, does the map of California start to take on its familiar appearance.

As the Farallon plate was consumed, the continent moved ever closer to the mid-ocean ridge. Thirty million years ago, North America was only a few miles from the ridge and was ready to overrun it too. Before that happened, however, there was another movement of crustal rock parallel to the California coast, and this movement would turn out to have life-and-death implications for Californians when the area was settled.

There was a thin ribbon of crust running between the main body of the Americas and the soon-to-be-destroyed ridge to the west. This strip of rock extended from what is now Bolivia to about the present U.S. border with Mexico. Before the oncoming juggernaut of North America consumed the mid-ocean ridge, this band of crust "made a break for it," one might say, up the narrow corridor between the ridge and the continent.

In the relatively brief time of 25 million years, this sliver of crust slipped northward some 300 to 500 miles. One part of it became Baja California, the long narrow tail of land that hangs down between Mexico and the Pacific. Another piece wedged itself against what is now southern California, just south of Los Angeles, pushing up the San Bernardino Mountains and the Transverse Ranges in the process. The third piece moved farthest north, to what is now the vicinity of San Francisco.*

* Though the advance of North America destroyed much of the Farallon plate, pieces of it survive in the eastern Pacific. The East Pacific Rise, for example, is descended from the Farallon plate. Ironically, the Farallon plate did not give rise to its namesakes, the Farallon Islands, a few miles west of the Golden Gate. These tiny islands, which are just barely visible from San Francisco on a clear day, are actually splinters of the North American mainland, broken off in the collision between the North American plate and the plates to the west. North America and the Pacific

Adding to the chaos along the California coast is the fact that California has now slid over the top of what was formerly the mid-ocean ridge. The result is a jumbled and bewildering geology—and a state highly prone to earthquakes.

The forces that made California also gave it a highly fractured crust. One of the cracks in the crust is the San Andreas Fault, which was created by the breakout of that ribbon of crust, starting some 25 million years ago. The San Andreas runs for more than 500 miles along the western border of California, and from the air it can be seen clearly near San Francisco as a series of lakes south of the city. These lakes occupy depressions created by the movement of the rocks along the fault. Just across the bay is one of the tributary faults that runs into the San Andreas. This fault is the Hayward Fault, and it runs along the whole eastern side of the bay. Further south, near Los Angeles, the San Andreas intersects with another fault, the Garlock Fault, which was created when a chunk of crustal rock sliding northward collided with North America in what is now the Mojave Desert. Where the San Andreas and Garlock come together, just north of Los Angeles, is a formation called the "Palmdale bulge." This is a vast elevation in the crust, roughly the size of Massachusetts, caused by slippage along the fault line. The rise in the land is not perceptible as one drives or walks across it, but sensitive instruments have measured a steady elevation of the surface over the last couple of decades. The bulge is thought to have been responsible for devastating tremors in the Los Angeles area in the past: the Fort Tejon earthquake of 1854, for example, and the killer San Fernando quake of 1971. The quakes were caused by the settling of the bulge. What will happen to Los Angeles

---

plate are still colliding, but not head on; the eastern edge of the Pacific plate is sliding northward, while the North American plate moves westward. This "glancing blow" accounts for the absence of a deep trench—the sign of direct collision and subduction—off the California coast.

when and if the bulge settles suddenly again, it is unpleasant to think; the area came within a few seconds of calamity in 1971, when the earthquake brought a dam near Los Angeles very close to failure.

Los Angeles is not the only section of the California coast where earthquakes have been tentatively predicted for the next few decades. Many geologists are willing to bet that when the next "big one" comes, it will hit San Francisco. As best we can estimate, major earthquakes strike the bay area about once every century or so on the average, and three-fourths of a century has elapsed since the great San Francisco earthquake of 1906.

That earthquake has been the subject of at least half a dozen American films, scores of books, and countless magazine articles, and so it is surprising to note that it was little more than a jiggle compared to many others in history along the Ring of Fire. Fewer than a thousand persons were killed in the San Francisco earthquake, and San Francisco was far luckier than most other cities around the Ring, in that it had the resources of one of the world's largest and richest nations to draw on as the city was being reconstructed. Compared to the Chinese earthquake of 1556 (more than 800,000 dead) and the Edo earthquake in Japan in 1803 (200,000 killed), the "great San Francisco earthquake" looks unimpressive.

It was frightening enough, however, for tenor Enrico Caruso, who was in San Francisco to perform in *Carmen*. Caruso was in his hotel room when the building started shaking. He was thrown to the floor, but got to his feet and searched frantically through his luggage for his most prized possession: an autographed photo of Theodore Roosevelt. Armed with the picture, he went out into the street when the tremor subsided, and began wandering aimlessly about the city. Caruso thought Roosevelt's picture would open all kinds of doors for him, and he was disappointed when the photo meant nothing to the people he showed it to.

Soon the portly tenor remembered he had a much better way of identifying himself. He made his way to the harbor and attempted to board a boat there, so as to escape any further shaking on the land. The crew of the boat was skeptical. Was this *really* Caruso? It looked like him, but . . .

Caruso put an end to their doubts quickly. He launched into an aria, and after a few bars the crew, convinced, welcomed their illustrious passenger aboard.

The city was full of celebrities on the day of the earthquake. John Barrymore was attending a private party when the earthquake began. When the tremor ceased, Barrymore, dressed to the nines, went outside for a walk. Along the way he met Caruso, who was highly amused by Barrymore's formal dress. "Mr. Barrymore," Caruso said, "you are the only man in the world who would dress for an earthquake."

But humor was scarce in the city that morning. The quake struck at 5:13 A.M. It lasted a minute and fifteen seconds. At the end of that period, several thousand buildings constructed on geologically unstable landfill were shaken down, trapping their occupants inside. Among the other casualties of the earthquake was San Francisco's recently constructed City Hall, one of the architectural masterpieces of the West. When the tremor was over, the ornamental columns on the building's face lay in the street like so many felled trees. The stone sheathing of the central tower peeled off and fell to the ground. What remained was a tubular framework of girders with the dome still perched on top, like some baroque spaceship ready for launch.

The gates of Stanford University crumbled, as did much of the school's library. A statue of the nineteenth-century naturalist Agassiz had been shaken out of its niche on a wall and buried itself on impact, upside down, about a foot deep in the pavement. Students were amused to see Agassiz standing on his head.

Most of the damage done to San Francisco, however, was done by fire rather than the tremor itself. Like Tokyo and Yokohama, whose turn for destruction came 17 years later, San Francisco was a massive firetrap, the result of more than half a century of construction with no thought to the hazards of fire. The National Board of Fire Underwriters had issued a gloomy report on the city's fire potential only half a year before the earthquake, and concluded it was a miracle that the city had not burned up already. The credit for that miracle was due entirely to the San Francisco Fire Department, which had performed valiantly under the command of Chief Dennis Sullivan. That underwriters' report warned, however, that the firemen could only be expected to forestall a disastrous fire for so long; and time ran out for the highly flammable city on April 18, when the earthquake struck.

The Fire Department was powerless to stop fires because its water supplies had been knocked out by the tremor. At first it looked as if the fire might stay contained in an area near the waterfront. But the firemen's hopes were shattered after the quake, when flames broke out on the other side of Van Ness Avenue.

Someone had decided that food was the best thing to restore one's spirits after disaster, and had lit a fire around 10 A.M., to cook breakfast. A defective chimney carried the fire to the rest of the building. Soon the neighborhood was ablaze; then the entire city.

Observers on the Oakland side of the bay watched as a cloud of smoke miles high rose above the city. Crews of explosives experts were setting charges, trying to collapse enough buildings to form a "firebreak," but their efforts were unsuccessful, and the fire burned for days. Chief Sullivan was killed in a burning building.

Most of the quake fatalities lived in brick or stone residences, which had no resiliency and thus crumbled under the tremors. Separate wooden structures, by contrast, swayed with the motion of the ground, and survived. Other patterns emerged from the destruction. Buildings on top of hills, where the "shear" (an engineer's expression for a building's proneness to slide during a quake) was least, generally came through the earthquake more or less intact. Buildings on hillsides suffered strong shear, and many were destroyed.

One clear lesson was learned in the San Francisco earthquake: building on landfill can mean disaster. The unconsolidated sediments that go into making landfill turn to something with the consistency of porridge during a severe earthquake, and buildings constructed on landfill have been known during tremors simply to lie down on their sides like exhausted horses. Sometimes the settling occurs so slowly that residents are able to walk down the sides of the building and jump safely to the ground, with no more trouble than getting off a streetcar.

One quarter of San Francisco was spared most of the ravages of fire. The Italian district contained several hundred thousand gallons of wine, in bottles and kegs, in home cellars. When the fire approached, the Italian-Americans simply carried the wine to the rooftops and poured it out on the shingles. The wet rooftops effectively put out any sparks that happened to land on them.

San Francisco may have had wine aplenty, but after the earthquake other foodstuffs were in short supply, and the market was ideal for profiteering . . . at least for a while. The price of a loaf of bread rose from something like ten cents to a dollar in several hours. Then the U.S. Army stepped in.

To discourage looting, martial law had been declared in San Francisco after the quake. Very often the soldiers patrolling the streets appointed themselves judge and jury when they found a suspected looter or profiteer. Reportedly, they appointed themselves executioners as well. There is a story of a grocer who was making himself a tidy profit by selling bread at a dollar a loaf. The soldiers saw him, and asked the price of his bread.

"One dollar," the grocer replied.

"What's the price of your bread?" a soldier repeated, this time pointing his gun at the businessman.

"A dollar a loaf," the merchant insisted.

Without a word, the soldiers took him off to one side, stood him up against a building, and shot him.*

With half a billion dollars in damages, more than 700 persons killed, and more than 2,000 acres of the city destroyed either by the tremor or by the fire that followed, one would have expected San Franciscans to have learned something about the fault line under their city. The existence of that fault was plain to see after the earthquake. The land was offset at least a few inches all along it south of the city. Fences were bent and twisted where they crossed it. Roadways were cracked where it had split them in two. Rows of trees in orchards showed clearly where the two crustal plates had moved relative to each other.

But San Franciscans were slow to learn from the earthquake. For years after the tremor, local businessmen were careful to refer to it as "the San Francisco *fire* of 1906," so as to conceal the real nature of the danger that lay under the city. They downplayed that danger so successfully that there is now a densely populated string of communities built right on top of the San Andreas Fault.

Take the Bay Area Rapid Transit train from San Francisco to Daly City, a southern suburb. Stand on the platform at the Daly City station, and all around you will see buildings, mostly private homes. There are prefabricated boxes with large plate-glass windows. There are pastel concrete atrocities from the fifties, and even here and there a Victorian house that somehow escaped the wrecker's ball. These homes are crowded together like the scales on a

---

* To be fair to the U.S. Army, this story may be apocryphal. Other versions have the soldiers persuading merchants, at gunpoint, to lower the prices of their wares. There were cold-blooded killings in San Francisco after the quake, but these appear to have been largely the work of private vigilante groups, not the Army.

fish. Wherever it is physically possible to put a house, someone has done so. They occupy plots so steep that they would seem incapable of supporting a home. Just a couple of hills over from the Daly City station is the San Andreas Fault.

Many lurid stories have been written about the day San Francisco has its next major quake. Authors have described whole neighborhoods sinking into the sea; cars hurtling off highways into thin air as overpasses and bridges collapse; men and women cut to ribbons by falling glass as skyscraper windows shatter down on pedestrians. A vast body of alarmist literature has contributed to the popular image of San Francisco as a city waiting to fall into the sea. In fact, San Francisco stands very little chance of getting submerged in the next big quake, because the San Andreas is what geologists call a "slip-strike fault": one along which two masses of crust slide horizontally, with little or no vertical motion. This lateral motion may create quakes, but is not likely to cause widespread subsidence.

Whether or not San Francisco stands to fall into the Pacific, however, it does stand to suffer billions of dollars in damage when the next major earthquake arrives. That day may be nearer than some residents of the area would like to think, if the seismological record along the San Andreas Fault is any indication.

Since 1979, compression has been relaxing along the fault; the plates of crustal rock are not pressing against each other quite as hard as they did in the 1970s. This development may sound reassuring at first, since we usually associate relaxation with safety. But here relaxation could mean disaster is just around the corner.

When the crustal plates press hard against each other, they tend to lock each other in place. Locked thus, the plates cannot move very much and the chance of a severe quake is small. But relaxation spells potential trouble, because the plates are then set free to shift; and movement along the fault is what causes killer quakes.

About the time relaxation started along the San Andreas, the earth under San Francisco started quivering noticeably. The year 1979 saw a series of disturbingly strong quakes there. San Francisco residents were reminded that the earth is unquiet under the bay, and that the date for another superquake is approaching.

Just when the tremor will occur, no one knows for sure; but hardly anyone denies that the next big quake is on the way. One television documentary on San Francisco called it "the city that waits to die." Most San Franciscans would disagree. They are confident their city will survive the approaching "big one" as it did in 1906. Indeed, the people of San Francisco seem almost proud of their city's record for seismic activity. Boston has beans, Chicago has hogs, San Francisco has earthquakes. And in a time when traditional values are crumbling and the future seems less certain every day, the coming earthquake—as one San Francisco writer pointed out in an article for the Baltimore *Sun* some years ago—at least gives the people around the bay "something to believe in."

XIV

To Warn or Not to Warn?

ONE OF CALIFORNIA'S more interesting cottage industries is occultism. The state abounds in astrologers, fortune-tellers, palm readers, astral body travelers, levitators, and experts on such subjects as reincarnation, time travel, telekinesis, telepathy, "psychic surgery," and so forth. For a small fee (or a large fee, depending on the fame of the practitioner), you may have your natal chart cast, with generalized predictions of your fortune for the coming year. You may even hire a specialist in reincarnation to give you an idea of what you did in past lives.

Of course, this proliferation of psychics and other dabblers in the occult makes California no different from most other parts of the United States. America holds a vast body of people who hunger for some hint of what the future holds for them, and so there is always a huge market everywhere for the psychics to tap.

But California has spawned a peculiar breed of psychic.

These occultists specialize in earthquakes.

Their methods of foretelling quakes vary. Some psychics claim they use their astral bodies to sense the vibrations of future events. They will tell you, when pressed for a coherent and rational explanation of this process, that it is "very difficult to explain." Indeed.

Astrologers at least have a method that they can explain. They believe that the time is ripest for earthquakes when the planets are arranged in certain patterns in the sky. Uranus is supposedly the big troublemaker. That planet is thought to govern sudden and catastrophic events, such as floods, earthquakes, and eruptions. And when Uranus forms a square (a 90-degree angle) or an opposition (a 180-degree angle) to some other powerful member of the solar system, such as the sun or Jupiter, look out: something awful may be about to strike from out of the blue—or from underground, as the case may be.

The psychics have made a profitable business out of warning of impending quakes. The problem with their warnings is, none of them to date appears to have come true; or if they have, the original prophecy was so vague and flexible that it might have been a description of any future event, almost anywhere.

The spiritual father of these fortune-tellers is a physician named Michel de Notredame, who lived from 1503 to 1566 and is better known by his professional name, Nostradamus. He was born in Provence, the wine-making district, and studied philosophy at the university in Avignon before taking a medical degree in 1529. He seems to have been a conscientious physician, and he is still remembered for his heroic efforts in fighting the plague in the 1540s.

Nostradamus's hobby was prophecy. Staring into a crystal ball or even a bowl of water, he would make woozy forecasts about future tyrants, apparent invasions from the heavens, and so forth. Eventually he collected a few hundred of his prophecies—written in rhyming verse—and had them published as a book called *Centuries*.

Nostradamus is often given credit for predicting the rise of Hitler, and there is a verse in *Centuries* that sounds very much like a description of Hitler: an absolute tyrant who "lifts up and casts down" the clergy and the lesser nobles of his land and time. But that description fits any number of other dictators, in Nostradamus's time as well as our own, and so the specificity of this prophecy is open to question.

Was Nostradamus sincere in his prophecies, or just a clever fraud who hoped to capitalize on the gullibility of the public? There is no question that he became a famous and influential man when now and again some of his predictions appeared to come true. He enjoyed the favor of Catherine de Medici and King Charles IX. When he died, his reputation as a prophet was just short of Isaiah's. It is hard to dismiss the suspicion that Nostradamus, like many psychics in our own time, saw occultism as a quick and easy road to fortune.

Nostradamus has had hordes of disciples and imitators over the centuries, and many of them are living in California today, juggling aspects and declinations and straining their astral bodies for a glimpse of the date of the next big earthquake. Their goal is prediction, and predictions they have made aplenty.

In 1968, for example, when a large number of psychics in the United States pointed to 1968 as the date of the long-awaited quake, hundreds of persons fled the California coast, for fear San Francisco and Los Angeles would fall into the ocean. Both cities were still there when 1969 began, and those who left the cities crept back home with their faith in psychics shaken.

Just over a decade later, in 1979, there was another prediction reported in the American media: the California earthquake was scheduled for sometime early in 1980. This time there was no exodus from California, because the

1968 fiasco was still fresh in mind. It turned out that there was no need to leave California; once again, the quake failed to materialize.

But the psychics keep trying. Many of them appear to operate on the scatter-shot principle: if you make a large number of reasonably specific predictions, then sooner or later events will prove you right. If you predict destructive earthquakes for a thousand locations in California over a period of a decade or two, chances are that at least one or two of these predictions will happen to be correct.

So far, the scientists' record is not much better than that of the psychics. There have been a few successful quake predictions by scientists in the last few years, and geologists seem confident—though perhaps not as confident as a few years ago—that we will have a reliable method of predicting earthquakes someday. (Progress in earthquake prediction has been covered extensively in the last decade, and anyone interested in the subject may consult the list of suggested readings at the end of this book.)

But even if we do develop a method of predicting quakes—that is, foretelling when and where they will occur, and how strong they will be—will we want to use it? A few years ago, the answer to that question would have been a resounding yes. Now it is an ambivalent maybe, because in recent years it has become clear that the damage done by an earthquake prediction may be as great as that of an earthquake itself.

That is the conclusion of a research group headed by two American scientists, Dennis S. Mileti of Colorado State University and J. Eugene Haas of the University of Colorado. Mileti and Haas have studied the possible social costs of earthquake prediction, as opposed to the physical damage done by the tremor; and their conclusions make one wonder if earthquake prediction is really the marvelous breakthrough one might think it to be.

The Haas-Mileti study of earthquake prediction covers

a wide range of possible reactions to a reasonably specific prediction of a tremor. The following scenario is based on their findings.

January (of a year not too far in the future) . A panel of professional seismologists announces that a major earthquake stands a 50 percent probability of striking the San Francisco Bay area about eleven months from now. The expected magnitude is 8.0 on the Richter scale, or approximately the same force as the San Francisco quake of 1906. The mayor of San Francisco condemns the announcement as "alarmism," and a flurry of lawsuits is filed against the panel and its individual members by local businessmen who think the announcement will hurt their profits.

February. Apartment and house rentals are down sharply from the previous few months—a strange situation in a town as short of housing as San Francisco. Landlords find that some of their tenants are simply packing up before their leases expire and leaving without notice. Civil-defense headquarters notes a sharp increase in the number of calls inquiring about protection from earthquakes, and books on the subject of seismology are sold out at local stores as fast as they are put on the shelves. The mayor of San Francisco and the governor of California plead with the public for a sane and levelheaded attitude toward the quake prediction, but their appeal has little effect: the word "earthquake" suddenly has about the same effect in California that the word "shark" has on a crowded beach.

March. The initial panic is over, and people in the bay area seem to be collecting themselves after a bad scare. Columnists and TV commentators point out the long history of unsuccessful earthquake predictions in California, and generally dismiss the chance that this forecast might prove accurate. "If you didn't leave during the scare of '68," one newspaperman tells his readers, "why should you leave now?"

April. A mild tremor shakes the San Francisco area. The

quake is not severe; just barely strong enough to rattle objects on the table for a few seconds. But the effect is dramatic and immediate. Men and women run into the street, trying to get outside in case the buildings should collapse. The worst result is the most colossal traffic jam in San Francisco's history as thousands of motorists jump into their cars and flee toward the mountains, convinced the predicted quake has arrived. Fifteen persons are killed on the highways, including one policeman run over by a speeding car. Disaster of a less dramatic kind is taking place in the real-estate business. A few months earlier, houses were easy to sell in San Francisco. Now no one wants to move into the area. Property values have fallen 35 percent since the earthquake prediction was made, and seem likely to drop still further.

May. San Franciscans are embarrassed at their behavior during the previous month's tremor, and now are resolved to avoid panic. This resolve takes the form of a sneering reply to any suggestion that the quake prediction might be accurate. Property values continue to drop, and the geologists who made the prediction are looking for ways to pay their staggering legal bills. One seismologist is denied tenure at his school as a result of his involvement in the controversy. The mayor of San Francisco tries to persuade several industries to locate in the San Francisco area, but the companies decide San Francisco is too big a risk in view of the quake potential, and decided to locate elsewhere. San Francisco loses 2,000 jobs as a result of that decision.

June. Quake insurance is now impossible to buy. Businesses and homeowners who could formerly insure against the effects of a possible quake now find themselves unguarded—and liable to lose everything if the expected earthquake does occur. Property values have sunk 60 percent since January. Several thousand homes in San Francisco stand abandoned by their occupants, and become targets for looters and arsonists. Sections of several neighborhoods go up in flames. Estimated damage: more than two million dollars.

July. The tourist business in San Francisco has declined precipitously in the previous half year. Hardly anyone wants to risk being caught in the city on a visit if an earthquake really is imminent. Local radio and television stations run special announcements telling the public how to prepare for and behave during an earthquake. Several dozen landlords declare bankruptcy because their tenants have moved away.

August. A suburban home blows up, killing the couple who owned it, as well as their three children. The reason: hoarding gasoline. The man and woman had been stockpiling gasoline in cans for use in the event an earthquake should make gas unavailable from stations. Stores record a shortage of items such as dried foods, toilet paper, and bottled water. People are stocking up against the possibility of a quake. Sales of guns and ammunition are up sharply, too, because of scare stories about the danger of rioters and looters running wild after a major tremor. "This town is going to be full of crazed maniacs after the earthquake," one gun owner tells an interviewer from a local radio station, "and I'll be ready for them." Owners of wood-frame homes, the kind most likely to survive a strong earthquake, are getting unbelievable offers for their properties. People are also willing to pay exorbitant prices for camping equipment—tents, sleeping bags, lanterns, and so on—that will come in handy if an earthquake shakes down houses and forces families to live outdoors. In Sacramento, authorities draw up contingency plans for use in case an earthquake strikes San Francisco and sends streams of homeless refugees outward from the stricken city, looking for shelter elsewhere.

September. San Francisco is economically a sick city. Businesses which would have been moving to the city a year before, are now shunning San Francisco as if a pestilence were raging there. The number of bankruptcies increases.

Property values have finally stabilized, but at an absurdly low figure: 30 percent of the previous year's. So many homes and stores are deserted, left behind by persons leaving the city, that the police simply lack the manpower to respond to all the calls reporting looting and vandalism. Some streets are covered almost entirely with broken glass from shattered store windows.

October. A theater located on a busy highway is shaken perceptibly one evening as a heavy truck passes. The building is full of moviegoers (attendance at theaters has risen recently as people try to distract themselves from thoughts of the predicted tremor) , and panic breaks out when someone mistaking the truck vibration for a quake screams, "The earthquake!" Three persons are crushed to death in the rush to get outside. Several of the geologists who issued the quake prediction back in January report they have received death threats, and one of the threats comes very close to becoming reality: a letter bomb goes off in the office of one of the geologists, who had the good luck to be down the hall at the time of the explosion.

November. As the date of the projected quake approaches, the exodus from the city picks up speed. Whole blocks of houses are virtually abandoned now, and many San Franciscans are selling their homes for little more than a cent on the dollar. The buyers are speculators who hope to make a fortune if the quake does not occur as predicted. The same goes for business properties. Some businessmen, their profits obliterated by the social effects of the quake prediction, sell their businesses and inventories for scarcely more than the air fare to a less quake-prone city.

December. This is the month when "earthquake day" is expected to arrive. Tent cities have appeared in the hills surrounding San Francisco as thousands of San Franciscans set up housekeeping in the open. Looking toward the city, the campers can see an occasional column of smoke rising: another house set on fire by arsonists, or touched off accidently by looters. Competition for space is intense in some of the tent cities, and there is no law enforcement to speak of in the makeshift communities. Violence is common; winter rains, chilly nights, overcrowding, and the suspense of waiting for the tremor wear nerves extremely thin. Sometimes quarrels are settled with fists, clubs, even guns. Local authorities try their best to get rid of the tent cities, but the campers merely settle somewhere else as soon as they are evicted from a site. Since the campsites have inadequate sanitary facilities, public-health authorities are worried about the possibility of epidemic disease. The National Guard is alerted in case the quake occurs.

Christmas Day. There is no festivity in San Francisco and its surrounding communities. The prediction of a major quake is starting to seem like so much fantasy to the people around the bay, and slowly the refugees from the city are returning. Why, they ask, did the eggheads make their pronouncement, if it was going to cause so much loss and inconvenience? Total economic damage to the city and its environs is difficult to estimate, but most guesses run well into the hundreds of millions of dollars—about as much as a major quake would have caused. Geologists are in very low esteem in San Francisco.

New Year's Day. Squiggles on a seismogram indicate that little quakes are taking place under San Francisco with unusual frequency, and getting stronger all the time. "Foreshocks," say the seismologists looking at the paper. "This could be the quake," they tell the mayor, the governor, and civil-defense authorities. "We think you should issue a warning." The warning goes out. No one listens. After the chaos and economic ruin of the previous few months, San Franciscans are in no mood to be scared again by some forecast of seismic doom.

January 2. An earthquake of magnitude 7.8 strikes San Francisco. The approaches to the Golden Gate Bridge collapse. So do some 25,000 homes in the city. A hundred thousand persons are injured. Fifty thousand are killed immediately. Ten thousand more die later of their injuries.

Total damage from the earthquake: somewhere in the billions.

What you have just read is fantasy, but it is based on sober predictions of what the social cost of quake predictions may be. In this scenario, the residents of San Francisco would probably have been better off if the alert had never occurred.

Of course, there are many different forms a quake warning might take, and therefore many possible responses to it. A short-term earthquake prediction—say, "A tremor is 60 percent likely to strike the city three weeks from now" —might leave little time to brace buildings and take other measures against physical damage from quakes; but the short warning time would also minimize the other social effects of the prediction, such as the drop in property values. A long-term warning, on the other hand—four or five years, perhaps—would probably save a lot of lives but have other disastrous consequences as people fled the area of the expected tremor.

Then there is the danger of false alarms. Suppose a quake warning was issued, the population of a major city was evacuated, and the earthquake did not occur. Would the populace be inclined to ignore the next warning, and suffer heavy casualties if the quake actually occurred?

Here the answer depends partly on the character of the society where the prediction takes place. The Chinese government, for example, controls the lives of its people so closely that when an earthquake was predicted for Haicheng in 1975, the authorities ordered the people out of the city and into the hills—and the public complied. The residents of the city shivered in the cold for two days before the earthquake occurred.

A highly regimented society like China might make such measures possible. In a less tightly controlled society such as ours or Italy or Spain, however, people might be disinclined to march when the government said to march. They might evacuate a city for one false alarm, but the next time they would be much more skeptical of the earthquake warning.

And there is always the danger of mass panic in the event of a specific earthquake prediction. Panic has resulted in many fatal accidents in history. In such comparatively small events as nightclub fires, hundreds have died as men and women have tried to evacuate a building and been crushed to death in the process. What might happen if thousands tried to evacuate *an entire city* without any guiding plan or sense of order? The casualties from such a stampede might equal those of an actual earthquake.

Quake prediction, then, is not the unqualified blessing we once imagined it would be, and if a reliable system for predicting quakes ever is developed, then government officials are going to face a difficult decision when the first predictions of major quakes come in. Which would be more in the public interest: a warning or silence?

XV

Deep Gas Power

THERE ARE HUNDREDS of mines along the Ring of Fire. They yield copper, cobalt, tungsten, tin, gold, silver, sulfur, and dozens of other economically important minerals concentrated along the Ring by vulcanism and hydrothermal activity.

As mineral deposits near the surface are exhausted, miners have to dig deeper into the crust to find fresh deposits. The deeper the mine, the more problems miners face in working it. One of those problems may turn out to be an important new source of energy, and is part of a story that involves mine disasters, earthquakes, fish kills, and a scientist who discovered the nineteenth century's equivalent of LSD.

When gold and silver were discovered in the Western United States in the nineteenth century, miners began digging into the roots of ancient volcanoes to extract the ores. Often the mines they dug were more impressive than modern skyscrapers. Some mines were three or four times deeper than the Sears Tower in Chicago is high. The mines also extended out horizontally in all directions, following the veins of ore wherever they led. It was not unusual for a mine to encompass ten cubic miles of rock. None of this vast underground construct showed on the surface, of course. The only visible indication of a mine aboveground might be a few buildings and a low steel tower housing the "cage," the elevator that took men and equipment down into the mine and back up to the open air.

Life in the mines was fraught with peril, with "firedamp"—hydrocarbon gas—as its most insidious enemy. Firedamp mixed with the air and exploded if the concentration was high enough. Ignition might come from a lamp, a spark, or any other heat source, but the result was always the same: an explosion.

In the early 1800s, the mining industry in Britain, desperate for a solution to the firedamp problem, turned for help to one of the most famous scientists of the time: Sir Humphrey Davy.

Born in Penzance, Cornwall, in 1778, and largely self-educated, Davy was a strikingly handsome man as well as an accomplished chemist. As lecturer for the Royal Institution, he was Europe's best known popularizer of science, and he would probably have had his own television show had he been born a century and a half later. He was known in scientific circles as "the poet," because he wrote fair verse, and he was also an enthusiastic sportsman.

His specialty was gases. At first he tried to find out what effect gases had when breathed in pure form. He breathed hydrogen and would probably have been killed instantly if anything had ignited the hydrogen-air mixture in his lungs. Davy also survived an attempt to breathe carbon dioxide. His most pleasant experiment concerned nitrous oxide, "laughing gas." He found it made him feel pleasantly drunk. Nitrous oxide soon became a popular high in Britain, and was supposed to work by "concentrating ideas," the nineteenth-century expression for mind expansion.

A man so experienced with gases was just what the British miners needed to solve the firedamp problem, and in 1815, after a holiday on the Continent, Davy tackled the miners' dilemma. The answer turned out to be surprisingly simple.

Firedamp was methane gas. Better known as "marsh gas," it is produced in swamps and salt marshes where bacteria break down organic material and release methane in the process. The formula for methane is CH_4: a carbon atom surrounded by four hydrogens. It is highly flammable and burns with a faint blue flame.

Davy knew that methane catches fire only when it reaches a certain temperature. So the answer to the miners' problem was to keep the methane from reaching that temperature.

Shortly, Davy had the solution. He surrounded a lamp with wire gauze. The gauze let light pass through but conducted heat away from the flame, so that methane in the surrounding air could not reach its ignition point. Davy's lamp was adopted immediately and helped to reduce the risk of firedamp explosions underground.

Firedamp remained a threat, however, because lamps were not the only source of ignition in the mines. Even a spark would set off the methane. So mining engineers worked on ways to ventilate the mines and remove the hydrocarbon gas before it could build up to an explosion.

It was a long time before anyone thought to wonder: What was marsh gas doing so far underground?

Paleontologists and chemists came up with a theory. The hydrocarbons found deep in the earth were thought to be derived from the dead animals of the earth's distant past. Just as trees were carbonized to form coal, plant and animal remains were believed to have been transformed by heat and pressure, deep underground, into hydrocarbons such as natural gas and petroleum.

That belief was modified when the theory of plate tectonics came to be widely accepted. Geologists realized that the boundaries of colliding crustal plates created a natural cauldron where organic matter could easily be cooked into hydrocarbon form. And this hypothesis has held up well in practice. All along the Ring of Fire, from Central America to southern California and westward to southeast Asia, there are hundreds of highly productive oil fields that bear witness to the petroleum-making potential of the Ring.

But there was a problem with the theory that petroleum and other hydrocarbons underground formed entirely from animal and plant debris. If all our hydrocarbon deposits formed from organic material, then one would expect natural methane reservoirs to be contaminated with other material from the original animal bodies that gave them birth, just as one expects beef stew to taste like beef.

But this is not always what one finds. Now and then one will tap a pocket of virtually pure methane, unsullied by other hydrocarbons. How do we account for the nearly pristine state of this methane if all the hydrocarbons underground had their origin in the bodies of ancient organisms?

Perhaps our model of methane formation is wrong. Maybe there are methane sources other than organic matter. And here we come to one of the most intriguing and exciting theories in modern geology.

The theory's author is Dr. Thomas Gold of Cornell University. Gold turned his attention some years ago to an obscure branch of geology dealing with a process largely ignored in the scientific literature: "outgassing." This is the term for what happened ages ago, when the earth's atmosphere formed from gases that leaked out of the earth itself.

That early atmosphere was different from what we breathe today. In the beginning, the earth's atmosphere appears to have been largely methane, like the atmosphere of Jupiter. We can tell much about the composition of this ancient atmosphere by looking at metal deposits in the crust. Here and there, deep in the stratigraphic record, are bands of unoxidized iron that were laid down long before life appeared on our planet. If the atmosphere had had more than a trace of oxygen then, that iron would have been oxidized into rust. The unaltered state of the iron tells us the atmosphere was almost free of oxygen at that time.

The oxygen we breathe came later, as microscopic plants and bacteria evolved with the ability to take the hydrocarbon gases out of the atmosphere and replace them with oxygen. These "anaerobic" organisms—so called because they did not need oxygen, as we do, to keep their metabolism running—gradually swept the earth's atmosphere clean of methane and created the life-sustaining oxygen atmosphere of today.*

So we are here, one might say, courtesy of a bunch of primitive microbes, and draw the breath of life from their "waste" oxygen.

(All that carbon-containing gas from the early atmosphere did not just disappear, of course. It wound up as carbonate rock—limestone, marble, and so forth—in the crust.)

The conventional wisdom of geology says that out-gassing has pretty much ceased. But what if it is still going on?

In that case, methane and other simple hydrocarbons seeping up from underground would get trapped in deposits of "biogenic" petroleum—formed from organic ma-

---

* Some anaerobic bacteria are still around. The organism that causes botulism in improperly canned foods, for example, cannot do its lethal work in the presence of oxygen.

terial—and dilute this "soup" of animal-derived hydro-carbons with non-biogenic methane from the earth's interior.

That would explain why dead animals and plants seem unable to account for *all* the petroleum and other hydro-carbons that lie under the surface. Outgassed methane seems to have been stretching the recipe, so to speak.

This is Thomas Gold's suggestion. He thinks methane left over from the formation of the earth (when our planet gradually came together from a huge cloud of dust and gas, including methane) may still be rising back to the surface, a whiff at a time. And if this hypothesis is correct, then many of the mysterious phenomena associated with the Ring of Fire may be easy to understand after all; and the world may have a tremendous new energy source, previously unsuspected, to supplement gas and coal and oil.

One of the weirdest phenomena associated with earthquakes is "earthquake light." This is a strange glow that may appear in the night sky before, during, or after an earthquake. It has been described on many occasions and supposedly photographed once or twice.

Scientists have been hard pressed to explain earthquake light, and many of them have just dismissed it as a fantasy. Those geologists who take the stories of earthquake light seriously have come up with some tentative—and not very convincing—theories involving electricity released from the ground.

But if methane is working its way back toward the surface, then earthquake light may be easy to explain as the glow from methane catching fire just aboveground. Flames shooting from the ground have been seen often during quakes (see *New Scientist,* June 9, 1978), and earthquake light may be methane seeping from the ground during tremors and being ignited by electrostatic potential in the air.

Quakes themselves may be easier to explain if methane

escaping from underground is a cause of tremors. There are many reports of quakes along the Ring of Fire where the sea appeared to be boiling. Here is an eyewitness account of what happened offshore during an earthquake in Japan in 1854:

> We felt the first shock at 9:15 A.M.; it was very strong . . . at the end of five minutes the water in the bay swelled and began boiling up, as if thousands of springs had suddenly broken out; the water was mixed with mud . . . and hurled itself upon the town and the land to either side with shocking force.

This description makes it sound as if large amounts of gases were released from the floor of the bay during the earthquake. Could this escaping gas have caused the earthquake itself? It could, if Gold's hypothesis turns out to be correct.

The escaping-methane hypothesis would also account for one odd characteristic of tsunamis. Many tsunamis seem too big for the quakes that supposedly spawned them. Let us imagine a wave 10 feet high generated by a quake in the Pacific. Water is incompressible, so that a 10-foot wave on the surface requires a 10-foot wave in the rocks on the sea floor underneath. It would take a titanic earthquake to create that kind of disturbance on the sea bottom, so we should look elsewhere for a mechanism that causes tsunamis.

What about big bubbles of methane rising up from the ocean floor? As they rise, the bubbles would make water pile up on top of them; a very large outburst of methane from the bottom could easily generate a 10-foot tsunami— at least in theory. This seems a plausible mechanism; and Gold, in a talk delivered at Imperial College in London in 1978, also suggested methane release from the seabed might explain another odd phenomenon associated with earthquakes along the Ring of Fire: massive fish kills. The conventional explanation is that the fish were killed

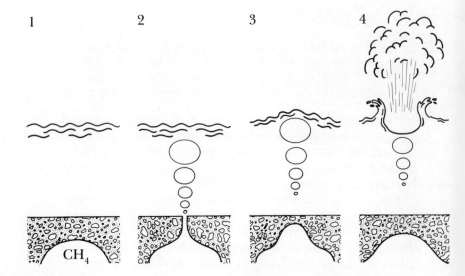

A METHANE ERUPTION: *This is an illustration of how a methane eruption from the bottom of the sea might generate a tsunami. A pocket of methane (CH_4) lies under the surface of the ocean bed. Some of that gas seeps out into the water and rises toward the surface in the form of large bubbles. When those bubbles reach the surface and break, they generate tsunamis.*

by shock waves from the tremor. But Gold's own experiments with fish in tanks indicate that even a tremor of the magnitude of the 1906 San Francisco earthquake did little more than startle the fish. An outburst of gas, on the other hand, might asphyxiate the fish—especially if the gas included toxic compounds such as hydrogen sulfide.

If this "outgassing" theory of earthquakes and tsunamis turns out to be correct (and it might easily be checked with the help of simple chemical sensors), then we may be sitting on top of a huge energy reserve, until now unsuspected. Some estimates put the amount of non-biogenic methane still trapped inside the earth at 90 percent or more of the original supply. Gold has suggested that even if the earth's internal supply of methane is nearly depleted, our planet still may contain enough of this fuel to meet our energy needs, at present levels of world energy consumption, for a million years or so. Perhaps non-biogenic methane will run our industrial society one day, with plenty of fuel for everyone, and the world will no longer need to fear the economic miseries caused by the arbitrary price hikes of a few favored nations.

XVI

Question Marks

THE RING OF FIRE is the edge of an ocean. It is the border of a crustal plate. It is also a vast set of mysteries.

Why, for example, is there vulcanism *inside* the Ring? The traditional theory of plate tectonics (nowadays science is developing so quickly that a revolutionary theory can become a tradition in less than twenty years) says that volcanic activity should be concentrated along the boundaries of crustal plates, not in their very hearts. Yet Hawaii, a volcanic island, rises from the Pacific floor thousands of miles from the edge of the Pacific plate— where theory says we should least expect it.

Is there some kind of "hot spot" under Hawaii generating a long string of volcanic islands as the moving Pacific plate slides slowly over it? If so, how can that hot spot be explained? Geologists have some hunches: an especially high concentration of heat from radionuclides, perhaps.

But the hot spots remain a mystery and probably will for years to come.

If we accept the "hot spot" theory of Hawaii's birth, it is easy to explain the long string of "seamounts" (submerged mountains) that string out to the northwest across the sea floor from Hawaii. The crust, in this case, has just been sliding across a stationary "plume" of magma and generating undersea volcanoes along the way.

But why does this underwater mountain chain make a sudden turn northward toward Siberia around the vicinity of Midway Island? The whole Pacific plate appears to have shifted direction abruptly about the time Midway was rising from the sea. Did the Americas, sliding westward after the opening of the Atlantic, shove the Pacific plate aside abruptly, changing the orientation of the island chain?

It would take a terrific push to move the entire Pacific plate off course, for the Pacific plate has almost as much mass as the moon. Where does that energy come from? Do convection cells in the asthenosphere supply *all* the motive force for the moving continents? That seems unlikely if our current estimates of the strength of those currents are correct. So where does the rest of the energy come from? Is there perhaps some "tidal force" like the one invoked by Wegener, shoving the crustal plates around in a way as yet unrecognized? Or have we just underestimated the forces at work in the upper mantle?

The asthenosphere, just a few miles from the surface of the earth, is one of the biggest mysteries underlying the Ring. (If one could drive a car straight down into the earth, the asthenosphere would be less than half an hour away.) Yet we know virtually nothing about this layer of the earth, compared to what we know of the distant stars and galaxies. We know, in a general way, what the mantle is made of; but volcanic eruptions along the Ring have spewed out tantalizing hints—in the form of bombs and tephra with widely different compositions—that the mantle may not have a uniform makeup, as we used to believe it did. The mantle may be as heterogeneous as a fruitcake.

Almost every day, some old and convenient idea about the earth we live on is knocked down by new discoveries. Indeed, the earth sciences are changing so fast that the knowledge given graduate students in geology today may be obsolete by the time they take their degrees.

In short, we are entering a whole new age in the earth sciences, thanks in part to discoveries made along the Ring of Fire. And what Churchill said about Russia's entry into World War II might well be said about modern geology:

"This is not the end. It is not even the beginning of the end. But it is, perhaps, the end of the beginning."

Suggested Reading

Many books on earthquakes and volcanoes discuss the Ring of Fire, and anyone interested in reading further on this subject may want to consult the books listed here. Kent Wilcoxson's *Chains of Fire* is an excellent introduction to the study of volcanoes, as is Peter Francis's small but highly informative book *Volcanoes*. Among coffee-table books on volcanoes, probably the most impressive is Fred Bullard's *Volcanoes of the Earth,* a well-illustrated survey of the world's volcanoes that is packed with information on everything from plate tectonics to the composition of volcanic ash. Walter Sullivan's classic *Continents in Motion* is one of the best introductions to the theory of plate tectonics, as is Ursula Marvin's *Continental Drift*. Dr. Robert Iacopi's *Earthquake Country* is a well-illustrated and clearly written guide to earthquakes in general and California quakes in particular. Peter Verney's *The Earthquake Handbook* is entertaining, and Preston Cloud's *Adventures in Earth Science,* while demanding for the average reader, is highly recommended.

Glossary

Aftershocks. Earthquakes which follow a more powerful earthquake in the same vicinity, decreasing in strength with time.

Albedo. The amount of sunlight reflected from an object, such as a planet. A light-colored object will have a high albedo, while dark objects have a low albedo.

Asthenosphere. The upper layer of the mantle, where plastic deformation of rocks allows convection currents to form.

Basal Wreck. The truncated cone left after the explosion and/or subsequent collapse of a volcano.

Basalt. A dark, fine-grained igneous rock commonly produced by volcanoes.

Billion. The billion used in this book is one followed by nine zeros, or, in scientific notation, 10^9.

Bomb. A solidified blob of molten rock ejected from a volcano.

Cenozoic. The so-called age of mammals, which began with the extinction of the dinosaurs at the end of the Mesozoic, some 65 million years ago.

Cinder Cone. A cone-shaped hill or rise or mountain formed by ash from a volcanic vent.

Clastic.   Broken up or fragmented. Sand is a clastic material.

Convection.   The rising of a fluid, such as air or water, over a heat source.

Cordillera.   A group of mountain ranges lined up in roughly the same direction. The Andes Mountains in South America are an example of a cordillera.

Core.   The dense nucleus of the earth, thought to be made up of nickel and iron.

Crust.   See LITHOSPHERE.

Epicenter.   The point on the earth's surface directly above the focus of an earthquake. See FOCUS.

Fault.   A fracture in the crust along which the rocks on either side have been moving with respect to one another.

Firedamp.   See METHANE.

Fissure.   A large crack in the crust through which magma may escape to form a volcano.

Focus.   The point of origin of an earthquake.

Fool's Gold.   See PYRITE.

Foreshocks.   Earthquakes which precede a larger quake at a given location.

Fossil Fuels.   Carbon-bearing fuels formed, in whole or in part, from the tissues of long-dead plants and/or animals. Coal and petroleum are the best-known fossil fuels.

Fractionation.   The process that occurs when a subducted slab of crustal rock starts melting on its way down into the asthenosphere, and the lighter components rise back to the surface before the heavier ones do.

Fumarole.   A hole in the ground through which steam or other hot gases may escape from underground. A geyser is an example of a fumarole.

Gondwana.   One of the two large initial fragments produced by the breakup of the supercontinent Pangaea. Gondwana, generally speaking, became the continents of the Southern Hemisphere.

Greenhouse Effect.   The trapping of heat in the atmosphere by carbon dioxide.

Hydrocarbons.   Molecules consisting of carbon chains with hydrogen atoms attached.

Hydrothermal Activity.   A catch-all term applied to the heating of underground water by rock, and the steam generated by that heating.

Igneous Rocks. Rocks formed directly by the cooling of molten rock. Basalt and granite are familiar examples of igneous rock.

Insolation. Any and all solar energy impinging on the earth.

Isostasy. The equilibrium theoretically achieved by blocks of crustal rock "floating" on the denser rocks below.

Lahar. A hot mudflow or flow of ash on the slopes of a volcano.

Laurussia. The northern fragment of Pangaea immediately after the supercontinent broke up. As a rule, Laurussia became the continents of the Northern Hemisphere.

Lava. Molten rock after it has flowed out onto the surface. See MAGMA.

Lithosphere. The outer shell of the earth, on which we live. The lithosphere is commonly called the "crust," and varies in thickness up to 50 miles or so.

Magma. Molten rock underground. Magma becomes lava if and when it flows out onto the surface.

Mantle. The intermediate layer of the earth, between the crust and the core.

Mesozoic. The so-called age of dinosaurs, between the Paleozoic, the earliest age of life on earth, and the Cenozoic, our present age of mammals.

Metamorphic Rocks. Rocks that have been transformed by heat and pressure. Limestone, for example, is metamorphosed into marble, and sandstone into quartzite.

Methane. A simple hydrocarbon gas, chemical formula CH_4, that is an important constituent of natural gas, Methane is also known as "firedamp" and "marsh gas."

Million. The million used in this book is one followed by six zeros, or 10^6.

Mother Lode. The main lode or vein in which metals or metal ores are found.

Obsidian. A black volcanic glass distributed widely in the American West.

Orogenesis. Generally speaking, mountain building; more accurately, the formation of mountains by thrusting and faulting. Also known as "orogeny."

Paleozoic. The earliest age of life on earth. The Paleozoic was the age of trilobites, marine anthropods of the extinct group *Trilobita,* similar in some ways to the modern horseshoe crab.

Pangaea. The supercontinent that is supposed to have existed some 225 million years ago, and to have broken up to form the pattern of continents we know today.

Panthalassa. The great world ocean that surrounded Pangaea.

Placer Deposits. Deposits of metal or metal ores that have been eroded out of their original location and deposited in sediments.

Pluton. An underground body of igneous rock younger than the rocks that surround it. A pluton is formed where molten rock oozes into a space between older rocks.

Pumice. A frothy gray volcanic rock formed when lava cools as the gases in it are bubbling out of solution.

Pyrite. The technical name for "fool's gold," iron sulfide. Pyrite is gold in color but can be distinguished from gold by its specific gravity and by the sulfurous smell it makes when heated.

Radionuclides. Radioactive atoms that break down and release heat.

St. Elmo's Fire. Visible discharges of static electricity in the air, specifically in the masts and rigging of a ship during storms.

Sedimentary Rocks. Rocks made up of clastic material—that is, bits of rock—eroded away from their parent material, carried away and deposited by wind and/or water, and then turned to solid rock.

Seismic Sea Wave. See TSUNAMI.

Seismicity. Essentially, how prone an area is to earthquakes.

Seismogram. The graphic record made by a seismograph.

Seismograph. A device for picking up earthquake vibrations and recording them on paper.

Seismology. The scientific study of earthquakes.

Sial. A relatively lightweight layer of rock that lies below the continents. Sial takes its name from two of its principal components, silicon (Si) and aluminum (Al).

Sima. The rock, slightly denser than sial, on which the sial floats. Sima takes its name from silicon and magnesium.

Subduction Zone. An area where a plate of crustal rock is drawn downward and back into the asthenosphere. Subduction zones are characterized by deep ocean trenches, frequent earthquakes, hydrothermal ore deposits, and ranges of volcanic mountains.

Tectonics. The study of the large-scale surface features of the earth and how they originated.

Telluride. A compound of tellurium and some other, usually more precious, element such as gold or silver.

Tephra. The collective name of all clastic material expelled from volcanoes during eruptions. Tephra may range in size from microscopic dust particles to chunks of rock 200 feet wide.

Tsunami. A large, long sea wave generated by some seismic disturbance in or underneath the water. Sometimes called, inaccurately, a "tidal wave."

Volcano. In the broadest sense, a fissure or vent in the crust through which molten rock rises to the surface; alternatively, the mountain produced by escape of molten rock.

Vulcanism. Volcanic activity of any kind.

Bibliography

Aaronson, S. "The Social Cost of Earthquake Prediction." *New Scientist,* March 17, 1977, pp. 634–636.

Adams, F. *Birth and Development of the Geological Sciences.* New York: Dover, 1938.

"After the Volcano." *The York Times,* May 25, 1980, p. 18E.

"Alaskan Atom Test—Why All the Furor." *U.S. News and World Report,* September 27, 1971, p. 38.

"Amchitka A–Test: Was It Worth It?" *U.S. News and World Report,* November 22, 1971, p. 72.

"Amchitka Bomb Goes Off." *Time,* November 15, 1971, p. 15.

American Geological Institute. *Dictionary of Geological Terms.* 2nd ed. Washington, D.C.: National Academy of Sciences, 1960.

Angeloff, S., ed. *Volcano: The Eruption of Mount St. Helens.* Seattle: Madrona, 1980.

"Ash Cloud Wafts Toward Virginia." Newport News, Virginia, *Times Herald,* May 20, 1980, p. 1.

"At Least 8 Dead As Peak Erupts; Worst Blast Yet." *The New York Times,* May 18, 1980, p. 1.

Bibliography

Ballard, R., and Grassle, J. "Return to Oases of the Deep." *National Geographic,* November, 1979, pp. 686–705.

Bank, T. *Birthplace of the Winds.* New York: Crowell, 1956.

Beerbower, J. *Search for the Past: An Introduction to Paleontology.* 2nd ed. Englewood Cliffs, New Jersey: Prentice-Hall, 1968.

Bird, J., and Isacks, B., eds. *Plate Tectonics: Selected Papers from the Journal of Geophysical Research.* Washington, D.C.: American Geophysical Union, 1972.

Bolt, B. *Earthquakes: A Primer.* New York: Freeman, 1978.

Boly, W. "Fire Mountain." *New West,* May 19, 1980, pp. 30–34.

Booth, B. "Predicting Eruptions." *New Scientist,* September 9, 1976, pp. 526–28.

————. "Volcanic Hazards." *New Scientist,* August 26, 1976, pp. 432–435.

Borton, H. *Japan's Modern Century.* New York: Ronald, 1955.

Brander, J. "The Iranian Earthquake: What Next?" *New Scientist,* September 28, 1978, pp. 930–31.

————, and Lewin, R. "Another Theory Shakes the Experts." *Ibid.,* October 12, 1978, p. 91.

Briggs, L. "When Mount Mazama Lost Its Top." *National Geographic,* July, 1962, pp. 128–133.

Briggs, P. *Will California Fall Into the Sea?* New York: McKay, 1972.

Brumdage, B. *Empire of the Inca.* Norman, Oklahoma: University of Oklahoma Press, 1963.

————. *Lords of Cuzco: A History and Description of the Inca People in their Final Days.* Norman, Oklahoma: University of Oklahoma Press, 1963.

Bullard, F. *Volcanoes of the Earth.* Austin: University of Texas Press, 1976.

Burke, J. *Connections.* New York: Macmillan, 1978.

Busch, N. *The Horizon Concise History of Japan.* New York: American Heritage, 1972.

"Can Catfish Forecast Earthquakes?" *Wall Street Journal,* March 6, 1978, p. 6.

"Carter Flies Over Barren Landscape of Mount St. Helens." *Washington Post,* May 23, 1980, p. 1.

Bibliography

"City Choking in a Storm of Ash." *Boston Globe,* May 21, 1980, p. 1.

Cloud, Preston, ed. *Adventures in Earth Science.* San Francisco: Freeman, 1970.

"Coincidence or the Tides?" *Boston Globe,* June 15, 1980, p. 1.

"The Convulsion of St. Helens." *Newsweek,* June 2, 1980, pp. 22–26.

"Costs for cleaning and rehabilitating clogged portions of the Columbia River channel and other waterways in the Pacific Northwest following eruption of Mount St. Helens may go as high as $219 million, the Army Corps of Engineers said." *Wall Street Journal,* June 2, 1980, p. 26.

"Crisis Brings People Together." *Boston Globe,* May 25, 1980, p. 8.

"Damage Adds Up Near Quake's Center." *San Francisco Chronicle,* August 8, 1979, p. 1.

"Damage by Volcano May Top $1.5 Billion." *The New York Times,* May 25, 1980, p. 1.

Dana, R. *Two Years Before the Mast and Twenty-Four Years After.* New York: Collier, 1909.

De Camp, L. *Lost Continents: The Atlantis Theme.* New York: Ballantine, 1975.

De Quille, D. *The Big Bonanza.* New York: Knopf, 1947.

"Doomsday in the Golden State." *Time,* April 11, 1969, p. 59.

Douglas, J. "Letter from Tokyo (6): Waiting for the 'Great Tokai Quake.'" *Science News,* April 29, 1978, pp. 282–3.

"Earthquake Forecasts: The Perils of Prediction." *Futurist,* June, 1979, p. 233.

"Eruption Kills 5—Gigantic Ash Cloud." *San Francisco Chronicle,* May 19, 1980, p. 1.

"Eruption of Mount St. Helens may cause disruption of area's economy for years." *Wall Street Journal,* June 16, 1980, p. 12.

"Even to Experts, Mount St. Helens Was Powerful Surprise." *The New York Times,* May 25, 1980, p. 18.

"Exploding Volcano: Full Impact Yet to Come." *U.S. News and World Report,* June 2, 1980, pp. 29–31.

"Extraordinary Lab for Volcano Scientists." *San Francisco Chronicle,* May 20, 1980, p. 6.

Bibliography

"Fears of Flooding from Volcano Ease." *The New York Times,*
May 22, 1980, p. Al.

"Fiery History Has Left Scars in Cascades." *San Francisco
Chronicle,* May 21, 1980, p. 4.

Francis, P. *Volcanoes.* New York: Penguin, 1976.

Fried, J. *Life Along the San Andreas Fault.* New York: Saturday Review Press, 1973.

"From Milrow to Cannikin: Amchitka Tests." *Science News,*
May 22, 1971, p. 350.

"From Topography to Daily Commerce, Some Things Have
Changed Irrevocably." *Boston Globe,* May 24, 1980, p. 5.

Galanopoulos, A. "Die aegyptischen Plagen und der Auszug
Israels aus geologischer Sucht." *Das Altertum* 10, 1964,
pp. 131–37.

Gibbons, B. "Risk and Reward on Alaska's Violent Gulf."
National Geographic, February, 1979, pp. 236–67.

Gibson, M. *The Rise of Japan.* New York: Putnam, 1972.

"God, I Want to Live!" *Time,* June 2, 1980, pp. 26–31.

Gold, T., and Sofer, S. "The Deep-Earth-Gas Hypothesis."
Scientific American, June, 1980, pp. 154–61.

Graves, W. "San Francisco Bay: The Westward Gate." *National Geographic,* November, 1969, pp. 593–637.

"Green Light on Cannikin." *Newsweek,* November 8, 1971,
p. 74.

Gribbin, J. *Our Changing Planet.* New York: Crowell, 1977.

Gruening, E., ed. *An Alaskan Reader.* New York: Meredith,
1966.

Halacy, D. *Earthquakes: A Natural History.* Indianapolis:
Bobbs-Merrill, 1974.

Hane, M. *Japan: A Historical Survey.* New York: Scribner,
1972.

"Harry: Riding High with his Grubstake?" *San Francisco Examiner,* May 19, 1980, p. C12.

Hindley, K. "An Earthquake Waiting to Happen?" *New
Scientist,* January 26, 1978. pp. 228–30.

———. "Beware the Big Wave." *Ibid.,* February 9, 1978,
pp. 346–47.

"Hot Spot: Volcano Specialist Gets 'Chance of a Lifetime' on
Mount St. Helens." *Wall Street Journal,* June 2, 1980,
p. 1.

Bibliography

"How One Town Cleaned Up Eruption of Mount St. Helens Near Yakima, Wash." *U.S. News and World Report.* June 23. 1980, p. 30.

"How Volcano Built Up to the Big Blast." *San Francisco Chronicle,* May 19, 1980, p. 2.

Iacopi, R. *Earthquake Country.* Menlo Park, California: Lane, 1973.

"In Krindjing, Java, the 'Glowing Cloud' Brings Rain of Death." *Wall Street Journal,* April 23, 1979, p. 1.

"In the Wake of Mount St. Helens." *Science News,* June 7, 1980, pp. 355–56.

"The Indian: 'We Just Go by What God Sends Us.' " *Washington Post,* May 23, 1980, p. 2.

"The Instant the Volcano Blew." *San Francisco Chronicle,* May 21, 1980, p. 1.

"Is This Blast Necessary?" *Time,* November 1, 1971, p. 99.

Jacobs, P. "The Coming Atomic Blast in Alaska." *New York Review of Books,* July 22, 1971, pp. 34–35.

"Java Eyes Dangerous Volcano." Richmond, Virginia, *News Leader,* June 5, 1980, p. 5.

Jones, S. "Danger: Tidal Wave." *Science Digest,* July, 1964, pp. 83–87.

Keating, B. *Alaska.* Washington, D.C.: National Geographic Society, 1971.

Kerr, R. "Earthquakes: Prediction Proving Elusive." *Science,* April 28, 1978, pp. 419–21.

———. "Prospects for Earthquake Prediction Wane." *Ibid.,* November 2, 1979, pp. 542–45.

Kummel, B. *History of the Earth.* 2nd ed. San Francisco: Freeman, 1970.

Leet, L., and Leet, F. *Earthquake: Discoveries in Seismology.* New York: Dell, 1964.

"Life After the Ashes." *Boston Globe,* May 27, 1980, p. 3.

"Life and Times of Mount St. Helens." *Science News,* May 3, 1980, p. 277–78.

"Life in Shadow of a Killer Volcano." *U.S. News and World Report,* June 9, 1980, p. 13.

Link, M. "Exploring the Drowned City of Port Royal." *National Geographic,* February, 1980, pp. 151–83.

Lynch, J. *Our Trembling Earth.* New York: Dodd, 1940.

Bibliography

Macelwane, J. *When the Earth Quakes.* Milwaukee: Bruce, 1947.

MacLean, A. *Goodbye California.* New York: Doubleday, 1978.

McIntyre, L. "The Lost Empire of the Incas." *National Geographic,* December, 1973, pp. 729–87.

Marvin, U. *Continental Drift: The Evolution of a Concept.* Washington, D.C.: Smithsonian Institution, 1973.

Melchior, F. *The Earth Tides.* Elmsford, New York: Pergammon, 1966.

Morgan, A. "Mount St. Helens Theology." *Christian Century,* July 2–9, 1980, pp. 694–95.

"Mount St. Helens Books and Other Volcano Tie-ins Sell Briskly." *Wall Street Journal,* August 21, 1980, p. 1.

"Mount St. Helens Erupts; At Least 5 Are Killed." *Washington Post,* June 21, 1980, p. 1.

"Mount St. Helens Explodes." *Boston Globe,* May 19, 1980, p. 1.

"Mount St. Helens Is Quiet As New Cleanup Begins." *The New York Times,* May 27, 1980, p. A20.

"Nature Packs a Wallop." *Boston Globe,* May 24, 1980, p. 14.

"Nuclear Test That May Fizzle: Cannikin Test." *Business Week,* September 25, 1971, pp. 117–18.

Oakeshott, G. *California's Changing Landscapes.* New York: McGraw-Hill, 1978.

"100 Missing in Gas, Ash." *Boston Globe,* May 21, 1980, p. 20.

Paterson, D. "Methane from the Bowels of the Earth." *New Scientist,* June 29, 1978, pp. 896–97.

Price, W. *The Japanese Miracle and Peril.* New York: John Day, 1971.

"Reading Entrails of Volcanoes Is Not Yet a Very Exact Science." *The New York Times,* May 25, 1980, p. 20E.

"Relatives Seek Survivors, Find Only Desolation." *Boston Globe,* May 24, 1980, p. 6.

Rensberger, B. *The Cult of the Wild.* New York: Anchor/Doubleday, 1977.

"Residents Say the Eruption 'Ruined the Country.'" *San Francisco Chronicle,* May 20, 1980, p. 7.

"Resort Owner May Be Victim of the Volcano." *The New York Times,* May 25, 1980, p. 19.

Bibliography

Richter, C. *Elementary Seismology*. San Francisco: Freeman, 1958.

"Ripe for a Big Quake . . . and the San Andreas Fault, Too." *Washington Post,* June 2, 1980, p. K10.

Robinson, R. "Duplex Origin of Petroleum." *Nature,* July 13, 1963, pp. 113–14.

Sagan, C. *Broca's Brain*. New York: Random, 1979.

"St. Helens Baffles Experts." *San Francisco Examiner,* May 26, 1980, p. 1.

"St. Helens Erupts: 5 Dead." *Philadelphia Inquirer,* May 19, 1980, p. 1.

"Search Among the Ashes." *Boston Globe,* May 20, 1980, p. 1.

"Shocking View of the Wasteland." *San Francisco Chronicle,* May 20, 1980, p. 1.

"Six Days Later, City Struggles to Free Itself of the Fallout." *Boston Globe,* May 24, 1980, p. 1.

Smith, F. *The Seas in Motion*. New York: Crowell, 1973.

Smith, R. "Waiting for the Other Plate to Drop in California." *Science,* February 24, 1978, p. 797.

"Steam, Ash, and an Unsettling Flight." *Boston Globe,* May 21, 1980, p. 17.

"Stifling Darkness Descended." *Washington Post,* May 25, 1980, p. 1.

Stommel, S., and Stommel, E. "The Year Without a Summer." *Scientific American,* July, 1979, pp. 176–80.

Sullivan, R., with Mustart, D., and Galehouse, J. "Living in Earthquake Country: A Survey of Residents Living Along the San Andreas Fault." *California Geology,* January, 1977, pp. 3–8.

Sullivan, W. *Continents in Motion*. New York: McGraw-Hill, 1974.

Tarling, D., and Tarling, M. *Continental Drift*. New York: Pelican, 1974.

Tazieff, H. *When the Earth Trembles*. New York: Harcourt, Brace, and World, 1964.

"Theory Explains Large U.S. Quakes." *The New York Times,* May 20, 1980, p. C1.

Thomas, G., and Witts, M. *The San Francisco Earthquake*. New York: Stein and Day, 1971.

Bibliography

Thompson, H. *The Great Shark Hunt*. New York: Summit, 1979.

Thompson, R. "Afloat on a Sea of Methane?" *Technology Review*, October, 1978, pp. 14–15.

Tiedemann, A. *An Introduction to Japanese Civilization*. New York: Columbia University Press, 1974.

"Tracking Tremors: Earthquake Prediction Comes Into Its Own but Still Isn't Reliable." *Wall Street Journal*, April 18, 1979, p. 1.

"U-2 Pilot Tells of 'Gruesome' Flight Over the Volcano." *The New York Times*, May 23, 1980, p. A12.

"U.S. Crops, Water Could Be Affected." *Boston Globe*, May 21, 1980, p. 16.

United States Geological Survey and National Oceanic and Atmospheric Administration. *The San Fernando, California, Earthquake of February 9, 1971*. Washington, D.C.: U.S. Government Printing Office, 1971.

"Vast Change Predicted for Coast of U.S." *The New York Times*, April 1, 1980, p. C1.

Velikovsky, I. *Worlds in Collision*. New York: Doubleday, 1950.

Verney, P. *The Earthquake Handbook*. London: Paddington, 1979.

"View from Above: A Study in Devastation." *Boston Globe*, May 24, 1980, p. 7.

"Violence from the 'Ring of Fire.'" *U.S. News and World Report*, June 2, 1980, p. 30.

"Volcanic Eruption Disrupts Air Traffic." *Aviation Week and Space Technology*, May 26, 1980, pp. 18–21.

"Volcanic Eruptions, Earthquakes Spark Financial Tremors in the Northwest." *Wall Street Journal*, June 12, 1980, p. 1.

"Volcano Continues to Snarl Air Traffic." *Aviation Week and Space Technology*, June 2, 1980, pp. 18–19.

"Volcano Cost May Be $2 Billion." *Boston Globe*, May 25, 1980, p. 1.

"Volcano Fallout Is Expected to Have Little Effect on Health or Crops." *The New York Times*, May 22, 1980, p. B12.

"Volcano Forecast: A Rainout in N.E." *Boston Globe*, May 21, 1980, p. 1.

Bibliography

"Voncanoes Fascinated Missing Peninsula Geologist." *San Francisco Chronicle*, May 20, 1980, p. 5.

"Volcanologist Was Gripped in Fatal Fascination." *Washington Post*, May 25, 1980, p. 2.

Weast, R., ed. *Handbook of Chemistry and Physics*. 55th ed. Cleveland: CRC Press, 1974.

Wegener, A. *The Origins of the Oceans and Continents*. New York: Methuen, 1967.

Wertenbaker, W. *The Floor of the Sea*. Boston: Little, Brown, 1974.

Wexler, H. "Volcanoes and World Climate." *Scientific American*, April, 1952, pp. 74–81.

"Whys and Hows of Eruption." *Boston Globe*, May 28, 1980, p. 2.

Wicker, T. "Out of the Ashes." *The New York Times*, May 26, 1980, p. 31.

Wilcoxson, K. *Chains of Fire*. Radnor, Pennsylvania: Chilton, 1966.

Wilford, J. "Right or Wrong, Thomas Gold Is Proving Provocative Again." *The New York Times*, October 7, 1980, p. C1.

Willenbecher, T. "The Quake As an Article of Faith in California." *Baltimore Sun*, July 20, 1980, p. K3.

"Windows Into the Restless Earth." *Time*, June 2, 1980, p. 34.

Wood, R. "Coming Apart at the Seams." *New Scientist*, January 24, 1980, pp. 252–56.

Index

Index

Index

Index

David Ritchie is a professional science writer who lives in Hampton, Virginia. He has a B.A. in environmental sciences from the University of Virginia (Charlottesville), and has written for numerous publications, including *Analog, Cavalier, Inquiry, Maine Life, Newsday, The Washington Post,* and *The Writer.* He is also a member of the Southern Science Writers' Association.